break into the Game Industry

How to get a job making video games

Ernest Adams

McGraw-Hill/Osborne

New York   Chicago   San Francisco   Lisbon   London   Madrid   Mexico City
Milan   New Delhi   San Juan   Seoul   Singapore   Sydney   Toronto

Publisher
Brandon A. Nordin

Vice President & Associate Publisher
Scott Rogers

Editorial Director
Gareth Hancock

Project Editor
Jennifer Malnick

Acquisitions Coordinator
Jessica Wilson

Technical Editor
Ellen Beeman

Copy Editor
Mike McGee

Proofreader
Claire Splan

Indexer
Rebecca Plunkett

Computer Designers
Tabitha M. Cagan
Lucie Ericksen

Illustrators
Melinda Lytle
Lyssa Wald

Series Design
Lyssa Wald
Peter F. Hancik

Cover Series Design
Jeff Weeks

McGraw-Hill/Osborne
2100 Powell Street, 10 Floor
Emeryville, California 94608
U.S.A.

To arrange bulk purchase discounts for sales promotions, premiums, or fund-raisers, please contact **McGraw-Hill**/Osborne at the above address. For information on translations or book distributors outside the U.S.A., please see the International Contact Information page immediately following the index of this book.

Break into the Game Industry: How to Get A Job Making Video Games

567890 DOC DOC 09876

ISBN 0-07-222660-9

This book was composed with Corel VENTURA™ Publisher.

Contents

EDICATION

This book is dedicated with love and gratitude to my parents, Bill and Nettie Adams, who taught me that I could be anything I wanted to when I grew up ... and successfully hid their surprise when I turned out to be a game developer.

And to my brother, Edward, whose generosity and selfless dedication to those less fortunate than him is a constant source of inspiration to me.

Acknowledgments

IN the course of my career in interactive entertainment, I have worked as a game designer, producer, and software engineer; but there are a great many other professions in which I have no personal experience. In order to write about them I have relied heavily on the advice and knowledge of my professional colleagues, without whom this book could not have been completed.

My first obligation is without question to Jason Della Rocca and the members of the IGDA Education Committee, for permission to reprint their Curriculum Framework document (Appendix B). Although it was not their primary intention for the Framework to be used as I have suggested, I believe its value to nascent game developers is greater than perhaps even the Committee realizes. Certainly this book would not be half so useful without it.

As I am a game developer, not a human resources person, I have relied heavily on the experience of Mary Margaret Walker, owner of Mary-margaret.com Recruiting and Business Services, for information about the process of jobhunting. Her advice, and that of her partner Robin McShaffry, has been of inestimable benefit.

It is with deep appreciation that I thank the many contributors whose wise and humorous words appear throughout this book, and indeed make it what it is. They are, in alphabetical order:

❯ Ellen Guon Beeman, Producer, Monolith Productions

❯ Kim Blake, Producer, Particle Systems

❯ David Bryson, Engine Programmer, Electronic Arts UK

❯ Charles Cecil, Managing Director, Revolution Software Ltd.

❯ Darryl Duncan, President, GameBeat Studios (www.gamebeat.com)

❯ Jon Gramlich, QA Analyst, Monolith Productions

❯ Robin Green, R&D Programmer, Sony Computer Entertainment of America

❯ Amy Kalson, Assistant Producer, Maxis

❯ Adele Kellett, Audio Lead, Electronic Arts UK

❯ Lauren Logan, Student, Full Sail

❯ Pascal Luban, Lead Designer, The Game Design Studio (www.gamedesignstudio.com)

❯ Christy Marx, Freelance Writer

❯ Kevin McGrath, Retired Game Programmer

❯ Clarinda Merripen, Human Resources Manger, Cyberlore

❯ Jake Neri, Founder and Partner, Blaze Games

❯ Susan O'Connor, Independent Interactive Scriptwriter

❯ Patricia Pizer, MMO Design Specialist, ubi.com

❯ Darrell Porcher, organizer of the Harlem Game Wizards

❯ Kent Quirk, President, CogniToy

❯ Keith Robinson, Cartoonist and Intellivision Programmer, Intellivisionlives.com

❯ Lee Rossini, Director of Marketing, Sierra Entertainment

❯ George Alistair Sanger, Legendary Audio Guy, The Fat Man

❯ Phil Sulak, Vice President, Westlake Interactive, Inc.

❯ Michelle Sullivan, Production Artist, Turbine Entertainment Software

❯ Mary Margaret Walker, Recruiter, Mary-margaret.com

❯ Gordon Walton, Vice President, Sony Online Entertainment

I must emphasize that while these people have contributed greatly to this book's virtues, its faults are entirely my responsibility.

Special thanks are due to Clarinda Merripen, Human Resources Manger of Cyberlore, and the many women of the IGDA's Women_dev mailing list, for their war stories and insights on being a woman in the game industry. I also owe a particular debt to Darrell Porcher of the Harlem Game Wizards; Darryl Duncan, President and Chief Composer of GameBeat Studios (www.gamebeat.com); and the members of the Culture Rock Network Yahoo Group for their thoughts concerning minorities in interactive entertainment. Both of these are subjects I was anxious to address but could not, in the nature of things, discuss from personal experience.

Alex Dunne, Editor-in-Chief of the incomparable Gamasutra developers' webzine, graciously gave me permission to include material from Gamasutra's educational and corporate databases. Michelle Sullivan, Ken Felton, and Leonard Paul all contributed valuable tips about art and audio tools. Kent Quirk and Tess Snider brought me up-to-date on modern coding practices; Tess in particular is my font of all wisdom to do with the homebrew, open source, and mod scenes.

I must express my gratitude to the following companies for kind permission to include screen shots of their products: Discreet, for *3ds max*; SN Systems, for *TUNER*; Metrowerks, for *CodeWarrior*; and Sonic Foundry, for *Sound Forge*. My former employers, Electronic Arts, also deserve a mention: It was their generous sabbatical policy that enabled me to begin work on this book.

My editors at McGraw-Hill/Osborne—Gareth Hancock, Jessica Wilson, and especially the ever-tolerant Jennifer Malnick—stood by me through missed deadlines, authorial tantrums about the proper use of gerunds, and indeed a substantial expansion of the book partway through its creation. Jawahara Saidullah, my agent, was instrumental in helping me find a publisher for the book. I owe them all much. Finally, special thanks and a big smooch go to my wife, Mary Ellen Foley, the World's Best Editor, who read many chapters and flagged many weaknesses and ambiguities in my prose before it ever left the house. She made my "official" editors' jobs much easier, though they never knew it.

Last and greatest of my benefactors is Ellen Guon Beeman, my technical editor and very old friend. Her touch, subtle but essential, is all over this book. It was she who recommended (and tracked down) many of my contributors; she who corrected my misconceptions when necessary; she who clarified glossary entries at six in the morning. Her experience is vast, her kindness and generosity immeasurable. I cannot thank her enough.

iNTRODUCTION

I was ten years old when I played my first computer game. It was a simulation of the starship Enterprise, and I played it on a Teletype, a clattering old printing terminal connected to a mainframe. Computers were rare and expensive back then; it cost me two whole weeks' allowance to use one for an hour. No pretty graphics, no awesome explosions—just text, slowly hammered out on a long roll of yellow paper.

It was the most exciting thing I had ever done in my life.

The game took place mostly in my imagination, but even so I felt as if I were in Captain Kirk's chair, directing phasers and photon torpedoes, shields and the warp drive, battling the Klingons. With each order I gave I held my breath, as I waited anxiously while the results were printed out. I was one with the machine: it was my ally and my adversary, both at the same time. I faced death at every turn, but victory was mine to achieve if I could master the weapons at my command.

In one hour the power and potential of computer gaming shone out of that rickety old Teletype like a searchlight, straight onto my face. I was dazzled, and at the age of ten I formed a resolution: I had to learn how to make these games for myself—maybe even make a career of it. But I had no idea how.

As I talk to people in my role as a consulting game designer, writer, and lecturer, I find that's a common experience. People who play games frequently want to make them as well. Creative people are attracted to the incredible power of computer and video games—the power to delight, to challenge, to amuse—in short, the power to entertain.

When I played my first computer game, there was no game industry; even the first arcade game, Pong, was two years in the future. Things are different now: It's a nine-billion-dollar business and there's a vast amount to know. But one thing is still the same: A lot of creative people want to make computer and video games, and, like me back then, they don't know how to educate themselves for it, or to get a job doing it.

That's why I wrote this book. Keep reading and I'll show you.

WHAT THIS BOOK IS ABOUT...

This book is intended for anyone who wants to learn about the interactive entertainment industry and is thinking of getting a job in it. It gives you the basic information you need to know about how games are built and sold, and what kinds of skills are needed and careers are available in the industry. I wrote it primarily for people who want to get jobs as game developers and game testers, but it will also be useful if you want to work in the marketing, sales, accounting, business development, or legal fields.

I don't expect you to know anything about programming or computer hardware, except to be familiar with the major elements of a personal computer: memory, hard disks, video displays, and so on. You don't have to know how these devices work, but you should understand the roles they play and be familiar with the terms used to describe them: kilobytes and megabytes of data storage, pixels of screen resolution, and things like that. If you've ever used a personal computer, you probably already know more than enough to understand everything in this book.

AND WHAT IT'S NOT ABOUT

Like most people interested in game development, you've probably got a great idea for a game in mind. Unfortunately, this book won't tell you how to build it. I'm not trying to teach you how to actually develop games—that would fill several books much thicker than this one. Rather, I'm going to show you what careers are available in game development, and how to go about preparing yourself for one. If you're a college student or a high school or even a middle school student, you'll find it helpful, but it's not only for young people. I got into the game industry when I was 29, after several years of programming chip-design tools for the electronics industry. Plenty of people switch to interactive entertainment from other careers. Getting a job in the business is a question of finding out what you need to learn (which is what this book tells you), then learning it, and finally getting yourself hired.

Another thing this book won't tell you is how to start your own game development company. If you're thinking of setting up a business, a lot of the material in here may be useful to you, but I'm not going to go into all the special issues that go with founding a company—writing a business plan, finding venture capital, getting incorporated, and so on. There are two reasons for this: First, I've never founded a game company, so I don't have any experience to give you the benefit of; second, it's too big a subject. People go to business school and earn MBA degrees to learn how to start a business, and even if I had all the answers I probably couldn't tell them to you in one book.

 A NOTE ABOUT TERMS

For the most part, we all know what we mean when we say "the movies" or "Hollywood." Of course, filmmaking techniques are used for a lot of things besides movies: TV shows, advertising, music videos, and so on. But on the whole, when people talk about "the movies," they're talking about feature-length movies shown at the cinema.

Not so with video games. When the term was first used, "video game" always meant a coin-operated arcade game—they were much more common than the early console machines. Then people began porting text-only games from mainframe computers to personal computers and calling them "computer games"; then personal computers got graphics and computer games began to be called "video games" as well. Now there are games available on mobile telephones and built into airplane seats; there are web-based games, handheld games, and electronic gambling machines. The whole situation is a real muddle.

I'm going to simplify things by adopting some uniform terminology. Unfortunately, there is no standard usage in the industry, but at least it'll be consistent throughout the book.

The term "video game" will be used to mean a game for either a personal computer or a game console (whether it's connected to a TV like the Sony Playstation or handheld like the Game Boy Advance), but not a coin-op game. When I need to distinguish between games on a personal computer and games on a console (there are important differences between them), I'll call the former PC games and the latter console games. If I need to differentiate between games for handheld devices and others, I'll call them—surprise!—handheld games. I won't use the term "computer game" except in a historical context.

Games that you put coins into are very different from games that you don't, and it's almost a separate industry, so I'll call them arcade games—unless you can win coins back again, in which case they're gambling machines.

A single-player game is a game designed to be played by only one person. A multiplayer game is a game that can be played by one or more people. If they play it over a network, it's a networked multiplayer game; if they all play it in the same room on one machine, it's a local multiplayer game. (A few games are single-player-only; a few are multiplayer-only; but many have both single-player and multiplayer modes.) An online game must be played over a network and cannot be played any other way. Web-based games can be played in a web browser and don't require the player to install any special software on her machine.

As you read more you'll discover that there are subtle differences between "games," "simulations," "software toys," and "persistent worlds," but for now they're all games.

ABOUT THE AUTHOR

Ernest Adams graduated from Stanford University with a degree in Philosophy in 1982. Initially, he worked as a software engineer in the electronics industry, but switched to game development in 1989, joining a company called Interactive Productions (later P.F.Magic). There he created the PC client for an early America Online game, *RabbitJack's Casino*. He also did the programming for a multiplayer party game called *Third Degree* for the short-lived CD-I player.

Moving to Electronic Arts in 1992, Adams became a game designer. He designed the first-ever CD-ROM edition of *John Madden Football* for the 3DO Multiplayer. For the next several years he served as the audio/video producer for the Madden series, and under his guidance Electronic Arts perfected the technique of assembling sentences from audio snippets to produce seamless play-by-play commentary. During this period Adams also helped to produce the Game Developers' Conference and founded the International Game Developers' Association, the first worldwide professional society for game developers.

In 1999, Adams moved to Great Britain to become a lead designer at Bullfrog Productions, a subsidiary of Electronic Arts. There he worked on two projects, *Genesis: The Hand of God* and *Dungeon Keeper 3*. Unfortunately, both were cancelled when the company refocused its attention on the *Harry Potter* series.

In 2000 Adams left Bullfrog to become a design consultant, joining the International Hobo consortium. Many of his projects are outside the mainstream, requiring a high degree of creativity. Among his clients have been the *Guinness Book of World Records* and Zoo Atlanta. He writes a regular column on game design called "The Designer's Notebook" for the Gamasutra developers' webzine, and has coauthored a book, *Andrew Rollings and Ernest Adams on Game Design*. He also lectures frequently on the subject at colleges, art festivals, and game conferences. His professional web site is at www.designersnotebook.com.

CHAPTER 1

A Brief History of Interactive Entertainment

BEFORE we get into how the video game industry operates —and how you can be part of it—we're going to

take a quick look at its history. Even though the industry isn't very old, certain events in the past had a profound effect on the way it does business. This may not sound like it has much to do with getting a job, but you'll appear more knowledgeable to a prospective employer if you understand not only how the business works, but how it got to where it is today. This chapter gives you that background information.

COMPUTER GAMES AND MAINFRAMES

Nobody knows exactly when the first computer game was written. The modern stored-program digital computer—to give it its full name—was developed during the Second World War, and computers first became commercially available in the 1950s. At that time, they had to be used in "batch mode"—you submitted your program on punched cards, and the machine ran it and printed out the results on a lineprinter. Obviously, this wasn't a good way to play games, although I actually wrote one once: each player typed up data cards and added them to the deck, then they went to the printer to see who had won. It wasn't terribly exciting.

The timesharing operating system, invented in the late 1960s, allowed people to use computers interactively via terminals rather than punched cards. It's likely that a number of computer games were written soon afterward. However, at that time, computers were still multimillion-dollar machines, available to only a few people. There was certainly no market for computer games, so the first games were developed by programmers just to amuse themselves. They passed them around freely and expanded on each others' work. Some games were written in FORTRAN, but many were written in a simple programming language called BASIC.

Throughout the rest of this chapter (and the next as well), you might find it useful to refer to Figure 1-1, which shows how video games evolved from their earliest beginnings to the present, and even includes some speculation about the future.

FIGURE 1-1

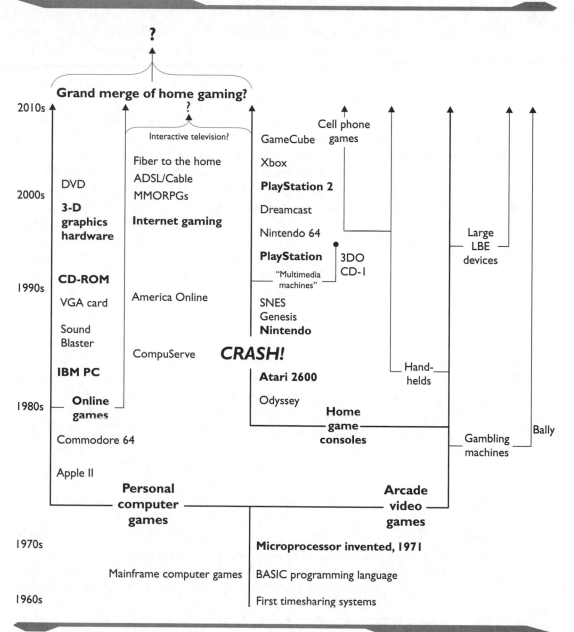

The evolution of video games

ARCADE GAMES AND CONSOLE GAMES

In 1971, Intel invented the microprocessor, and changed the nature of computing—and, indeed, all of society—forever. Because microprocessors were cheap, and could be manufactured in large quantities, they made it possible to use computing power in all kinds of ways that had never been tried before. Two of the earliest were a coin-operated video game named *Pong*, and a home console version of essentially the same game, the Magnavox Odyssey. Video gaming was a huge success, and a new form of mass-market entertainment was born. The earliest consoles could only play one or two games that were hardwired into them, but in 1976, Fairchild Camera and Instrument introduced a machine that accepted ROM cartridges. This important advance enabled players to buy new games without having to buy a whole new machine.

By the 1980s, the market for the games was growing at a tremendous rate, and there were several different home console machines available. The two most popular were Atari's 2600 and Mattel's Intellivision. Anyone could make ROM cartridges for these machines, so new publishers were springing up overnight. The programmers often earned royalties on their games, and some of them became immensely rich making such classic titles as *Pitfall* and *Chopper Command*. The games had to fit within 4K of memory, so this was truly "programming on the bare metal"—no fancy object-oriented programming languages for them!—but on the other hand it was possible for one person to write an entire game in just a few months. There were few specialized musicians or artists on the projects; the programmers did it all. But within the early publishers' success were the seeds of their downfall. They kept producing new games faster and faster in order to meet the demand, and in doing so they began to sacrifice quality. The games were buggy, too much like one another, and just not that much fun. In 1983, the public started to lose interest.

The industry, which had been spending money assuming that the extraordinary rate of growth would continue indefinitely, crashed. Atari and Mattel nearly went out of business. Imagic, a publisher which made games for both those machines, was within three days of going public on the stock exchange when Atari announced that it was losing money. Imagic's initial public offering was withdrawn, and within a few months they were bankrupt. Throughout 1984 and 1985, the home video game industry was nearly dead, although arcade machines continued to be successful at a slower pace.

ENTER THE PERSONAL COMPUTER

Now we have to go back to 1971 again to look at a whole other branch of gaming: personal computer games. When the microprocessor was invented, electronics hobbyists seized on it with delight. Building a computer's central processing unit was too big a project for most hobbyists, but the microprocessor allowed them to buy the CPU off the shelf, then add the memory and peripherals necessary to turn it into a general-purpose computer. In 1975, the first microcomputer went on the market: the Altair 8800, which was sold as a kit. Soon after that, preassembled micros began to appear. The early ones were too small to do much with, and the general public paid them little attention. Large mainframes running timesharing systems were still the preferred computer for any serious work.

Because microcomputers—which later began to be called personal computers—were first adopted by hobbyists, a culture of sharing information and helping each other grew up around them. The owners of a particular machine would establish a user group that met on a regular basis to exchange tips and software (usually programs that their members had written). Although the Internet has reduced the need for user groups, the culture of sharing and mutual support is still very much part of the personal computing world.

As soon as personal computers became available, people began writing games for them. Radio Shack's TRS-80 was one of the most popular machines, as was the Commodore PET, which I owned. Most early machines were able to run BASIC programs, so some games were ported over from the mainframes. The (completely unauthorized) Star Trek game I mentioned in the Introduction was among the best. Computing magazines of the late '70s and early '80s often published entire printouts of game programs written in BASIC. Small game companies appeared, selling their games on floppy disks or cassette tapes stuck inside a zip-lock bag with a photocopied page of instructions.

The early computer game industry grew slowly. The machines were small and expensive, and, more importantly, most of them could only display text or rudimentary graphics. Most people felt no need to own one and couldn't imagine what they would do with it if they did. If kids wanted interactive entertainment, they could go down to the arcade or play on their home console machines, which offered a much more exciting experience.

WAR STORIES

Back in the old days, the genres were not as well defined; the teams were smaller and more intimate. You knew we were part of something revolutionary in bringing interactive entertainment to people. Most people involved were passionate, naïve, and idealistic, and you did not see as much of the hard-nosed business tactics prevalent today. You could bring a game to market in a 9-to-18-month period, and do it with under 10 man years of effort (current projects can be 100–300 man years of effort). It was a narrow hobbyist market, aimed at the smart, early adopter, high-tech consumers.

—Gordon Walton, Vice President, Maxis/Electronic Arts

THE REBIRTH OF CONSOLE GAMES

In 1986, two years after the crash of the console game industry, a Japanese company, little-known in America, brought out a new home console machine called the Nintendo Entertainment System. The retailers were skeptical, but in the end, Nintendo almost single-handedly rebuilt the home console industry and made their name synonymous with video games. People who have never heard of a Microsoft Xbox or a Sony Playstation will immediately know what you're talking about if you say the words "Nintendo machine."

Nintendo made three important changes to the way that the games were produced and sold. First, they strictly controlled who could and could not make games for their machine. Nintendo does not allow just anyone to publish for their systems: they want to know that the publisher is reputable and will stand behind its products. There will never be any fly-by-night publishers for Nintendo systems (as there were for the Atari).

Second, they instituted quality standards. It's not enough just to have a license from Nintendo; if you publish for their machine, you must submit your game to them for rigorous testing before they will allow it to be sold. Many independent publishers grumble about this, since Nintendo also publishes games of their own and the testing process gives them an advance look at what their competitors are doing. Nevertheless, Nintendo considers that their own reputation is at stake with every game. They won't allow shoddy, buggy products to go out with their logo on them.

Third, Nintendo instituted content standards. Not unlike Walt Disney, they wanted to be perceived as producers of entertainment for children. When people thought "Nintendo," the company wanted them to think "safe for kids" at the same time. To that end, for many years they had a strict policy against showing any blood, and they limited the kinds of violence that could be depicted. Again, independent publishers fretted under these regulations.

A by-product of these rules is that they tend to restrict the total number of games for the Nintendo that are on the market at any given time. If there were a glut of Nintendo games, all very similar to one another, it would drive down prices and could potentially lead to another crash just like the first one.

These policies were the path to Nintendo's fortune, and the home console game industry was reborn. In the years since then, every company making a console machine has adopted similar rules, and the industry has continued to grow. At this point, another crash seems unlikely; or if there is one, it will be caused by different factors.

THE IBM PC ARRIVES

The personal computer side of the game industry continued to grow slowly in the late 1970s. The Apple II, Commodore 64, and Amiga helped a lot; they were popular, well-designed machines with color displays. But because relatively few people felt they needed a computer in their lives, home computers were still considered luxuries (if they were expensive) or toys (if they were cheap). One famous name was missing from the personal computing world.

IBM finally introduced its microcomputer in 1982, primarily as a machine for small businesses, and at last the general public began to take personal computing seriously. People who wouldn't have considered buying a computer before then were willing to do so if it had IBM's name on it. And since the IBM machine had an open standard, its design could be copied by others. This made the IBM PC (and its clones) a runaway success.

Unfortunately, the original PC was badly designed for gaming. It was introduced with a very weak color graphics board and no sound capability except a speaker that could only beep. On the other hand, it was a 16-bit machine when the others around it were 8-bit machines, so it was capable of addressing more RAM and running a good deal faster than its competition. And it was too popular to ignore.

The Macintosh has never been that popular a machine for games, despite the fact that its hardware and operating system are extraordinarily well designed. The first Macs had small black and white screens, and this worked against using them for gaming. The Mac was also a good deal more expensive than the PC. Despite the introduction of color and full-size screens a few years later, the Mac has never caught on with the gamers in the same way that the PC did.

With the introduction of better color graphics cards for the PC, and also a new digital sound card, personal computer game development took off. PC games were still nowhere near as profitable as console games, but they remained solid sellers throughout the 1980s, aimed at a somewhat different market than console games. Home consoles were still definitely considered toys, and the games for them were correspondingly simpler and more focused on action than strategy.

THE CD-ROM CHANGES EVERYTHING

In the early 1990s, a great change swept through the personal computer industry. The compact disc arrived as a data storage medium.

INSIDE iNFO The difference between then and now is this: Back in The Day, people would say, "George, we're going to make a great game." Then, one day, they started saying, "George, we're going to make a demo that's going to blow those investors away." Demo-making for investors is a totally different activity than game-making.
—*George Alistair Sanger, Legendary Audio Guy, The Fat Man*

Up to that time, the standard portable storage device was the floppy disk, which holds a little over a megabyte of information. The compact disc can store over 650 megabytes of data, and it can be manufactured more quickly and cheaply than a floppy can. Since they weren't writeable (at the time), compact discs weren't of any use to the consumer for storing their own data, but for software publishers, they were an ideal distribution medium. They also had the advantage (again, at the time) of being uncopyable. For a while, they virtually eliminated the kind of casual piracy that was common among computer owners.

CD-ROMs changed the PC game landscape enormously and, a little later, the console game landscape as well. It was now possible to create really large games. About the largest number of floppy disks ever shipped with a game was 12, for *Ultima Underworld II*, which together amounted to 25 megabytes of data once they were all decompressed. Today, a single compact disc can hold 26 times that much information, even without data compression. CD-ROMs allowed games to include photorealistic graphics, high-quality sound, and even small movies. One of the first games to take advantage of this new technology was called *The 7th Guest,* and it was so spectacular in its day that people bought CD-ROM drives just to be able to play it.

INTERACTIVE MOVIES COME ... AND GO

In the mid 1990s, a number of Hollywood studios entered the game business. They already owned a lot of audiovisual content from their movies and television shows, and they thought that computer games would be an easy way for them to make more money out of this material. It was not the first time that Hollywood had gotten into the game industry. During the video game boom of the late 1970s, several movie studios had started game development divisions, but most of them got their fingers burned in the crash and never came back. By 1994, some were ready to try again. A number of people in the game industry were quite excited about the prospect of working with Hollywood, and so a new game concept was born, the "interactive movie." A number of interactive movies were produced, and some of them met with considerable financial success. Taking advantage of the CD-ROM, they presented pictures and sound that were better than anything seen before.

After the initial excitement was over, however, the interactive movie was abandoned as a product concept. The biggest problem was the cost of producing all the video needed for a branching storyline. Back when games were all text you could write large numbers of scenes for very little money, but when it became necessary to film them all, the cost was prohibitive. In addition, the CD-ROM, large as it is, still doesn't have enough room for all the video that a truly branching storyline requires. As a result, the storylines of most interactive movies didn't branch very much—which meant that they weren't really very interactive. The term "interactive movie" oversold the concept without really delivering on its promise, and nowadays few games are called that. Today, video is used mostly for the opening and closing sequences in a game, or as transitions between levels.

3-D GRAPHICS HARDWARE REINVENTS ACTION GAMING

Until the mid 1990s, the only games to use 3-D environments were vehicle simulations: flight simulators and the occasional racing game. A few games "faked it" successfully, most notably *Doom*. But displaying a true 3-D environment, in which you can move and look in all directions, requires a lot of computing power. Action games avoided using them because they needed the CPU for other things. The standard of the day was the side-scroller, a game in which a character moved from left to right in a two-dimensional world.

3-D graphics hardware, adopted first by the PC and then by console machines, changed all that. In a 3-D accelerator, a special-purpose processor takes over the work of computing and displaying the environment. This frees up the CPU to do other things, so games can be richer and deeper. 3-D accelerators were a boon to vehicle simulators, but their greatest benefit was to action games such as *Quake* and *Half-Life*. Instead of watching a character move left and right in a flat space, players could run around fully three-dimensional worlds at high speed, viewing the landscape in the first person. The technology makes games more immersive; it gives players the sense of being *in* the world rather than just looking at it.

THE ONLINE EXPLOSION

In the mid 1980s, a few PC games began to allow networked play. Most only supported two players, and required them to phone each other directly via modem. Unfortunately, incompatibilities between modem settings made this process awkward and error-prone. A few other games could be played over local area networks, but at the time, LANs only existed in offices, so this was not an important selling point. The most common networked games of the day were specialized ones built to work with proprietary information services like America Online and CompuServe. (I worked on one of these myself, *RabbitJack's Casino* for America Online, a suite of four games that allowed players to play poker, blackjack, bingo, and even a slot machine together.) The networks charged high prices (sometimes as much as $18 an hour) to use them.

The Internet changed all that dramatically and forever. The Internet wasn't designed for gaming, so it has some technical disadvantages over proprietary game networks, but these are more than made up for by its wide availability. The Internet gave game developers a common worldwide standard for data communications, and relieved the publishers of the burden of designing and maintaining their own networks. Networked gaming suddenly became easy and cheap. Now you can play dozens of online games for free on the World Wide Web, and it's easy to find opponents with Internet-based matchmaking services like Battle.Net.

The next big step forward was the creation of the massively-multiplayer online role-playing game (MMORPG), sometimes also called a *persistent world* because they continue to exist even while you're logged off. People have been playing online role-playing games (multi-user dungeons, or MUDs) for many years, but most of them are text-based and that limits their appeal. 3DO, a publisher, created the first graphical online RPG, *Meridian 59,* but the first big success was Electronic Arts' *Ultima Online.* Based on a universe that was already familiar to many gamers, UO was a runaway hit and demand for it almost overwhelmed EA's ability to support the game. Not long after that, Sony introduced *EverQuest* and Microsoft offered up *Asheron's Call*, both highly popular. Another new type of interactive entertainment was born.

WRAP-UP

You've probably noticed that most of these changes have been brought about by new hardware of one kind or another: first the microprocessor, then the CD-ROM, the graphics accelerator, and the Internet. The game industry has had purely creative advances as well, but they haven't been so dramatic.

There are two reasons why hardware makes such an impact. First, the computer is such a new entertainment medium that any change to it has a big effect on the kinds of things we can do. By comparison, the movies have had 80 years to settle into a fairly stable format: 35mm film. While filmmaking still undergoes advances, they don't dramatically redefine the way movies look every single year. The game industry is still where the movies were when they first moved from the nickelodeon to the screen. We're inventing new techniques all the time, and it's reflected in the games we play.

Second, games are primarily about interactivity, and computing hardware is what makes interactivity possible. Since the power of the hardware is growing at a rapid rate, it makes sense that interactivity itself is changing rapidly as well. The CD-ROM gave us mass storage; the graphics accelerator gave us spectacular sights; the Internet allowed us to play together conveniently. Who knows what the next big advance will be?

As I said at the beginning of this chapter, the history of the game business explains why it works the way it does—why PC game programmers tend to share information and console programmers don't, why not just anybody can make a console game, and why full-motion video, once seen as the most desirable feature of video gaming, is now out of fashion. Now that you're familiar with its background, we can move on to the next part of the story: the game industry today.

CHAPTER

2

A World of Games

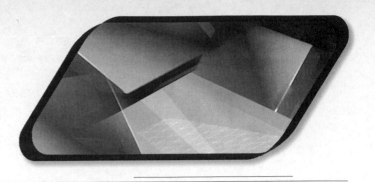

THE interactive entertainment industry is actually composed of several different businesses, and some of them have little contact with the others. "Interactive entertainment" can mean anything from $5 handheld devices to multimillion-dollar installations in a theme park. They differ in a variety of ways: how they're manufactured, how they're distributed, what they cost and who buys them. What matters to you, however, is the fact that they all need game developers to design and build the games. If you want to get a job in the industry, you need to know what kinds of products there are, because you might prefer to work with one kind over another.

PERSONAL COMPUTER GAMES

PC games have a lot in common with their near cousins, home console games, but there are some important differences as well. As we saw in Chapter 1, the two kinds of devices originated in two different ways, and this has some influence on the way they're developed, even today. PC games were first created by individual programmers for fun, often in a spirit of cooperation. Console games were first created by toy and arcade-game companies—both fiercely competitive industries—very much for profit.

A PC game runs on a machine that costs anywhere from $500 to $4000. That means that the machine is not a toy, and although it may be used exclusively by a kid, an adult, or at least a teenager, was involved in its purchase. You can't let a small child use a PC unsupervised; it's too fragile. In the home, PCs are normally installed in a home office or den. This is one of the most important things that distinguishes the personal computer from the home video game console. A PC is designed to be used by one person at a time. It's usually set up with a viewing distance of 12 to 24 inches in mind, generally on a desk with a single chair in front of it. A game console, on the other hand, is usually in a living room (or a kid's bedroom) attached to a TV that's placed so several people can see it at once. This important distinction has a major effect on the kinds of games that are designed for the two types of machines.

As a gaming device, the PC has certain important advantages. It always has a hard disk—a large, writeable storage medium. It also has a keyboard and a mouse, which means you can design a game with a fairly complex user interface; almost certainly a modem; and a high-resolution screen—generally quite a lot higher resolution than a color TV set. In addition, you can usually count on the machine having a reasonably fast processor and a fair amount of RAM. Although there are variations, most PCs are more powerful computers than the console machines available at the same time.

Another important technical advantage that PC games have over home console games is that they can be updated or patched. Since the game resides on the hard drive, it's easy for the player to download bug fixes and add-on modules over the Internet. The hard disk also means that the game program can actually be larger than the available memory on the machine: segments of it can be swapped in and out at high speed.

From a creative standpoint, the greatest benefit of the personal computer is that anyone can write a game for it. On the PC, you don't have to obtain the approval of the machine's manufacturer. PC developers are free to explore themes and subject matter that a console manufacturer would never allow.

The great Achilles' heel of personal computers, as far as game developers are concerned, is that they don't have a standard set of features. Games written for personal computers have to run on processors of different speeds, with varying amounts of RAM and varying video resolutions. Ever since the 3-D hardware accelerator was introduced, more and more games have taken advantage of this useful piece of equipment, but they, too, vary considerably in speed and power. Even with Direct X, the standard hardware interface provided by Microsoft Windows, it's not uncommon for a game to break down with a given piece of hardware. The manufacturer's drivers can be buggy, or the game can be trying to do something that that particular card doesn't do very well.

Because the Macintosh's hardware and operating system are both designed by the same company, it doesn't have this problem as often. Unfortunately, the Mac is nowhere near as big a market for games as the PC.

Both PC games and home console games are generally sold in retail stores to the end user. That means that marketing and distributing them is fairly similar, but the games themselves tend to be somewhat different because of the different features of the machines. The following table shows a comparison:

	Personal Computers	Home Game Consoles
Hardware standardization	Some	Strict
Manufacturer approval	Not required	Required
Data storage media	Large	Small or nonexistent
Display device	High-resolution monitor	Color TV
Basic input devices	Keyboard, mouse, joystick, controller (less common)	Standardized controller
Network capability	Modems to broadband	Modems, broadband coming

	Personal Computers	Home Game Consoles
Usage profile	Awkward for more than one person to use	Easy for more than one person to use
Distribution media	DVDs, CDs, the Internet	DVDs, CDs, cartridges
Distribution mechanisms	Retail, bundling, shareware	Retail, rentals

HOME CONSOLE GAMES

The home console video game is the most common and most financially successful form of interactive entertainment in the world. If a game exists in both a personal computer version and a home console version, chances are the home console version will out-sell the PC version by three to ten times as much—even if the price is the same or higher for the home console version. The main explanation for this is that there are simply more console machines in homes around the world than there are personal computers. A home console machine costs between $100 and $300. Personal computers cost five to ten times that much. As a result, more families can afford home consoles, and they can afford more games for them.

There are two reasons why home console machines cost so much less than PCs. The first, and most important, reason is that the manufacturers are not trying to make money on the sales of the machines themselves. They sell the machines to retailers at very near their cost in order to get as many of them out to the public as possible. This way, the manufacturers make their money on the games that go into the machines instead. It's the same principle as giving away razors, but selling the blades. And even if the manufacturer does not publish all the games themselves—and none of them do—they charge the other publishers a license to be allowed to publish games for their machine. That way they make money even if another publisher's games sell better than the manufacturer's own ones do.

The second reason is that home console video game machines are designed to be as inexpensive as possible while still meeting the performance criteria needed for a successful product. The machines have no floppy drive, no keyboard, and no monitor, and as of this writing only the Xbox includes a hard disk drive. They usually have less RAM than the average PC—typically 64 megabytes or less, while most modern PCs have 128 megabytes or more. Their sound hardware is less versatile. And in particular, they contain much less powerful microprocessors. The fastest console available today, the Xbox, uses a 733MHz processor. The fastest PCs sold at the consumer level use a 3GHz processor, and it's more sophisticated besides.

Home console machines used to use ROM cartridges as their distribution media, but these have been replaced by CDs and DVDs in the current generation of consoles.

Cartridges are slow and expensive to manufacture, and hold only a fraction of the amount of data that an optical disc can. Their big advantage is that they are rugged, which makes them ideal for children, and comparatively difficult to pirate. The cost difference, however, is unanswerable. Nintendo continued to hold out for cartridges through the previous generation of consoles, but they finally abandoned them for the GameCube.

Developing for home console machines is somewhat different than developing for personal computers. To start with, the machine is not itself a general-purpose computer, so you can't write the program on the machine you're programming for, as you would on a PC. Instead, you have to buy a "development station"—typically a specialized version of the machine that contains hardware for communicating with a PC. You write the game on the PC, then download it into the development station over the hardware link. These "dev stations," as they're called, can cost from $5,000 to $25,000. This puts them out of reach of most amateurs, and they're further out of reach because the hardware manufacturers will only sell them to developers whom they have licensed to produce games for their machines. In short, it's almost impossible for an ordinary person to develop commercial games for home console machines. Sony has recently begun to allow you to program the PS2 using their Linux kit, but since an ordinary PS2 does not run Linux, you can't sell the programs to the general public.

INSIDE iNFO Until recently, it was impossible to get experience programming a console machine without a dev station. However, the Microsoft Xbox is based on Windows and PC technology, so PC programming is good preperation for Xbox development. Sony is also beginning to allow unlicensed PS2 programming using their Linux kit. The whole situation is in a state of flux, but don't worry too much about this. As a new programmer, it's more important that you get a thorough grounding in the key game programming specialties—graphics, AI, user interfaces, networking, and so on—than it is to gain experience on a particular machine.

Unlike a personal computer, home console machines typically have a more rudimentary operating system, stored in the machine's ROM. Anyone programming a console machine is somewhat closer to the "bare metal" than they are with a PC, which has both advantages and disadvantages. Since you are guaranteed that all consoles will have exactly the same hardware, programmers don't face the compatibility problems that they do on PCs. However, it does mean that the programming is more tricky and time-consuming.

Games in the International Market

Video games are an international phenomenon. The United States is the largest single market for them in the world, but the big manufacturers and publishers are all multinational. Sony and Nintendo are, of course, Japanese companies. Eidos, publisher of the *Tomb Raider* line, is British, and Infogrames is French. For a game to be a true blockbuster, it must be a success in Europe and Asia as well as America. The process of modifying a game to make it suitable for a different country is called "localization," and is a task often given to companies that specialize in it. There are both technical and cultural implications.

Technical

Because home game consoles use a television as their video output device, they have to be manufactured in different ways for different parts of the world. The television standard used in the United States and Japan is called NTSC, which stands for National Television Standards Committee, the American organization that originally defined it. It displays 525 horizontal lines approximately 30 times a second to make up an image. The standard used in most of the rest of the world is called PAL (for Phase Alternation Lines), and it displays 625 lines 25 times a second. The shape of the screen is the same in either case, so PAL television looks better because it shows finer detail—in computer terms, its pixels are smaller. However, it flickers more. Also, PAL comes in several variants that aren't fully compatible, and France and many former French possessions use yet another standard called SECAM, a further complication.

The other big technical issue is language. English and other western languages can be stored with one byte per character, but many Asian languages require two. If a western company wants to publish its games in Asia, its programmers have to prepare for this in advance. It's also important not to build any text directly into the graphics, because there's no way to change it afterward. And, of course, any voiceover narration must be supplied in different versions for different languages.

Cultural

You might think that video gaming is so new that it hasn't had time to form divergent cultures in different countries, but you would be wrong. For one thing, there are cultural motifs that are much older than games but still apply to them. For example, in the West, black is the color of death, but in China it's white. Red denotes good luck in China, and has a particular significance in certain contexts.

There are also cultural variations in the kinds of games that people prefer. Online games are hugely popular in South Korea, even more so than single-player games, but they're mostly played in Internet cafés rather than at home. Japanese games seem to have much richer storylines than their American equivalents. In Germany, intricately detailed management games are especially popular, while the French are much more tolerant of nudity than Americans are, and so on. If you want to make a truly multi-national game, there's a great deal to know.

The hardware of a home console machine has usually been designed to minimize components and maximize cost savings. As a result, developing for them is often further complicated by shortcuts taken by the hardware designers. For example, the Sega CD player, which was an add-on device to the original Sega Genesis, had no way of directly informing the program when a new batch of data had been read off the CD. In a personal computer, this is handled by something called an "interrupt line"—a special wire from the CD drive to the microprocessor to inform it that some new data is ready. On the Sega CD, there was no such line. Instead, the microprocessor had to constantly "poll"—that is, ask the CD drive—whether the new data was ready or not. Obviously, this takes time out from whatever the program is really supposed to be doing. If the hardware designers had included an interrupt line, the program wouldn't have had to poll, and it would have run faster. But the extra interrupt line would have added a few cents to the cost of the machine. With each little design change, the costs add up.

Finally, because a home console machine typically uses an inexpensive microprocessor (no 3GHz Intel Pentium 4s here!), the developer has to write more code to do the same amount of work that a more expensive processor could do with less code.

You would think, with all these disadvantages for the developer and publisher, that they would shy away from home console machines. But the lure of the money is well worth it. When you can sell three to ten times as many copies of a game by putting it on a console, it's worth the trouble.

How the Xbox Changed the Rules

The Microsoft Xbox is the first home console to be designed in the United States since the Atari Jaguar in the mid '90s—and the Jaguar was a flop. Microsoft defied a lot of conventional wisdom with the Xbox. Since it's a PC-oriented company, they decided to make a PC-oriented console. The Xbox's microprocessor is functionally identical to a 733MHz Pentium III, and it runs a special version of the Windows operating system. It has a faster CPU and more RAM than any other console today, and it includes Universal Serial Bus and network connections normally only found on PCs. The Xbox is also the only one of the current generation of consoles that can display graphics at HDTV resolutions. Most importantly of all, the Xbox comes with a hard disk drive, which means that it can be put to other uses as well. It wouldn't be hard to convert an Xbox into a digital video recorder, for example.

Microsoft went to all this trouble because they knew they were taking on giants in the console business. If they were going to beat Sony and Nintendo in the marketplace, they had to have a lot of great games for the Xbox, fast. To achieve this, Microsoft's strategy was to build a machine that was easy and familiar to develop for. The Xbox isn't really a conventional console at all, but a PC sitting inside a console-shaped case. However, that doesn't guarantee sales with consumers. For the most part, they don't care what's inside the machine as long as the games look great and there are plenty of them. Only time will tell if the Xbox can survive the console wars.

ARCADE GAMES

Arcade games are still popular despite the prevalence of home video games, because the video arcade has a social aspect as well as a game-playing aspect. It gives kids a place to go, play games, and hang around together without their parents. Arcade machines are also common anywhere that kids might be stuck with nothing to do, such as airports and hotels, and they're popular moneymakers for resorts and theme parks as well.

The people who buy arcade games—that is, the machines themselves—are really only interested in one thing, the amount of money that they make in a given time. Arcade game design is strongly driven by this consideration. An arcade game should take no longer than three to ten minutes to play, and unlike its predecessor, the pinball machine, it gets harder as you play.

Arcade games also have to be reasonably easy to learn, although the machine can make a lot of money by making its players learn the hard way. The designer has to carefully balance this—if the game is too frustrating at first, people simply won't play it and the game will be a commercial failure; if it's too easy, people will be able to play for a long time without putting any more coins in. In any case, it can't be the kind of game that requires a manual or much detailed explanation. Arcade games are a special subset of video games in general, because there are so many constraints on their design. Shigeru Miyamoto, who invented Donkey Kong (and with it the whole Mario universe), switched from arcade machines to console machines because he found the requirement to generate "coin-drop" to be too limiting.

Developers in the arcade game industry need many of the same talents and skills as in the retail game industry, but the two businesses are otherwise quite different. Since arcade games are sold to arcade owners rather than to end users, they have separate trade shows and other professional events.

ONLINE GAMES

Online games—that is, games which can *only* be played online—are a rapidly growing segment of the market. People like the social interaction of playing with other people, and they like the challenge of playing against a human rather than an artificial opponent. There is an enormous number of game-show style games available for free on the Internet; they're cheap to develop and quick to download. Most of them make their money through advertising, because they don't offer a rich enough experience to charge for.

The other branch of proprietary online games is the persistent world that I talked about in the last chapter. These require vast investments to build, and ongoing expenses to maintain, and they make their money through monthly subscriptions. Persistent worlds need just about every skill the game industry uses: ordinary game programmers and also programmers skilled at working with networks and servers; artists, animators, and musicians; game designers, level designers, and writers. And unlike retail games, where the developers usually move on to another project as soon as the previous one is done, persistent worlds need people on a continuing basis. It's a little like the difference between a movie and a theme park: the cast and crew of a movie can go home once the filming is done, but a theme park needs employees every day that it's open—and it needs to change and expand from time to time to keep people coming in.

Online games present a number of design and development challenges that don't exist in games that are only played on one machine. The game must be scrupulously fair, and it should not be possible for players to manipulate the system to gain an unfair advantage. It also needs to respond well to the sudden disappearance of one of the players, since people can log on and off at any time. Online games require facilities for people to get together and talk about the game, "brag boards" that show who are the best players, customer service agents to help solve problems and moderate disputes, and a great many other features that non-networked video games don't have to bother with.

Now that game consoles are starting to have modems, online games will become important for them as well. However, the primary reason for playing an online game is to communicate with other people, and at the moment that still means typing. Since consoles don't routinely come with keyboards, this will limit their appeal. As customers move to broadband Internet connections, we can expect to see voice communication between online players, but that is still a few years off. In any case, online games for consoles are in their infancy at the moment, and promise to be an area of significant growth in the years to come.

HANDHELD DEVICES

The category of handheld devices can be broken down into several subspecies: toys that only play one game; programmable machines like the Game Boy; personal digital assistants (PDAs) such as the Palm Pilot; even cellular telephones. What they have in common is that they're small. They have a slow CPU, a small amount of RAM, and a small screen. Their buttons are built into the device instead of being on a detachable controller. This also means that the games for them tend to be single-player games: like the PC, handhelds are optimized for one person to use at a time.

The market for games for handheld devices is growing steadily, and they remain an important source of employment for developers. However, the games are severely limited by their hardware. If your goal is to work on big, spectacular (and expensive) products, you'd be better off with a different kind of game, such as…

LOCATION-BASED ENTERTAINMENT

Location-based entertainment (LBE) is a catchall term for computerized entertainment that the customer goes to, rather than purchasing and taking home. Taken broadly, location-based entertainment could include arcades, but the term is really used to mean something larger and more specialized. One kind of LBE is the BattleTech Centers. These are storefront operations that players come to, usually in small groups. The BattleTech Center consists of a number of enclosed capsules that simulate the driver's seat of a kind of tank; the players' machines are all networked together, and they can play cooperatively or competitively as they choose. Another kind of LBE is a theme park attraction with a large computerized component. This kind of equipment is highly specialized, often unique, and extremely expensive. Frequently, it has been commissioned for a specific location. A good example is the "ride" at the Luxor Hotel in Las Vegas, which involves sitting in a bank of seats mounted on hydraulic pistons while watching a movie. The sudden swoops and jerks of the seats are timed to accompany the events taking place in the movie.

The customer for the LBE experience is, of course, the end user, but the customer for the equipment itself is the company that is running the attraction. What they want to deliver is a highly intense experience in a short amount of time that they can move a lot of people through—essentially, an electronic roller coaster. The owner of an LBE has to balance a number of factors. The experience can't be too short, or the player won't feel he's gotten his money's worth; it can't be too long, or the line will move too slowly and the people waiting will get frustrated. It has to cost a lot because the initial investment and maintenance costs are so high, but not so much that people don't come. And, of course, it has to be in a convenient location.

In my experience, most LBEs are extremely action-packed, fast-paced experiences. This appeals to the kids who are their primary customers, but it has a secondary, pragmatic value. If you're going to offer an entertainment that lasts, say, ten minutes at the most, it needs to be packed with thrills every second of the way. It should be almost exhausting—so intense that you wouldn't even *want* to be in it any longer than that. That way the customer leaves feeling certain he's gotten his money's worth.

GAMBLING EQUIPMENT

Gambling (or, as the gambling industry prefers to call it, "gaming") equipment is a specialized market of its own. Video poker and other kinds of electronic gambling games are not manufactured by the same people who publish video games, and obviously they're only purchased by casinos in places where gambling is legal. These machines have a number of specialized requirements. For one thing, they have to be extremely rugged. The games are designed to be played very quickly indeed—a typical game lasts a few seconds at most. Finally, the games are very carefully regulated by government authorities to make sure they're fair. If a video blackjack machine states that it plays single-deck blackjack, it must really simulate a 52-card deck, going all the way through before reshuffling. Even the software that generates the random numbers used for the shuffle must be approved by the casino regulators, to make sure it remains truly random and doesn't fall into a predictable pattern.

MISCELLANEOUS GAMES

Video games are turning up in a variety of other places: in seat backs in airplanes and in built-in entertainment centers in cars. There have also been efforts to set up in-air gambling systems that use an airline passenger's credit card number as a source of money. As publicly available computers appear in more and more places, we can expect to see games in them as well. These are usually considered specialty or niche markets, but they're all part of the industry's growth, and represent job opportunities for game developers.

GAMES VERSUS MULTIMEDIA

Once the CD-ROM was developed and it was possible to ship 650 megabytes of data at a time, many new kinds of software products arose. Whole encyclopedias could be put on CDs, as well as all kinds of other libraries. Pictures, movies, and music could all be incorporated into software without raising the cost of the distribution medium. Thus was the multimedia industry born.

Unfortunately, over the course of the next few years, it became clear that the market for specialized libraries of content was pretty limited. If you were interested in the music of Antonio Vivaldi, for instance, you probably already owned several music CDs with recordings of his. If you were interested in his life, you might already own a book about him. For most people, there was no need to buy a piece of software about Vivaldi as well. After an initial period of explosive growth, the multimedia industry shrank considerably, and a good many providers went out of business.

The other thing that severely challenged the multimedia business was the World Wide Web. As soon as it became possible to look up information for free on the Web, people stopped buying CDs that contained the same information. Nowadays, the majority of multimedia products are widely used reference works: encyclopedias, dictionaries, atlases and almanacs. Often, they are copyrighted works, like the *Encyclopaedia Britannica,* which aren't available on the Web, or are only available on a subscription basis. For highly graphics-intensive applications, like maps or libraries of photographs, it can still be more convenient to have that information on a CD than to download it over the net. And for travelers who don't always have access to the Net, it can be very convenient to use a CD. But for specialized reference works, the Web is nearly always faster and cheaper.

Although the game and multimedia industries have certain things in common—they both produce mass-market retail software products, and both use a lot of graphics and sound—their customers and their retail strategies are quite different. Games are entertainment, and they require a lot of software engineering to create the simulation and the artificial intelligence they require. Multimedia is really about presentation of data. Ninety percent of the work of developing a multimedia product goes into developing an efficient user interface.

I won't be discussing multimedia products further in this book. Getting a job as a developer in the multimedia industry is not that different from getting a job as a developer in the game industry.

WRAP-UP

As you can see, the term "video game" actually encompasses several different kinds of games and different markets where they're sold. The interactive entertainment industry consists of many businesses, some of which have very little contact with the others. What they have in common is the fact that they all use the same technology to entertain people: a computer running a game program. To build that software, as well as all its art and animation, music and sound, these companies need game developers: people like you.

The market is growing rapidly for PC games as more PCs enter the home, especially online games of various kinds. The popularity of consoles continues to increase as well, though perhaps not quite so quickly, but there are already so many consoles in homes that you can't expect the same rate of growth. Handhelds, too, earn steadily even though the games aren't as sophisticated. There's considerable uncertainty in the short term about cell phone games, although in the longer term, especially with the new 3G "always connected" phones, the handheld and cell phone may merge into a single device. The emergence of Indian casinos has created a growing demand for gambling machines. About the only part of gaming that seems fairly flat is arcade games.

It's a good time to become a game developer!

CHAPTER

3

How the Game Industry Functions

BEFORE you walk into an interview, you should have a general idea of how the game industry functions. A lot

of things about the industry only make sense if you know where the money comes from and where it goes to. And although you're probably interested in interactive entertainment because it's fun to play and fun to build, the person interviewing you for a job will be used to thinking about it as a commercial enterprise. The more you know about the business aspects of the game industry, the better you'll look to them.

SOME FUNDAMENTALS

For our purposes I'm going to talk about the retail video game industry rather than arcade games, gambling machines, and so on, because the retail business is the largest segment of the market. It's also the most complicated. Before we get into the essentials, though, there are three important facts to keep in mind.

 **INSIDE INFO** Fact #1: The game industry is not a technology business, but an entertainment business with a technology component.

This is an important distinction. Technology businesses are those which depend primarily on technological advancement for their prosperity. They include engineering firms, silicon chip fabricators, electronic equipment manufacturers, and tool vendors of various kinds. For the most part, these companies sell their products to other industries, not to the general public—for example, companies that make medical diagnostic equipment sell it to hospitals. The fortunes of technology businesses are often interrelated. If there's a shortage of gallium arsenide, a key component of semiconductor electronics, chip manufacturers will suffer, and this can create a ripple effect throughout the rest of the high-technology industry.

Video games are different. New technology certainly helps us build bigger and better games, but if there were no advances in technology for a while, the publishers would continue to produce new products. That's because this is an entertainment business, and it's driven by creativity as well as technology. Working in the game industry has certain things in common with high technology, but it also has things in common with movies and television. This melding of creativity and technology makes the video game uniquely powerful as an entertainment medium, but uniquely difficult to develop as well.

 **Fact #2: The game business in the U.S. and Europe has a seasonal cycle based on Christmas.**

This is another way in which the interactive entertainment business is different from the high-technology business. People don't give lab equipment as Christmas gifts, so the people who sell lab equipment don't have to worry about what time of year it's released. But the game business is a lot like the toy business in this respect. Nearly 50 percent of the game industry's revenues come from pre-Christmas sales, and this imposes a schedule on game development for the rest of the year.

In practical terms, this means that a game should be shipped and on store shelves by the Friday after Thanksgiving, the biggest shopping day of the year in the United States. With this as a requirement, we can design a schedule by working backward (I've included one in Chapter 4). Of course, in countries where they don't have Thanksgiving, the Christmas shopping season starts at different times; and in countries where Christmas is not observed, the ideal ship date may be at another time of year altogether. However, it's true as a general rule that game sales don't do as well in the summer as they do in the winter, because people are enjoying outdoor activities rather than looking for ways to entertain themselves indoors.

Publishers don't schedule all their games to ship at Thanksgiving, of course; they need income all year round and not just in one quarter. They will look at their financial forecasts and decide on a ship date based on when they feel they need the money (among other factors). But if a game is supposed to ship for Christmas and doesn't for some reason, it's usually a serious problem.

There is one other class of games that doesn't ship at Thanksgiving, and that is sports games. Consumer interest in sports games closely parallels the sport that they're simulating, so ideally a game should ship a few weeks before the start of the game's regular season. A pro football simulation should ship in August, and a pro baseball simulation should ship in March.

The cyclical nature of the business imposes quite a burden on game development, for reasons that are explained in Fact #3.

 **Fact #3: The key difference between interactive media and non-interactive media is that interactive media require *engineering*.**

Engineering is a process of finding new ways to accomplish tasks. Most of the linear media don't require engineering. Books certainly don't, and although TV and movies do use engineering from time to time, especially in creating special effects, it's not an absolute requirement of the medium. It's possible to make a brilliant movie with good actors, a good script, a camcorder, and a sunny day.

But interactive entertainment is different. You cannot make *any* video game without doing engineering. Software engineering is the first and the most essential task of the game developer. It's the hub around which everything else revolves. If we apply a movie metaphor, the software is the projector, the means by which the pictures and the sound make it to the screen and the speakers. But unlike a movie projector, the software is different for each game. Imagine what moviemaking would be like if it were necessary to build a different, unique projector for each movie!

Worse yet, engineering is problem-solving, and problem-solving knows no timetable. Nobody really knows how long a given problem will take to solve. We can make educated guesses based on experience, but that's as close as we can get. And software engineering is particularly unpredictable, because as a discipline it's only about 50 years old and there are very few standard ways of doing anything. Ask ten software engineers how to solve a given problem and you will get ten different answers—or twenty. This uncertainty is one of the reasons that the Christmas timetable creates such problems for the game industry. In ordinary high technology, unaffected by Christmas, you ship a product when the engineering is finished—whenever that is. But in the game industry, you must complete a game in one year, or two years at the most, because you can't afford to miss Christmas. The Christmas selling season imposes an artificial deadline on what is essentially a process of indeterminate length.

The true nature of engineering—the unpredictability of problem-solving—is an issue that you *must* understand if you want to be a game developer. Video games may be entertainment just as books and movies and television are entertainment, but the game development process is fundamentally governed by the need to do engineering. Books and movies have more in common with one another than they do with video games.

TRACING A GAME TO ITS SOURCE

The path that a game takes, from its creation to the software store shelves, is a little like a river flowing to the sea. It starts as a small creek, and along the way various tributary streams flow into it. In order to explain the game business, I'm going to explore this river by traveling upstream, following the game back to its source. See Figure 3-1 for an illustration.

The Customer

The customer is someone who wants to buy a video game. You're probably one yourself. (If you aren't, and you've never bought a video game, you should consider

FIGURE 3-1

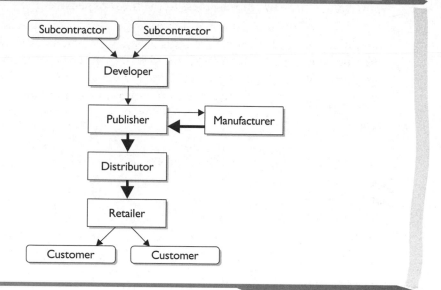

The game river

another career. Game companies like their employees to be enthusiastic gamers.) The customer either wants to buy the game for himself, or he wants to buy it as a present for someone else. Typically, he's going to spend between $20 and $70 on a first-class game, although there are smaller games that are cheaper and you can often find games a year or two old in a "bargain bin" going for $5–15.

This price range puts a video game in a certain class of entertainment. It's far more expensive than a box of dominoes, a deck of cards, or a jigsaw puzzle. It's a little more expensive than a board game. It's about the same price as a trip to the movies for the whole family, if you buy them all popcorn and soft drinks as well. It's cheaper than taking them to a baseball game, and much cheaper than taking them to a football game. On the other hand, it's much more expensive than watching broadcast TV, which is free at the point of delivery (the TV set). (We all pay for TV by purchasing advertised products, because the cost of the TV shows is built into the cost of the products.)

Video games normally give about 20–40 hours' worth of entertainment—some many more than that—which means that the cost of the entertainment is $1–2 an hour. This is a pretty good rate of return, given that the movie or the baseball game will be over in two or three hours but you can go on playing the video game for weeks if you want to, and your roommates and friends can play it, too.

The following table gives you a good idea of the relative cost of various forms of entertainment, from the cheapest to the most expensive:

	Cost to Buy/Play	Hours of Use	Cost/Hour
Playing cards	$2	∞	$0
Board game	$25	∞	$0
Broadcast TV	$0	∞	$0
Online game	$10/month	120/month (4 hours a day)	$0.08
Cable TV	$40/month	120/month (4 hours a day)	$0.33
Paperback book	$5	5	$1.00
Video game	$40	40	$1.00
Movie rental	$2	2	$1.00
Movie at cinema	$8.50/ticket	2	$4.25
Baseball game	$20/ticket	3	$6.67
Arcade game	$0.50/play	0.05/play (3 minutes)	$10.00
Live theater	$20/ticket	2	$10.00
Slot machine (adjusted for winnings)	$0.01/play	0.0008 (3 seconds)	$12.50
Pro football game	$50/ticket	3	$16.67
Opera	$100/ticket	3	$33.33

The Retailer

Most of the time, the customer buys the game from a retailer, although it is becoming more common for people to order games directly from the publishers. The retailer has bought the video game from a publisher or distributor (we'll get to them later) for a wholesale price that's about half the manufacturer's suggested retail price (MSRP), but the MSRP is always inflated. In practice, the retailer has typically marked up the price of the game from 10 to 50 percent above wholesale. The retailers can negotiate themselves a better wholesale price if they buy in really large quantities. A mom-and-pop store has to pay the full price, but a chain like Wal-Mart can get a better deal. Retailers have a lot of expenses. They have to pay not only for the game, but also to have it shipped to them; then they have to provide a warm, dry, secure, well-lit, attractive store to keep it in, and (theoretically) knowledgeable staff to help sell it. They have to use good judgment to guess which of the thousands of games available they want to sell. If a game turns out to be a dog, it'll sit there taking up shelf space that some other, more lucrative, product might be using.

Retailers expect that the publisher or distributor will spend a certain amount to market the game, and they may insist on some evidence of it before making a purchase. When a retailer is ordering copies of a game, they don't just want to know how cool it is, but also how much money the publisher is planning to put into TV and magazine advertising.

Retailers work with the publishers in other ways besides simply purchasing their games. The publishers often supply posters, fliers, stand-up displays, and other store decorations to the retailers free of charge. They may pay the retailer money to guarantee that their products are on the shelves at eye-level, not down near the floor. Publishers will also help pay for the retailer's newspaper ads and mass-mailings if their games are featured prominently. These kinds of deals are known as "co-marketing arrangements." Unlike an ordinary consumer purchase, where the deal is pretty much "take it or leave it," retailers' and wholesalers' business dealings are infinitely variable. The bigger the retailer is, the more likely they are to win concessions from the publishers.

There are, very roughly, three kinds of retailer: mail-order vendors, general merchandise stores, and software stores. *also online/streaming*

Mail-Order

Mail-order vendors offer the game at the cheapest price because they have no storefronts, only warehouses, and no customer service staff. If you buy from them, you can't ask their advice or look closely at the boxes. You also can't walk out with the game in your hand. Buying mail-order is definitely the best deal for the consumers, but only if they know exactly what they want and don't mind waiting three or four days to get it.

General Merchandise Stores

The next kind of retailer is a store that sells video games along with other products, and these can be either large or small. Wal-Mart, Office Depot, and even drugstores sometimes sell software. With them you often get a pretty fair price, and you can browse among the games and take one home with you immediately. However, they seldom have a big selection and they won't special order games that are out of stock. Also, their staff usually know nothing about the games, so you're still on your own as far as knowledgeable sales advice is concerned.

Software Stores

A specialty shop that only sells video games, or perhaps computer software in general, offers the best service and the widest selection to the customer. The sales people are specifically interested in computers, and it's their business to know which games are fun for what age groups and things like that. You'll probably pay a higher price if you shop at one of these stores, but you'll also have the opportunity to chat with someone knowledgeable and maybe even get to see a demo of the game before you buy it. The other advantage of specialty shops is that they will have the very latest games the first day they're available. For stores like Wal-Mart and Target, games are only a small part of their business and they don't have much incentive to carry up-to-the-minute stock. But specialty shops want to attract the hardcore gamers, and the hardcore gamers want the games as soon as they're out. If you have to have the very latest thing, go to a specialty shop.

A lot of people in the game industry started their careers working in such specialty shops. Selling video games isn't very glamorous, but it's an excellent way to learn a lot about games. A good many game testers and customer service representatives start off as sales people in computer stores, and both those jobs can be stepping stones into game development.

The Distributor

So who does the retailer buy the games from? Usually, it's the game's publisher, but sometimes it's an intermediate company called a distributor. A distributor is a company that does not either develop or publish games. That is, they don't build them, market them, or manufacture them, nor do they directly fund any of these activities. A distributor is a company that sells games to retailers on behalf of small publishers. The distributor also provides the warehouse space and the shipping. They take no credit for making the game, and they provide no after-sale service. They're purely middlemen. In fact, if there are any legal problems with the game, the publisher specifically agrees to indemnify the distributor in the event of a lawsuit. Since they have nothing to do with creating its content, the distributor isn't held accountable for it.

Publishers use distributors when they can't afford to have their own warehouse space, sales staff, and fulfillment operation. Using a distributor allows the publisher to concentrate on getting the games to market. The publisher turns the actual handling and selling over to the distributor and gives up a percentage of the wholesale price. If a publisher is small, this is often the only way they can get their products into stores. Distributors have long-term relationships with retailers that small publishers don't have, and can bring a game to the attention of a buyer for a big chain who might not make time for a small publisher.

Electronic Arts: A Game Industry Giant

It's worth taking a closer look at Electronic Arts, because it's one of the game industry's bigger success stories, and it does several different things at once.

EA was established as a publisher in 1982 by its charismatic founder, William "Trip" Hawkins. It sought out excellent game developers, signed contracts with them, and produced some truly groundbreaking early games: *Archon, Pinball Construction Set, Dr. J and Larry Bird Go One-on-One,* and others. Trip's motto was "simple, hot, and deep": games should be easy to learn to play (simple), exciting (hot), and provide rich, long-lasting gameplay, with new things to see and learn (deep).

Before long, however, EA began to hire developers to work in-house. They set up programming, art, and music departments and staffed them with some of the best people they could find. Sometimes they bought small development companies outright. They didn't stop doing contracts with external developers, however; they adopted a mixed approach, often doing their most valuable projects in-house where they could keep a close eye on them.

In the late '80s, Electronic Arts decided to capitalize on the strength of their sales force and enter the distribution business as well. If they were so good at selling their own games, why not sell other publishers' as well, in exchange for a cut of the revenue? They signed distribution deals with Lucasfilm Games (now LucasArts Entertainment), Strategic Simulations Inc., and a variety of other small publishers. So they actually occupied three different parts of the chain: development, publication, and distribution.

The two areas that EA *hasn't* gone into are retail sales, at one end, and hardware manufacturing at the other. They don't own software stores, and they never tried to build a game console of their own. Nor have they ever signed a deal to produce games exclusively for one machine. This way they're not dependent on a hardware manufacturer; if a console flops, as the Sega Saturn did, they can simply stop supporting it and carry on building games for its competitor.

EA has had its failures on occasion. They established a children's software group, EA*Kids, that was poorly managed and had to be shut down. They tried to get into the arcade game business, spent several million dollars, and got out again after their development efforts bogged down. They also backed Trip Hawkins' new company 3DO, which made a machine called the 3DO Multiplayer that turned out to be an over-hyped, overpriced failure. But EA has never bet so much money on one of these projects that it really hurt the company when it failed; and, in fact, by selling their 3DO stock at a judicious moment, they actually made money on the deal.

In recent years, EA has taken to buying up other publishers—Origin, Maxis, and Kesmai to name just a few—and then adding those companies' products to their own lineup. They've also gotten some great licensing deals, making games with the *Harry Potter, Lord of the Rings,* and *James Bond* brands. EA still doesn't have the money and power of a console manufacturer like Nintendo, but they are the largest independent publisher in America.

The Publisher

A publisher is a company that funds the development of new games and advertises them to the public. Of all the various company names which may appear on the game box, theirs will be the largest and the one that they want the customers to remember. So far as the publisher and the general public is concerned, it is *their* game—they paid for it to be developed; they put it on the market; they're held responsible for its content and ultimately, for its success or failure. Also, even if a different company developed it, it's very likely the publisher actually owns the copyright on the source code and the artwork—it is literally their property.

The publisher is the financial—though not necessarily the creative—heart of the game industry. They're the equivalent of book publishers in the book industry, or movie studios in the film industry. They decide what games will be funded for development. They also have the final word on content: since the publisher is paying for the game, they get to decide what's in it. Publisher employees who oversee the development process, and keep it on track, are called *producers,* and I'll talk about them and their jobs in the next chapter.

Some publishers develop their games themselves—that is, they have an in-house team of programmers, artists, audio engineers, and so on who actually build the games. This is called *internal development.* Other publishers have no developers on staff, preferring to publish games done by development companies under a contract, a process called *external development*. Many publishers work both ways at once, using internal development teams for some projects, and contracting with external developers for others.

So the customer buys from a retailer, the retailer buys from a distributor or publisher, and the publisher buys from—whom? Well, the publisher doesn't actually *buy* a game; rather, it pays for a game to be developed, and then it hires a manufacturer to produce copies of the game in quantity. If the publisher develops the game internally, it's paying the salaries of its employees; if the publisher uses an external development company, it pays them according to their contract. Usually the publisher pays the developer just enough money to build the game, with nothing left over (no profits), and then gives the developer a *royalty*—a percentage of the price of each copy that the publisher sells to the retailer. That way if the game is a huge hit, the developer stands to make a fortune on royalty payments. (It's actually more complicated than this, but I'll discuss development contracts in more detail in Chapter 4.)

The Internal/External Cycle

In my experience, publishers go through cycles of preferring internal and external developers. What usually happens is this. Suppose a publisher uses almost exclusively external developers. This is financially very convenient, but robs the publisher of control, because the programmers aren't in-house where the publisher can keep an eye on them. Sometimes developers miss deadlines, which screws up the publisher's shipping schedule and causes them to break promises to the retailers, who are expecting to get the game by a given date. In extreme cases, the developer may go out of business, leaving the publisher with a half-finished game and no way to complete it. The publisher says, "We've got to get some control back here—keep this process where we can see it on a day-to-day basis. Let's bring all our development in-house."

So the publisher goes out and hires a lot of programmers and writers and artists and musicians, and everything goes along well for a while until somebody notes that there is a huge number of people on staff, all drawing pay and consuming office space and taking vacations and requiring benefits and wanting stock options and bonuses. It's costing the company a fortune. So this person says to the management, "You know, there are people out there who would work for half this much money if we pay them on contract. We wouldn't have to provide all these nice benefits; we can give them just barely enough to stay alive with a promise of royalties when the game turns a profit. They'll work their guts out for the prospect of getting rich, and we won't have all this overhead." Management likes the idea, they duly get rid of all their in-house developers, and the cycle starts all over again.

This cycle typically takes about two to five years to run, and it depends on how good the management's corporate memory is. If someone suggests it too soon, there will be someone else around who says, "Oh, no, we had that system [whichever system] a year ago and it was a nightmare." But if there's turnover in the senior staff, then the new ones don't know that it was a nightmare, and they go round again.

The Developer

Here at last is the source of the river: the place where the games come from. Development companies exist to do one thing: design and build video games. In the early days of the personal computer game business, the developer was usually just one person, a programmer, who did all the art and music (what there was of it) himself. Nowadays, most first-class games require teams of 10 to 50 people, and a development company is a full-scale business with administrators and a personnel department.

If a developer is big enough, it may have several projects going on at once, possibly for several different publishers. Publishers tend to be a bit leery of developers who work with more than one publisher at once, since they're afraid that the program code they're paying for may find its way into another publisher's products. However, if the developer is good enough, the publisher will either overlook this, or try to give the developer so much work that they don't have time to work for anyone else.

Development companies tend to be small, rarely more than 200 people, all of them usually highly dedicated to making great games, and most of them more interested in the fun aspects of the game industry rather than in the business and moneymaking aspects. These tend to be more relaxed and less "corporate" places to work, with inflatable sharks hanging from the ceiling and Nerf ball fights in the hallways. Because they don't normally sell anything, there aren't any sales or marketing people around, only programmers, writers, artists, musicians, animators, and similar folks. If you want to make games in a place where you'll be surrounded by creative people, a development company is the place to be.

However, being small, development companies can't offer the same benefits that publishers can. The pay and facilities aren't usually as good. Development companies survive from year to year on their development contracts with publishers, and as soon as one project is finished it has to scramble to get a contract for another one, or it'll have to start laying people off. Developers often make use of *subcontractors*—small, independent companies that concentrate on one thing, like animation or music—in order to do part of the work. That way they don't have to carry these people on their books as employees year-round; they only pay them when they need them. In a way, a subcontractor is to a developer what a developer is to a publisher: a way of saving money by moving the work out of house.

Because it doesn't have as reliable a source of income as a publisher, a development company is unlikely to go public on the stock exchange. If you need the benefits and stability of a large company, you're better off working for a publisher; if you like the freedom and crazy atmosphere of a bunch of wildly creative people in a small office, then go for a developer.

Converting Games to Other Platforms

Often a publisher will develop a game for a specific machine in-house, but later decide to make that game available on another machine. This is called "porting" or "converting" the game. When they do this, publishers often contract the work out to another company, usually a developer that specializes in conversions. This is a good idea if the publisher's own programmers don't have a lot of experience with the second machine. Also, publishers see themselves as creators of new intellectual property. A conversion doesn't create a new game, but only moves an existing game to a new hardware platform. The publisher may prefer not to tie up its top creative talent doing a conversion. By the same token, the developers that specialize in doing conversions may be excellent at understanding their hardware, but poor at devising new intellectual property. By contracting out the work, a convenient synergy is obtained.

Conversion work requires great programmers who really understand gaming hardware. If you're a hotshot programmer who's more interested in the technical details of coding than in devising new games, you might consider working for a company that specializes in doing conversions.

RELATED BUSINESSES

In addition to the businesses I've already mentioned, there is a variety of other companies that provide specialized services. In this section, we'll look at a few of them.

Console Manufacturers

You probably noticed that some important people got left out of the previous section: the companies that build the game consoles themselves. What role do Sony, Nintendo, and Microsoft play in the game business?

Well, to begin with, it's important to realize that the hardware itself is not really the way they make their money. Sony sells the PlayStation 2 to the retailers for just a little more than what it costs them to build it in the first place. That's because the real profit isn't in the machines, but in the games. Each customer only needs one PlayStation, after all. What Sony is hoping is that those customers will each buy dozens of games for it.

Console manufacturers make their money by charging the publishers a fee for each copy of every game published for their machine. You're not allowed to publish a game for the Nintendo GameCube, for example, unless you sign a contract with Nintendo authorizing you to do so, and specifying how much you'll pay them for every copy that is manufacured. In order to make sure they make a profit—whether or not the players buy the game—the console manufacturers retain the exclusive right to manufacture the games themselves. Only the console manufacturer can press the special CDs or DVDs required, and they charge the publisher about $9 or $10 per copy. (If the publisher agrees to make games for *only* that machine, they can negotiate a better deal.)

Console manufacturers are also publishers in their own right, doing deals with external developers and maintaining internal development teams. They have their own lines of games, often with highly recognizable characters like Mario and Sonic the Hedgehog. These help them establish a brand identity and make sure there are games available for the console as soon as it comes out.

Console manufacturers are the most powerful companies in the business, but they're also the ones taking the biggest risks. It costs hundreds of millions of dollars to design and bring a new console machine to market, and experience shows that there's really only room for about three of them at any one time: two main competitors and an also-ran. Once it was the Sega Genesis and Super Nintendo, with the Neo-Geo in third place. Then it was the Sony PlayStation and Nintendo 64, with the Sega Saturn in third place. Now it seems to be the Sony PlayStation 2 and Microsoft Xbox, with the Nintendo GameCube bringing up the rear. (After the failure of the Dreamcast, Sega abandoned hardware manufacturing altogether and decided to stick to publishing.) Before people buy a console, they want to be sure that there will be a lot of games for it. If the publishers spread their efforts over six or seven different machines, there wouldn't be enough games on any one of them for the machine to really take hold.

Add-on Manufacturers

There's also a vast secondary market for add-on devices of one kind or another: joysticks, dance mats, steering wheels, "light guns," memory cards, cables … even "fishing rods." The list is nearly endless. Most of this stuff is manufactured by third parties under license to the console manufacturers (unless it's for the PC, in which case no license is needed). These manufacturers don't develop games, but often work with developers to encourage them to build in support for specific add-ons. A company that makes a force-feedback steering wheel, for example, will work with programmers building a highly anticipated racing game to make sure their device works with the new game. Sometimes they'll even offer to help with the programming.

Product Manufacturers

Once development of a game is complete, obviously somebody has to manufacture the CDs or DVDs that it's shipped on, print the manuals, build the boxes, and assemble it all for shipment. In the case of console games, as I said earlier, it's the console manufacturer. But for PC games, this work is done by product manufacturers, who are under contract to the publishers. Product manufacturers never even see the developers or the customers, and they're not much interested in the games themselves; it's just a disc in a box to them. But they're part of the game industry, too.

Each copy of a game typically costs $5 or so to manufacture: this number is called the *cost of goods*. In other words, out of the $40 or so that you pay as a customer, only $5 actually goes for the physical objects that you're purchasing. All the rest is paying for developing, publishing, marketing, and license fees. The CD or DVD itself costs less than a dollar to make; the other $4 goes into that brightly colored, embossed cardboard box that the game comes in. About ten years ago there was a fad for really fancy boxes with strange shapes—you might remember *Tomb Raider's* pyramidal box, or *Ultrabots,* which came in a huge box with two telescoping sections. The retailers complained that they took up too much room on the shelves, however, and since then the boxes have gotten smaller and smaller as the publishers have tried to save money on cost of goods; the coming standard is a DVD box. The manuals, too, have shrunk from thick paperback books filled with background material down to little pamphlets held together with staples.

Publishers are often concerned about a product manufacturer's data security. As soon as the master copy of a game leaves the publisher's offices, there's a risk that it could be copied and pirated. Sometimes pirate copies of a game start circulating

WAR STORIES

Manufacturing a game is usually fairly boring, but one time it became very interesting! I was working at Origin as the Project Director for the Wing Commander mission packs. We were in Beta test for one of these mini-games when I got a phone call from the lady in charge of customer service. In a very strained voice, she said that she had a tech support call that she wanted me to handle personally. I agreed, as I often personally handled the more challenging tech support calls for my own projects, and then realized what was so peculiar: the guy on the phone was asking for help on a product we hadn't shipped yet!

I talked to him for a few minutes, made sure to get all of his contact information, then told him that he needed to hold for another minute, while I transferred him to someone else.

That person was Origin's General Manager, Fred Schmidt. Fred found out what had happened. The guy had received the game from someone at the disk duplication company we were using to make disks for Beta-testers and game reviewers. Origin stopped using that duplicating service, and I presume the caller's "friend" at the duplication company ended up looking for a job!

—Ellen Guon Beeman, Producer, Monolith Productions

around the world even before the legitimate one is released. This usually happens because there's a leak somewhere, either at the developer, the publisher, or the product manufacturer. Nowadays, publishers have to make individually numbered copies of their master game disks, and be sure they know who has each one at all times. Piracy costs the game industry billions of dollars a year.

OTHER DISTRIBUTION CHANNELS

The retail and mail-order businesses are the traditional ways to sell software to consumers, but they are beginning to get serious competition from other distribution channels.

Online

Online distribution is an increasingly popular mechanism for small programs, and I believe that eventually almost all software will be distributed this way. After all, a computer program is nothing more than a very long string of bytes. When you want to transfer that string of bytes from one place to another, it's a bit ridiculous to press them on a plastic CD, put the CD into a cardboard box, ship it around the country, and require the customer to drive down to the retail store to pick it up and take it home. It makes a lot more sense to send the bytes directly over a wire between the vendor and the customer's computers. The process doesn't generate any trash, and you don't have to use air-polluting vehicles to transport the bytes. Right now, this isn't possible for large software products, because most people's network access is too slow to download 650 megabytes of data at a time. However, as broadband access to the Internet becomes more and more common, people will routinely purchase software this way, including games. There will be piracy problems, of course, but then there are already piracy problems. Through the use of encryption and other mechanisms, they will be solved in time. The fact that some major software publishers such as Symantec already sell their software in downloadable form suggests that they have confidence in the process.

There are some downsides to distributing games electronically. Many games are bought as Christmas presents for someone else, and people like to see boxes under the tree, not just slips of paper with a web address on them. People also like to browse when shopping, and buying online doesn't let you pick up the boxes and look at them side by side. Finally, although you can get a great deal of information from a company's web site, you still can't ask questions of a knowledgeable sales clerk. That's a level of support you can only get by going to a retail store.

In the end, however, I think the costs associated with retail software sales will outweigh the benefits, and most distribution will be online. For the time being, it's an excellent way for publishers of small games to distribute their products.

Shareware

Shareware is a good way for small developers to sell PC games: they give the game away for free, let the users pass it on as much as they like, and they hope that if people like it enough, they'll pay for it. If you want to make little games for fun, and you're not really concerned about making a lot of money from them, then shareware is a good way to go. It also has the advantage that every penny comes back to you: there are no publishers, distributors, or retailers taking a cut, and, of course, no manufacturers building boxes.

The problem with distributing fully functional games as shareware is that people are unlikely to pay you for them. Unlike software utilities or other applications, people usually stop playing a given game after a short while. If they've already seen all that the game has to offer for free, why pay for it? A much more common approach is to distribute just part of the game, and make people pay if they want the whole thing. Id Software made a vast amount of money this way with *Doom*. This is, in effect, what happens with game demos already, although they're not normally referred to as "shareware." For PC games, demos are now almost obligatory as a way of generating demand before the complete game is released.

Rental

Rental of computer software other than video games is illegal in many places because too many people were using it as a means of making pirate copies of the software. But rental of video game CDs is quite common, and a good way to let a customer get a taste of a game without having to pay for the whole thing.

On the whole, the industry doesn't like rentals much. Just as the public library lets dozens of people read a single copy of a book, the rental store lets dozens of people play a single copy of a video game. Since games have a limited life anyway—few people really want to keep and play a video game for the rest of their lives—there isn't a lot of point in owning one if you can just rent it until you've played it all the way through. The publishers, however, would much rather that you bought it.

Bundling

When you buy a new piece of computer hardware, especially a video card or sound card, it's common to get a free copy of a game bundled in with the hardware. It usually doesn't have the nice manual and box that you would get if you bought it at retail, and often it's not one of the very latest games, but it's still a free game. Hardware manufacturers like to make bundling deals with publishers because it helps them sell their gear. Sometimes the hardware manufacturers will even help fund the development of a game if the publisher will make sure it runs well on their particular piece of equipment.

Bundling deals are also a good way for a publisher to continue to make some money out of a game that isn't selling well any more. They don't make as much money selling it to the hardware manufacturer as they would selling it at retail, but on the other hand they get a large volume sale at one time, and they don't have to do any marketing.

"Unsold Returns": A Game Industry Scam

It used to be that if a game didn't sell well, the retailer was stuck with all of the unsold copies. But after a while the big retail chains got enough clout that they began to insist on the right to get a refund from the publisher for any games they couldn't sell. These unsold copies are called *returns*, and the publisher can either pay to have them shipped back, or allow the retailer to destroy them. (Remember, the cost of goods is only $3–4, so it's seldom worth the publisher's trouble to have them shipped back again.) Since the publisher can no longer count on a sale being final, it has to keep a fund of money, called a *reserve*, around to pay the retailers back with. Part of this money has to come out of the developer's royalties, because the developer shouldn't receive royalties for games that the retailer has returned for a refund. So, even though the developer is supposed to get, say, 15 percent of the wholesale price of every copy sold, the publisher hangs on to as much as a fourth of that, keeping that money (along with more of the publisher's own money) in the reserve fund to repay retailers for returned copies.

There's nothing wrong with this system if nobody buys the games and the retailer really does destroy the unsold copies. The problem is with the definition of that little word "destroy." Most wholesale contracts don't actually state how the game is to be destroyed, and the publishers don't have the time and energy to enforce it anyway. Unfortunately, a few unscrupulous retailers have been known to get their money back on a return, then mark the game down and stick it in a bargain bin instead of destroying it. The retailer gets the game for free, the customer gets a bargain, and neither the publisher nor the developer sees a penny for it.

GAMER DEMOGRAPHICS AND MARKETS

So who actually plays video games? It's difficult to tell for sure, because interactive entertainment is such a big, sprawling business. Gamers vary from little kids playing with battery-powered handhelds in the back seat of the car to grandmothers playing bridge over the Internet in the retirement home. Unlike the movies, where you can watch who goes in and out of the cinema, it's not easy to tell who's playing games, especially online games.

You can categorize the players of video games any number of ways, but I'm going to pick just three, and compare how they affect our understanding of the market. I'll look at children and adults, males and females, and hardcore and casual gamers. Each of these distinctions is the basis of a stereotype about gamers, and like most stereotypes they're either outdated or were never really true in the first place.

"Video Games Are for Kids"

This one has a basis in historical reality, because the first home consoles were chiefly marketed as toys, and the games were too simple to have themes of interest to adults. Children and teens still make up a large part of the player base of video games: 34 percent of PC gamers and 45 percent of console gamers are under 18. However, this doesn't mean they're the ones actually purchasing the games. Only 4 percent of console game buyers are under 18, and only 10 percent of PC game buyers. Parents are very involved in determining what games kids play.

Video games are clearly no longer just for kids, though. The market has changed. There are now people in their 30s and 40s who grew up playing video games, and the age of the average gamer is now 28. Adults who grew up with video games want grown-up stories and characters. It can be hard to provide them, sometimes—the victory/defeat metaphor doesn't always lend itself to conveying the subtlety of adult situations—but developers are working on it. As the market ages, so its tastes are changing as well.

"Video Games Are for Boys (and Nerdy Men)"

This, too, arises out of the history of games: the early computer games were played by computer programmers on mainframes or their home-built machines, and these people were almost entirely male. All these years later, the stereotype persists that video games are a primarily male preserve. In reality, 43 percent of American game players are female, and their average age is 27.

This stereotype persists for a variety of reasons. Many of the top-selling games are designed to appeal to men, and those are the ones that get the most attention in the press. The majority of game developers are still male, and they tend to make games that they themselves would like. The industry is still trying to figure out how to make games more appealing to women and girls, because while a great many women *play* games, a rather smaller number is prepared to *buy* them, and that's what we really need.

Casual Versus Hardcore

When people hear the word "gamer," they often think of a crazed teenager who spends hours in his room doing nothing but playing games, and has no other social life—the classic hardcore player. Such people do exist, naturally, and they treat gaming as a hobby rather than just entertainment; it's a pursuit that they're willing to devote substantial amounts of their leisure time and money to. They're awed by spectacular graphics and they tend to play the latest, goriest action games. When they're not actually playing games, they're reading magazines about them or building fan web sites dedicated to their favorites.

Game publishers make serious efforts to reach and keep the hardcore market, because they're extremely reliable customers: they often buy one or two games a month, or even more. But there are fewer hardcore gamers than their reputation suggests. There are far more casual players—ordinary people who like to play for a few hours per day or per week, but don't let it consume their lives. *The Sims* is the best-selling PC game of all time, and it's about the most prosaic subject imaginable: looking after people in a suburban house and making sure they get the dishes washed and the plants watered. To a hardcore gamer, this is not what constitutes exciting gameplay. Casual gamers made *The Sims* a worldwide mega-hit.

As a game developer, you're likely to be surrounded by hardcore gamers; you may already be one yourself. That seems to be the kind of person who goes into game development, especially programming. But never forget the casual player. If you build a game that only appeals to the hardcore type, you're automatically limiting the size of your market.

GAME GENRES

Just as television has its sitcoms, cop shows, science fiction dramas, and soap operas, commercial video games have their genres, too. They appeal to different kinds of players—and different kinds of developers too, for that matter. I'll take a quick look at these categories, because if you get a job in the game industry, the chances are that you'll end up working on a game in one or another of them. Of course, these certainly aren't the only kinds of games available, and many games include elements from more than one genre. *Dungeon Keeper,* for example, was partly a construction and management simulation and partly a war game. But when a publisher is planning their product line, they're likely to want a certain number of games that fit neatly into one pigeonhole or another.

Action

If a game requires quick reflexes and good hand-eye coordination, it's an action game. The one exception to this rule is vehicle simulations like driving and flying games, but those actually depend more on fine control—steering—rather than reflexes. Action games are the oldest of all video games, beginning with *Spacewar* in 1961 and then *Pong* in 1974. Because they rely on speed and frenetic activity, they're ideal for games of short duration like arcade machines.

Action games can be divided into several subcategories:

> **First-person shooters (FPSs)**   Sometimes called point-of-view (POV) shooters. *Quake, Half-Life,* and *Unreal Tournament* are classic examples. They're far and away the most popular PC action games, especially if played in multi-player mode over networks.

> **Third-person games**   In these games, you can see your avatar on the screen, usually from behind. *Mario Sunshine, Banjo-Kazooie,* and the *Tomb Raider* series are all third-person games. Shooting is a bit trickier in these games because the avatar is often obscuring part of the target from the player's view.

> **Fighting games**   These require players to learn complicated sequences of button-presses on the controllers. In multi-player mode, there's a distinct psychological element, too, as players bluff and feint.

> **Dance simulations**   This subgenre of games is a Japanese import and only a few years old, but they've already made a powerful impression on the American market. Their gameplay comes from challenging the player's sense of rhythm rather than simple reflexes.

> **Action-adventures**   A hybrid genre made possible by today's powerful machines. In traditional action games, the plot is usually trivial and players

must meet the game's challenges by skill alone. Few action games require much thought. In traditional adventure games, the plots are complex and almost all the obstacles are puzzles of one kind or another; physical skill is seldom needed. Action-adventures combine these qualities into a single game with some action elements (typically not too demanding) and some puzzles (typically not too obscure). Good examples of this type of game are *The Legend of Zelda* for the Nintendo 64, and *Indiana Jones and the Infernal Machine* for the PC.

) **Platform games**   Also called side-scrollers, these are the classic action games from the early '90s—*Super Mario, Sonic the Hedgehog,* and others. They've largely been supplanted by 3-D designs, but people still have a certain nostalgia for them. Although games like *Crash Bandicoot* now use 3-D engines, their linear gameplay path has its historical roots in platform gaming.

To get an idea of the importance of action games in the console game market, take a look at Figure 3-2.

Strategy and War Games

A decade ago, war games were almost a dead genre, enjoyed only by die-hard aficionados who didn't mind playing simple turn-based variants of board games. All that changed with the invention of the *real-time strategy game* (*RTS*) of which the *Warcraft* and *Command & Conquer* series are the best known. The introduction of time pressure, along with good sound effects and attractive animation, opened up this market to a new generation of enthusiastic players. Strategy games tend to require complicated user interfaces, and for that reason they're mostly found on the PC.

FIGURE 3-2

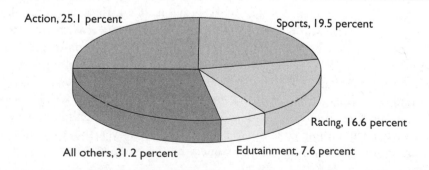

Action, 25.1 percent   Sports, 19.5 percent

Racing, 16.6 percent

All others, 31.2 percent   Edutainment, 7.6 percent

The top-selling console game genres of 2002
(*source: IDSA*)

Sports Games

From their early, ugly beginnings, sports games have grown into a hugely successful class of games. They're the best-selling genre of game on console machines, surpassing even action games. The new subgenre of extreme sports games—*Tony Hawk* and others—have strongly boosted the popularity of this perennial favorite.

Game designers find working on sports games a little less appealing, because after all, most of the game is already designed. However, they offer great challenges to artists, animators and artificial intelligence programmers. Sports and car racing games are the only genres where players can directly compare the game with real life. Nobody has ever really led an army of elves into battle, but everybody knows what a star quarterback is supposed to do. It's the sports game developer's job to make it seem as real as Sunday afternoon at the stadium.

Vehicle Simulators

Vehicle simulators are games about driving or flying—cars, motorcycles, civilian and military aircraft, tanks, and science-fiction vehicles all qualify in this category. Even a game like *Drakkan,* which was about flying around on a dragon, is essentially a vehicle simulator. They vary considerably, of course, from the extreme realism of a military flight simulator like *F-16 Falcon* to the lighthearted silliness of *Mario Kart.* Some of them are first-person and some are third-person, but most are switchable so the player can choose the camera angle she's most comfortable with. The main point about vehicle simulators is that they're about controlling something mechanical. The avatar is a vehicle, not a person or an irradiated hedgehog.

Construction and Management Simulations

Sim City, the *Caesar* series, *Roller Coaster Tycoon,* and all the other games in which you build a world and try to make it run efficiently belong to a class called construction and management simulations. Like real-time strategy games, these tend to have complicated user interfaces, and work best on PCs rather than consoles. They're more popular with adults than children, and more popular with women than most other kinds of games. Because they're not games of high adrenaline, they don't make as much of a splash in the press when they come out, but they belong to an enduringly successful genre. Part of their appeal is the creative aspect of the gameplay. Players get to build something to their own specifications, or try to at least, within the constraints of the game. Construction and management systems often don't have a victory condition—a particular thing you have to do to "win." However, they often have a loss condition: if you run out of money, or some other resource, you can't go on playing.

A subgenre of construction and management simulations is the *god game,* a game in which the player takes on the role of the god of a group of (usually tribal) people. His godly powers are usually proportional to the numbers and prosperity of his worshippers, so it's up to him to look after them, while smiting the unbelievers with fire and brimstone. Most construction and management simulations tend to be rather businesslike; god games add a fantasy element and appeal to the megalomaniac in us.

Graphic Adventures

Adventure games are slow-paced games, filled with puzzles, in which the player typically follows a plot or storyline, often a fairly intricate one. The earliest ones were text-based, but adventure games quickly adopted graphics and their visual artistry is an important part of their appeal. Faster-paced games tend to stick with simple environments because there's not much point in creating beautiful backgrounds if the players are just going to move through them as quickly as possible. Lushly illustrated adventure games give you time—and a reason—to admire the scenery. They're particularly popular with female players, who often enjoy the exploration and puzzle-solving aspects without the frustration of having to try a tricky action move over and over before getting it right.

There was a time when adventure games were the best-looking and best-selling PC games on the market, but in recent years they have largely been surpassed by other genres.

Fantasy Role-Playing Games

Fantasy role-playing games, often abbreviated FRPs or RPGs, are a steady staple of the game industry. The object is to take a group of weak characters and, through exploration and (usually) combat, build them into strong characters with powerful abilities. RPG's are, of course, inspired by pencil-and-paper role-playing games like *Dungeons & Dragons,* whose mechanics translate over to the computer pretty well. Like construction and management simulations, they encourage the player to build and customize something, but in this case it's a character rather than a city or a theme park. There's also a strong element of exploration and usually a storyline of some sort, although it's seldom as sophisticated as those in adventure games. RPGs are most commonly found on the PC because they tend to have a lot of options that are more easily managed with a mouse than a controller. However, the *Final Fantasy* series, hugely successful in the console market, is a notable exception.

Online Role-Playing Games

Massively-multiplayer online role-playing games (MMORPGs, also called *persistent worlds*) have experienced phenomenal success in the last few years. As in RPGs, you're trying to build up a character through exploration and combat, but you're doing it in an online world filled with other players, a situation offering all kinds of opportunities for social interactions—both pleasant and otherwise—that single-player RPGs don't have. As software, RPGs consist of two parts: a *server* program that runs on the publisher's computer and simulates the game world for all the players, and a *client* program that runs on each player's computer and is the means by which he interacts with the game world. The client and the server talk to each other over the Internet.

Persistent worlds are sold on a subscription model, although the players often have to buy the client software from a retailer first. Such games are incredibly expensive for a publisher to build and maintain because, unlike an offline game, they require constant updating and a large number of server computers to simulate the game world. There are substantial bandwidth costs as well, since every change in the game world must be transmitted back and forth between the player's client software and the server. On the other hand, instead of getting the player's money just once, the publisher gets more every month and it comes directly to them, not through a middleman.

Puzzle Games and Software Toys

Puzzle games are usually collections of puzzles of several different kinds. But don't think in terms of puzzle toys, like sliding little tiles around. Computers can use the power of the machine to create much more interesting challenges. In *Mind Rover*, for example, you build a robot out of standard parts and set it to do battle against another robot. In *Marble Drop*, you drop colored marbles through a wonderfully complicated contraption, and try to get them to come out at the bottom in the right order. Many computerized puzzle games use sound, animation, and beautiful background screens to make them attractive even if the puzzles themselves aren't especially intricate.

If a video game doesn't have a well-defined victory condition, and it's just something you fool around with for fun, it's called a "software toy." Construction and management simulations like *Railroad Tycoon* often don't have victory conditions either, but they do have challenges to meet and problems to solve. A software toy is more free-form. There's no real way to win or lose, just different things to do. Good examples are the artificial life programs like *Creatures* and the *Petz* series, or children's painting programs.

Children's Games

Games designed specifically for children shouldn't be considered a genre, strictly speaking, because they can be about all different kinds of things. Nevertheless, the market—that is, the retailers—tend to treat children's games as a distinct category of product. Games for young children are, of course, easier, requiring less hand-eye coordination, and often are shorter than games for teenagers and adults. They resemble children's books, with bright, simple artwork, and avoid violence or morally ambiguous situations. This doesn't mean they have to be dull, though. Children's games are often full of things that make sounds and animate when you click on them. They reward curiosity and exploration.

THE GAME PRESS AND WEB SITES

Yet another ancillary business in the game industry is the press, including both print media and companies that run web sites for gamers. Serious players follow events in the game industry (and want information about forthcoming games) with all the enthusiasm of sports fans or movie buffs.

Players' Magazines and Web Sites

Players can choose from a vast number of magazines dedicated to video gaming. A few, like *Edge,* try to cover all the different platforms at once, but most specialize in a particular console (or the PC or Macintosh), realizing that a player is unlikely to want information about games for a machine that she doesn't own. Magazines are a good source of information about upcoming products, and often come with CDs full of demos attached so you can try out some of the games without having to download hundreds of megabytes from the Internet. However, the mechanics of magazine publishing are such that they can't include the most up-to-the-minute information; for that, you'll have to look on the Web. On the whole, there are more magazines about PC gaming than about console gaming, because the kind of dedicated gamer who wants to buy magazines about games tends to prefer the PC as a platform.

Unfortunately, the game press doesn't have a very good reputation for objectivity, because it depends very heavily on advertising revenues from game publishers. It's rare to find a gamer magazine that gives a game a really bad review. Also, some of the console-oriented magazines are actually published by the console manufacturers themselves, so they're really more of a marketing tool than an impartial observer of the game scene.

Video game web sites are huge. From the all-inclusive *HappyPuppy.com* down to individual gamers' fan sites (and complaint sites too!), you can find a colossal amount of information about video games on the Internet. Many of them have message boards where people can discuss their favorite games, and passionate debate rages. On the whole, the web sites are a little more objective than the magazines, and, of course, web sites always have the latest information. Most magazines now have associated web sites as well.

Industry Publications and Web Sites

There's only one major U.S. magazine that's specifically intended for all game developers, and that is, not surprisingly, *Game Developer*. In the UK, there's *Develop*. But a number of others are dedicated to the industry in general. *ieMagazine,* for example, is intended for publishers and retailers in America, as is *MCV* in Britain. They give you a perspective that you don't usually see as a developer; they're mostly concerned with prices, ship dates, and the amount of money the publisher is spending on its marketing campaign.

The best industry web site devoted to game development is *Gamasutra,* although I have to admit to some bias in saying this; I've been writing a column there for the last five years. It is specifically about development, not retailing or marketing, and includes features on all aspects of building games: programming, art, animation, music, design, testing, and so on.

Gamasutra's nearest competitor is *GameDev.net,* although it's aimed more toward the small-time developer and programmer than to large industry projects. GameDev.net offers a large collection of tools and tutorials for the beginning developer.

There are many other web sites devoted to game development, mostly run by individuals working on games in their spare time. As with early homebrew computers, a culture of cooperation and helpfulness accompanies small-time development. If you're trying to design or build games on your own, you can always find people on the Internet to talk to about it and get advice from.

WRAP-UP

Now you should have a better idea of how the game industry actually functions—where games come from, how they flow down to the customer, and what each different company does with them along the way. In the next chapter, I'll talk about something that affects you directly as a potential developer: how games are actually built.

CHAPTER

4

Inside the
Fun Factory

IN the previous chapter, I traced games back to their origins: a team of game developers, working either for a development company or a publisher. In this chapter, we'll go inside that team and see how games are actually built, from initial concept to shipping product.

iNTERNAL OR EXTERNAL DEVELOPMENT?

As I mentioned in Chapter 3, publishers either hire their own developers to work in-house (internal development) or they sign a contract with a development company (external development) to build a game. This has certain implications for the development process, depending on the approach used. The financial and administrative details tend to be rather different, so as I describe each stage of development, I'll break out the differences into separate subsections.

STAGE 1: THE BRILLIANT IDEA

A game begins as an idea. You've probably got a great idea yourself, or several of them. Every game developer in the whole industry has ideas for games, and they think and talk and argue about them with their colleagues whenever they have free time. There's very little point in trying to keep a game idea secret; the chances that you have a completely unique idea, never before thought of by anyone, are incredibly small.

 "Ideas are easy, production is hard." What matters is the ability to build and complete a high quality, compelling, marketable game.
—*Ellen Guon Beeman, Producer, Monolith Productions*

Evolutionary or Revolutionary?

The vast majority of games in the industry are "evolved" from earlier games. Their creative, and often their technical, content—what you might call their genetic material—is a mixture of ideas that have gone before. Certain groups of characteristics are especially popular with the players, so games have evolved into different "breeds"— the genres I talked about in Chapter 3.

If a game idea has evolved from earlier games or other entertainment media, it is easily understandable to anyone who hears about it. For example, a friend and I once pitched an idea to a producer as "*Diablo* meets *The X-Files* in 3-D." If you were to cross *Diablo* (fairly fast combat action from an aerial perspective above a small party of people) with *The X-Files* (mysterious supernatural conspiracies set in the present day) you would get our game, which we had decided to call *Psychic Warriors*. We hoped that, by summarizing the game idea in a single, crisp sentence (known as a "high concept"), it would appeal to the producer and the marketing people whose job it would be to sell the game to the public. The longer it takes to explain an idea, the more likely you are to lose someone's attention and interest.

As you can imagine, this evolutionary approach has given rise to a world of games that look somewhat alike. Some are even derisively called "clones"—games with identical play mechanics and nothing but some new graphics slapped on. During the heyday of the Super Nintendo console, a few publishers became notorious for producing clones: side-scrolling games that were all alike except for their appearance.

The alternative, a revolutionary game, is much harder to persuade a publisher to build, and even if they do build it, it's harder to sell to the public. Players like their cozy, familiar genres. When a player puts down his money for a role-playing game or flight simulator, he knows what to expect: what sorts of challenges he will face, decisions he will make, and actions he will take. Asking a player to buy a revolutionary game—a type of game the world has never seen before—is asking him to gamble $50 or so on a game that he may end up hating.

But when the revolution succeeds, the rewards are enormous. Power, glory, riches! A new kind of game is born and you were part of it. To a creative person there is no finer feeling. *The Sims* is such a game—a runaway bestseller whose publisher never really believed in it until its colossal popularity showed them how wrong they were. Electronic Arts only grudgingly allowed Will Wright, the designer, to make *The Sims* because he already had a string of hit games. Interestingly, *The Sims* was *not* the first game of its kind. It borrows a number of ideas from a much earlier game called *Little Computer People*, but *Little Computer People* was ahead of its time; the public wasn't ready for it. Which brings up a point: Sometimes you can only have a revolution when the conditions are right.

How Publishers Hear about Game Ideas

To begin with, whoever has the idea (I'll assume it's you for the moment) has to persuade a publisher to think about it. Not to develop it—we're still a long way from that stage—but just to think about it. Getting a publisher's attention is the first hurdle, and you can imagine, there are an awful lot of people clamoring for it. Publishers get unsolicited submissions—"bluebirds"—sent to them in the mail all the time, but they seldom take them seriously. (In fact, for legal reasons, most publishers won't accept unsolicited submissions. If you do want to send your game idea to a publisher, you should contact them first to find out whether they will accept your game proposals.)

More frequently, an external development company whom a publisher has already worked with, or has heard of—someone like Monolith, for example, with a track record of creating successful games—phones up a producer and says, "Hey, we've got a great idea for a game that we want to talk to you about." If the development company has a good reputation and the producer isn't too busy, he'll set up a meeting for the developers to come and deliver their pitch.

But publishers don't just wait for ideas to come to them, either. They have a product plan that specifies what kinds of games they want to release in the next year or two, and how much money they want to spend on developing and marketing them. If a publisher is large enough, it usually has several product lines or brands that it's planning to produce games for. In this case, they already know what they want to build, and they go looking for developers to do the work. Sometimes they'll use their own in-house teams; other times they'll contact development companies and offer them the job.

Internal Development

If you work for a publisher, it's not that hard to get someone to at least listen to your idea, because they work in the same office with you. If it meets their product needs they may ask you to do some further work on it; if they really like it, they may even assign a few developers to work with you.

External Development

If you work for an external developer, you can of course talk to your bosses about your idea, but your company is unlikely to have the money to develop it themselves. If they like it enough, though, they may decide to pitch it to a publisher.

Pitching the Game

Since this is a book about how to get a job, not how to get a publishing deal, I'll just give brief highlights of pitching a game. First you have to find someone who's interested and willing to talk to you in person—just mailing them some documents isn't going to cut it. Second, that person has to either have some decision-making authority herself, or have the ear of someone who does. There's no point in pitching your game to a testing intern. Ideally, the pitch should be made to a producer or executive producer.

Pitching a game is more than just talking about it. You should have a prepared presentation, with PowerPoint slides and handouts. You should bring along some early, "high-concept" design documents and some concept drawings that show key visual elements in the game, especially anything radically new. You might have some animations already, a short video to show, some working code, or ideally, a playable prototype. Obviously, the farther along a game is in development, the more interested the publisher is going to be, because it means they have to invest that much less money to finish it. In rare cases, a developer has actually got a complete game that's ready to ship. Financially, that's the best scenario of all, although few publishers will ship a game without insisting on a few changes.

A pitch is not just a lot of blue-sky enthusiasm about new technology and innovative gameplay, however. You have to convince the publisher that there is a market for the game and it will make them a lot of money. You also have to show them that you can build the game on time and under budget. A well-prepared pitch includes cost estimates and a proposed schedule. You can't do a pitch without being able to demonstrate these things; no matter how brilliant the idea may be, what the publisher wants to know is how feasible and profitable it is.

STAGE 2: PRE-PRODUCTION

If the pitch has gone well, the publisher likes the idea, and they are interested in working with whoever is proposing to do it, then pre-production begins. At this point, the publisher still isn't fully committed to producing and marketing the game. (In fact, a publisher is never entirely committed to publishing a game until it has been built and tested and they've started the marketing for it, for reasons I'll explain later in this chapter.) For the time being they only want to explore the idea, but they're prepared to spend a little money to do so.

There was a time when a publisher said, "Yes, go!" and a developer dived into coding the game the very next day. That time ended about 1985, when a game still cost between fifty and a hundred thousand dollars to develop. It was never good practice even then, and nowadays, with development costs in the millions of dollars, it would be a disaster. Any large project, whether it's building a skyscraper, filming a movie, or developing a computer game requires pre-production: an exploratory and planning stage. It's absolutely essential for building a game on time and within budget.

Once a publisher has decided to go into pre-production, they will assign a producer to it. This person is an employee of the publisher whose job it is to make sure the idea turns into the game the publisher wants. The producer is responsible for making sure it's a fun and, above all, marketable product. I'll discuss his vital role in the development process later, in Chapter 5.

Design Work

The first thing that's needed is a design document, although one may already exist. The developer may have written it on spec, and shown it to the publisher to get their interest, or someone at the publisher may have written one. In most cases, the design will be incomplete, because there's no point in fleshing out every detail until you know the publisher is interested. Now is the time to finish that work. I'm not going to describe it in detail here, but in addition to thinking about how the game should look, sound, and, most importantly, play, the designer does a certain amount of competitive analysis, checking to see how similar games work, and doing background research—for instance, familiarizing herself with the subject matter of the game. If it's a military flight simulator, for example, she'll go to the public library and check out *Jane's All the World's Aircraft* for inspiration.

Internal Development

Within a publishing house, the producer might write the design document himself, but more likely he will assign an experienced game designer to do it. A producer has other tasks, and modern games are too large and complex to be designed on a part-time basis. Even though the work is taking place in-house, the publisher is already spending money on the project: the designer and producers' salaries.

External Development

Whether the developer has pitched an idea to the publisher, or the publisher has sought out a developer for a project they already have in mind, the publisher will then give the developer a small amount of money—between five and twenty thousand dollars—to write a design document and produce some concept sketches. In the meantime, the producer will be visiting the developer, looking over their facilities and their previous work, talking to their artists and programmers, and trying to get an idea of whether they'll be able to do the job. At this point, a lot hinges on the personal relationships between the people involved. If either side feels they can't trust the other, or just doesn't like the other's way of working, the process can break down right here.

Technical Research and Prototyping

The pre-production phase includes more than just design, however. It's also a time to identify the risks involved in the project, and to do research to minimize those risks when possible. To this end, the publisher will usually ask the developers to assemble a small team, seldom more than ten people, to identify the key challenges in developing the game and start work on them.

Risks fall into three categories: *technical risks*, *production risks*, and *creative risks*.

Technical Risks

Any video game that is not a direct clone of another requires new programming. All new programming represents some technical risk, but certain areas, such as new graphics technology or artificial intelligence, are particularly tricky. Two or three programmers will build a small demonstration program (sometimes called a *proof of concept*) to test out the new ideas. A proof of concept is not a game at all. It's just a demo, often using "programmer graphics" (old graphic scrap or even just colored dots), that is written to illustrate the correct behavior. The proof of concept is used to show the publisher that the technical issues facing the team are surmountable.

Production Risks

Can the developer's team actually complete the project? This will also need to be demonstrated. Usually, the developer's internal producer/project manager will assemble a document describing the experience of the team, their production methodology, their ability to meet milestones and handle change requests, and other elements that will prove there is a minimal completion risk.

Creative Risks

No one can really be sure what the public is going to like, but if a game design calls for a new kind of user interface, or a type of gameplay never before seen, the publisher is likely to want to try it out before giving the go-ahead for the project. Likewise, they will want to see what the game is going to look like, and maybe even get an idea of how it will feel to play. This is where prototyping comes in. A prototype is a partially working model of the game, normally constructed by a handful of people: a few programmers, maybe a couple of artists, a designer, and a team leader. It doesn't even have to be a stand-alone application; a prototype can be built in Shockwave or Flash as long as it conveys the general idea; though some publishers will insist on more.

In addition to devising a prototype, the artists will be creating concept drawings, a few 3-D models, animations, and backgrounds, and looking in art books and on the Web for background material. It's always valuable to have a lot of pictures around during the prototype phase, to help inspire the team and give everyone a shared sense of what you're aiming to achieve.

WAR STORIES

At one point in my career, I was a lead game designer at Bullfrog Productions, which I had joined because they were famous for some of the most innovative PC games ever made. I was given a prototype team to research a new god game (a subgenre of real-time strategy games) called Genesis (nothing to do with the Sega Genesis, by the way). It was to be set in a world of pre-industrial tribal peoples, somewhat like the earlier Populous games. I had three programmers (two working on technical proofs-of-concept and one on the prototype), an artist, and a level designer to help me with design work.

I wanted our game to have spectacular and realistic-looking landscapes, so at our first group meeting I brought big color photographs of actual jungles, deserts, mountain ranges, seacoasts, prairies, and other dramatic geographical features. I told them, "One of our goals is to make our game look like this," which pleased the artist

and made the graphics programmers look rather thoughtful. We hung them all around the walls of our bullpen (Bullfrog had no cubicles) so everyone who worked there, and everyone who walked by, could see them. My artist, Alex Godsill, got into the spirit of the thing and began

posting the results of his research as well: pictures of the clothing and weaponry of native peoples all over the world. The place looked amazing, a visual riot of spears and shields, tunics and turbans.

Genesis never went beyond the prototype stage, unfortunately—the company

secured the Harry Potter license and realized, quite correctly, that that would be a much more lucrative game to publish. But everybody in the building could tell what the Genesis project was about, and we all had a collective idea of how it would look to be in our imaginary world.

Project Planning

The third aspect of pre-production is project planning. This is an unexciting but absolutely vital part of the process. It's also a black art that can only be learned with experience. Project planning is normally done by the producer working together with a project manager. They'll define the scope of the project: how big and complicated the program will be, and how much artwork, animation, and audio the game will require. From those assumptions, they'll then estimate the size of the staff required to develop the game, and how long it will take.

Internal Development

Obviously, a key consideration at this point is whether the publisher is going to have the internal development resources to do the job. Planning the project will include looking to see what other projects are winding up, so you know which people will soon be available. If they don't have the necessary people on board already, and the project looks like a sure thing, that's good news for you: they'll start hiring!

External Development

Project planning is the responsibility of the development company, but it's also very much a process of negotiation. This is because the plan they come up with will be the basis for a very important business agreement: the development contract between the publisher and the developer. The developer will consider everything carefully, then add a certain percentage for slippage, profits, and bargaining room, and tell the publisher that the game will take two years, require 40 people, and cost three million dollars to develop. The publisher will reply that this is totally unacceptable and that any competent development house could do it with 20 people in 12 months for 1.5 million. The developer will remonstrate and point to all the things required by the design document. The publisher will say that the designer was letting her imagination run away with her, cut a few things out, and raise their offer a little. The developers will reluctantly admit that they don't *really* have to hire the London Symphony Orchestra to record the music, and lower their demands a little. The process will go back and forth until both sides have a budget and schedule they can live with, which will form part of their development contract.

Whether they actually succeed in keeping to either one depends greatly on the quality of their project planning and management.

Going to Full Production

The length of time a project spends in pre-production can vary from about one to six months, depending on just how much design work, technical research, and prototyping needs to be done. If the game is a sequel whose codebase is largely complete, pre-production might take no longer than is required to do the project planning.

Whether internal or external, pre-production ends with the development team giving a presentation to the publisher to show what they've done, and trying to persuade them to "green-light" the product—take it into full production. This presentation is similar to the original pitch, except that now there should be a lot more to show. It's a key moment for the developers, because if the publisher goes for it, they will eat, sleep, and breathe the game for the next year or more of their lives.

Internal Development

Apart from considering the merits of the game as a product, a publisher has to decide if developing it in-house is the best use of its available people. This usually isn't a difficult decision if the prospective development team has been on-staff for a while, because the company knows them and their strengths and weaknesses. If the publisher really likes the product but not the available team, they can always look for an external developer instead.

External Development

Going to full production with external developers is a much more tricky decision for the publisher, because at this point they're preparing to commit hundreds of thousands or even millions of dollars to an outsider whom they have little control over. But before they do that, the two parties must reach agreement on a development contract. The development contract contains far more than just the development budget and the schedule hammered out in the project-planning phase. You can't understand the game business without at least a passing acquaintance with development contracts, so I've written a special section just about them.

The Development Contract

There are two kinds of development contracts; each uses different terms and each is intended to serve different purposes. The first, and by far the most common in developing new games, is called a *publishing contract*. The other is called a *work-for-hire contract*. I'll describe each in turn.

The Publishing Contract

A game publishing contract is, in essence, very much like a book-publishing contract, although there are many differences in the details.

Advances   In a publishing contract, the publisher agrees to *advance* money to the developer throughout the development period to cover the cost of building the game. Book publishers do the same with authors: they advance them money to cover the cost of writing the book. But an advance is neither an outright payment for work accomplished (which is what happens in a work-for-hire contract), nor is it a loan that creates a debt from the developer to the publisher. It is, in fact, an advance payment as part of the total deal. Just as you have to pay a building contractor part of his fee in advance so he can buy construction materials, so a publisher pays a developer in advance so he can work on the game.

Royalties   The other key part of the contract states that the developer will get *royalties* from wholesale (not retail) sales of the game; that is, a percentage of the money the publisher makes from selling the game to retailers after it's finished. This amount varies enormously, from as little as 7 or 8 percent of the wholesale price up to 40 percent or more in very special cases. 10 to 20 percent is a fairly common range.

However, the publisher doesn't pay royalties to the developer right from the first unit shipped. Since they've already given the developer advance payments, the publisher keeps the money until the amount of royalties earned matches the amount already advanced. Only when that happens does the developer start receiving royalty payments. The exact same thing occurs in book publishing. Once the advances have been repaid out of the royalties, the game, or book, is said to have *earned out*. The whole scheme is called *advances against royalties*.

Here's a simple example. Suppose Publisher P advances Developer D $2 million to make a game. Publisher P has agreed to pay Developer D a 20 percent royalty on wholesale sales of the game, which they'll be selling at $25 apiece. Twenty percent of $25 is $5, so the developer will receive $5 for each copy of the game shipped. However, the publisher needs to recoup their advances first. So they'll withhold the royalties until that $2 million has been paid off. That means the publisher has to sell 400,000 copies of the game before the developer starts receiving royalty money. (This is all in theory. In practice, it's somewhat different, for reasons I'll describe later.)

Milestones   The advance money is not all paid in one lump sum at the beginning of the development; rather, it's doled out a little at a time as the project progresses. The development contract will include a schedule with a series of *milestones*—dates by which certain features must be in the game. On the milestone date, the development company will send a copy of the work in progress to the producer at the publisher. If the producer agrees that the required features are in fact present in the game and working properly, then he'll authorize the next milestone payment to the developer. If he doesn't agree, he'll point out what's wrong. This is one of the touchiest areas of publisher-developer relations. Publishers and developers often disagree on whether a feature has been implemented properly. The publisher withholds the milestone payment, the developer thinks they're being unfair, and a squabble ensues. If the developer is absolutely depending on the money coming in, the publisher can drive them out of business (and kill the project) by not making the payment. On the other hand, sometimes publishers make milestone payments even when they're not really satisfied with the quality of the work, because they can't afford to let the developer go out of business. Even if they could find another developer to take over the project in the middle, it will almost certainly be very late and screw up the publisher's product planning.

Settling on the Numbers   The amount of the advance and the size of the royalty percentage depends on a great many factors, not the least of which is the negotiating skill of the developer. However, there are a couple of rules of thumb that help to determine their size. If some of the development work is already done when the publisher agrees to publish the game, then the amount of advance money needed to complete it is smaller, and the royalty percentage is correspondingly larger. For example, the developer may already have a software engine that allows them to build the game very quickly. If the developer has done all the work on their own nickel and the publisher doesn't need to pay *any* advances, then the royalty rate is the highest of all because the publisher's financial risk is correspondingly lower. However, this situation is very rare. Most often, little or none of the work has been done, and the publisher has to pay large advances to complete it.

Another thing that affects the royalty percentage is the developer's track record and technological skill. If the publisher has worked with the developer before and has made several hit games with them, the royalty rate is bound to be much higher than if the developer is new and the publisher doesn't know them well. First-class developers are rare and a valuable asset to any publishing company. A publisher who has a relationship with a development company that they like will do a lot to keep it happy and working with them. If the developer becomes *so* vital to the publisher that the publisher's business success would be threatened if the developer started to work with someone else, the publisher might actually buy the developer's company and make it a division of their own.

Finally, royalty percentages aren't always fixed for the life of the product. They often contain escalator clauses that mean the developer gets a higher royalty once the game has sold a certain number of copies. Publishers may also offer bonus percentage points for getting the game done ahead of schedule.

The advances against royalties aren't usually much more than what it will cost to build the game in the first place—there isn't a fat profit built into them for the developer. That's because the developer is hoping to make their real money on the royalties afterward. If the game is a hit, the developer can make millions. On the other hand, if the game is a flop, at least they got paid while they were making it. Unfortunately, it's a sad reality that most games today never earn out (recoup their advances), so the developer never sees any royalties at all. They cost a great deal to develop, and they don't sell well enough to repay those costs. On the other hand, in a few cases, they do fabulously well and the developers make millions. As in Hollywood, the hits subsidize the misses.

What if the Game Gets Cancelled or Doesn't Sell?   It's important to realize that the advances are not actually a debt owed by the developer back to the publisher. They're simply an advance payment against anticipated future earnings. If the publisher decides not to publish the product after all, the developer doesn't owe the advances back. Or if the publisher fails to sell enough units to recoup all the advances, the developer doesn't have to pay the difference. Creating the game is the developer's job; selling it is the publisher's. If the developer has done their part, they are entitled to keep the advance money. If the publisher fails to sell the game, that's their fault, so they assume the risk if losing their advance money.

What if the Development Company Wants Out?   If the development company doesn't want to finish the project for some reason, they can usually back out by repaying all the advances they have received so far. However, in practical terms this is seldom possible. The developer has been spending that money to pay its employees and subcontractors to build the game; they don't have it to give back. The publisher is counting on them to deliver, so the contractual terms are designed to make sure they do. Of course, terribly managed developers do occasionally go bankrupt, leaving the publisher in the lurch. Back when development companies consisted of only one or two people, they were also known to simply disappear—vanish into thin air, taking the source code for the game with them!

The Fine Print   The preceding example gives the bare bones of the advances-against-royalties system. Most arrangements are not that simple, and there are a lot of other things that go into a game development contract as well. Games are big business, and where a lot of money is involved you will always find smart lawyers and fine print. For example, a publisher could try to sell more games by offering a deal to the retailers: buy one game for $30 and get a second game for a penny. If the second game happens to be your game, the publisher could claim that the wholesale price was one cent, and you would get royalties of 20 percent of 1 cent! Wise developers make sure there are clauses in the development contract that prevent this kind of thing.

There are other things to be aware of as well. As I mentioned in Chapter 3, publishers never actually pay a developer the full amount of the royalties specified by the percentage, because they have to keep a reserve fund of money around in case the retailers want to return the games and get their money back. So although the contract states that the development company will receive 20 percent of the wholesale price of every game sold, after the reserves are deducted this could be 15 percent or even less. This means that it takes even longer for a product to earn out.

Occasionally developers need help from the publisher: assistance with knotty programming problems, or specialized services like motion capture that the developer can't do for themselves. All this costs money, and depending on the terms of the contract, the publisher may consider any money they spend on such things to be part of the developer's advance, having to be recouped later. After all, creating the game is the development company's job; if they need help with it, then should be the ones to pay for that help (goes the theory). But occasionally publishers can be pretty insistent about offering their "help," and an unscrupulous publisher might even overcharge a developer for the value of this "help"—whether they need it or not.

But Don't Worry about It!   You're probably wondering why I'm dumping all this rather grim business stuff on you when all you want to do is get a cool job in the game industry and realize your creative potential making great games. The reason is that, although you don't have to negotiate these deals in person, they still affect your day-to-day life as a game developer working for an external development company. When the boss comes in and says, "We hit our milestone two days early! Free beer for everybody!" you'll know what she's talking about. At this point in your career you don't have to *worry* about these things—but what you see go on around you at a game company will make a lot more sense if you *understand* them.

The Work-for-Hire Contract

A work-for-hire contract is a far simpler deal. In this case, there are no advances and no royalty payments. Instead, the publisher simply pays the developer a negotiated fee—again, spread out over a series of milestones—to do the work. This fee is usually higher than the amount a developer receives in advances in a publishing contract, because the developer is giving up the chance to earn royalties. If the game turns out to be a colossal hit, the developer doesn't share in its success.

Publishers seldom sign work-for-hire contracts for original game development. Work-for-hire contracts tend to be used for particular projects like converting an existing game to work on a new platform, or localizing a game into a new language.

These sorts of tasks are often undertaken by development companies that specialize in them. Since they're not contributing to the game's creative content, they aren't really entitled to share in the rewards of having a hit.

STAGE 3: PRODUCTION

The project is off and running! The development team, whether internal or external, has gotten the green light—that is, received approval to execute the development plan. At this point, the company staffs the project, deciding on all the programmers, writers, artists, animators, musicians, sound engineers, and other creative and technical people that will need to be on board. They may be coming from other projects that have just been completed, or (and this is where you come in!) they may be hired to work on the game. Take a look at Figure 4-1 to see how development teams grow and shrink during the production process. This is only an example; different companies use different approaches.

At this point everyone is working hard. Typically, it'll continue that way for the next 12 to 18 months. Equipped with a task sheet, the project manager will go around making sure people have done the work they're supposed to, and know what they're supposed to do next.

FIGURE 4-1

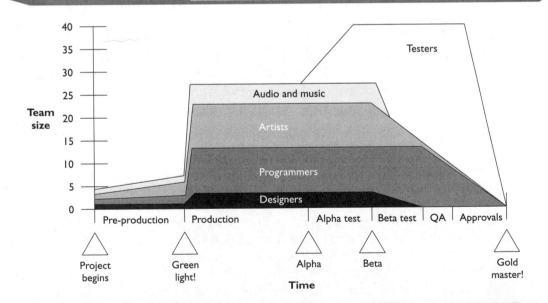

A plot of team size versus time for a hypothetical product

The Production Process (and Why It's Not Your Problem Yet)

There's an old adage than managing programmers is like herding cats: they're wayward, individualistic, and unpredictable. The field of software engineering is only about 50 years old, so we aren't yet sure how it's really supposed to be done. (Civil engineering, by comparison, is almost 5000 years old, which dates back to the Pyramids.) Game development is even worse, because in the game industry we have to build lots of stuff besides program code: still images, 3-D models and animations, music, sound effects, user interface elements, and so on. Each of these things requires a different procedure to make, so they all take different amounts of time to complete.

It used to be that project managers flew by the seat of their pants, making up schedules and deadlines out of thin air and based on hunches. That kind of approach doesn't work any more. The projects are too big and too complicated to manage by instinct alone, and now we need formal methods. Many smart people have written many large books on the subject. If you're particularly interested, you might read *Game Architecture and Design*, by Andrew Rollings and Dave Morris (now out of print, but there should be plenty of used copies available; a new edition is in the works), and *Rapid Development*, by Steve McConnell.

However, as a newcomer, you really don't have to worry about it now. You're not going to be hired in as a full producer or project manager. If your employers know their business, they will have thought carefully about how they want to run the project, and as it enters full production, they'll be putting their plan into practice. *Your* job will simply be to do your own work.

Jobhunting Tip: Avoiding Incompetent Employers

If all you want is a job, any job, and you don't really care whether the people you work for are competent or not, then you can ignore this (but be warned: companies with incompetent management tend to be short-lived!). On the other hand, if you want to find out if you'll be working for professionals, ask your prospective boss to describe the development plan for the product you're being interviewed for. Don't give him a grilling; just say that you're learning about the business and you'd like to understand his approach. If he seems surprised by the question, or gives you a lot of hand-waving, you'll know he hasn't really thought about it. That's a warning sign that there may be trouble ahead. Conversely, if he draws a neat timeline on the board and explains where the milestones are and who else will be on the team, then you can feel a little more confident. Of course, you don't have any way of knowing if the plan is realistic or not, but at least they *have* a plan. It's a sure way to separate the amateurs from the pros: pros make a plan.

> **WAR STORIES**
>
> At some point in every day there is a moment when we all try to let loose and do something out of the ordinary. When I was at EA, in the early days of my career, we would have shooting contests for money in the lobby with a Fisher-Price basketball hoop that we bought. This would get everyone together, and while most of the people had no ability to shoot, it didn't really matter. A dollar on the line is worth the fun of breaking away and laughing as a team. At Konami, our guys quickly switched this to producer baseball. I, being inept at baseball, didn't have as much success as the others, but it was fun nonetheless, and an important part of our day. Never underestimate the importance of team bonding. A key part of our morale can be directly traced to the bonding that went on as a group.
>
> — Jake Neri, Founder and Partner, Blaze Games

Meetings, Meetings, Meetings!

Every week throughout the production period there will be regular meetings. Subsets of the team, like all the animators, will get together with their lead to discuss issues specifically related to their role. All the leads will get together with the project manager to report on their respective departments. From time to time, the whole team will get together as a group, both for people to learn what the others are doing, and for management to give them information. And these are just the regular meetings. Often, a problem will come up during a larger meeting that requires only two or three people to solve. It's a waste of the others' time to try to solve it there, so the people involved will schedule another meeting to get together and deal with it. And then there are the ad-hoc meetings that arise spontaneously: "Hey, Pat! Let's grab Sandy and Chris and figure out how much disk space we can afford for voiceover audio." A surprising amount of a game developer's life—in extreme cases, 40 percent of a programmer or artist's time and 80 percent of a manager's—is actually spent sitting around a conference table rather than at her desk. Game development is an intensely collaborative activity.

Marketing Activities

Although this is a book for prospective game *developers*, it's useful for you to understand what's involved in *marketing* a game as well. Long ago, all a publisher had to do was buy ads in some gamer magazines, because those were the only media available. Nowadays, there are many more ways to reach gamers, and the marketing department has to cover them all. Here's a list of approaches modern game marketers use:

❭ **Print advertising**   Still the mainstay of game marketing, the marketing department will devise an ad campaign and purchase space in magazines they think will best reach their market. In special cases, they may even buy space in non-gamer magazines and newspapers as well, if they feel a game has a broad enough appeal to justify it.

❭ **Web sites**   Any forthcoming game has to have a web site full of screenshots, information about the game, interviews with the designers, and downloadable items: desktop themes, audio clips, movies, and, above all, a playable demo once the game is complete enough to play.

❭ **Co-marketing activities**   Publishers will often work with retailers to help them sell the game, by providing displays and decorations for their stores and fliers and other material about the games. The publisher may also help to pay for the store's own advertising. Retailers now have enough clout to demand this; a publisher who doesn't provide it may find their games on the bottom shelf, back in the least-accessible corner of the store!

❭ **Trade shows**   A trade show isn't really marketing aimed at the consumer; rather, it's an event intended for the retailers. The Electronic Entertainment Expo (E3) is the big game trade show in the United States. Publishers will spend hundreds of thousands of dollars building a fancy booth and flying their marketing staff and senior developers to a trade show to demonstrate their products to distributors, retailers, and the press. E3 allows consumers in on the last day, so those who want to can get an early look. E3 can be a great opportunity for someone seeking a game development job, but keep in mind that the publishers are spending big bucks to be there to cut deals with distributors and retailers, not necessarily to talk to job applicants.

❭ **Press events**   In addition to buying print advertising, a publisher will also try to get press coverage of the game in as many magazines as possible. They'll invite reporters to visit their offices and send them *press kits*—fliers and CDs full of images and other information the magazine could use if it writes an article about the game. They'll send out early versions for previews to just about everybody they can think of, as well as distribute another version to magazines and other media sources near its release to facilitate reviews.

❭ **Television advertising**   Only used for the biggest of the big hits, such as a surefire winner like *Madden NFL Football*. TV advertising is incredibly expensive just to produce, much less buy.

❭ **Public events**   These are particularly common with sports games, because they can be held in conjunction with major sporting events like the NBA playoffs. The publisher holds a big party, hires celebrities to come and play their game, and, of course, invites the press to attend.

❯ **Box design** The design of a game's box is important to help sell the game, so this is traditionally a marketing activity. They'll take all the pictures and lay out the text. In some cases, the marketing department considers everything except the contents of the CD or DVD itself their responsibility, so they'll write the manual, too.

INSIDE INFO You know those "designer diaries" you see online? If one is being produced by a small development company or a one-person shop, it's probably more or less real and tells the unvarnished truth. But if it's on a big publisher's web site, it's essentially a marketing gimmick, letting the public think it's getting a peek into the internals of the design process. Trust me, if there was a colossal screw-up on the project and half the animations had to be reworked, it wouldn't appear in a big publisher's "designer diary." That kind of thing could hurt the stock price!

Marketing a big product is hugely expensive. The general rule of thumb for an ordinary, run-of-the-mill PC game is that the publisher should spend the same amount of money marketing it as they did developing it. But for their AAA products, the top-of-the-line blockbusters, they'll spend three or four times that much—many millions of dollars.

STAGE 4: TESTING

Once the game has gotten to the point where large parts of it are playable, testing begins. Testing is an absolutely essential, but rather unglamorous, part of developing any game. It involves no creativity, only hour upon hour of trying out different features in different combinations to make sure they all work.

Informal testing goes on throughout the development process, as programmers run their code and producers check it over at milestones. Formal testing is normally divided into phases called *alpha*, *beta*, and *quality assurance* (QA). I'll discuss each here in turn.

Alpha Testing

Testing may begin on a game long before the whole thing is assembled and playable; testers can test parts of it as development progresses. But when the game reaches the point that all its *features* are present—even if all its *content* is not—then the game is said to be "at alpha" and ready for alpha testing. Alpha occurs when all parts of the game are functional but not all the graphics or data are necessarily available. For example, in a flight simulator, the plane may be fully functional but not all the landscapes are ready yet. In a football game, the game may be playable, but not all the stadiums or teams yet created. As a general rule, though, about 80 percent of the content ought to be done, because most of your team's effort after alpha is spent on tuning and bugfixing. There's not enough time left to be creating large amounts of new material.

Alpha is a make-or-break point for the game. For external developers, it's normally an important milestone and triggers a big payment. The publisher's next step will be to commit a lot of resources to testing the game, and to start ramping up the marketing. Before they take that step, they are likely to take a long, hard look and make sure that the game is really fun enough to succeed in the marketplace. A fair number of projects make it all the way to alpha and get killed because, even though they're competently built, the publisher doesn't believe they can compete. Remember, the amount the publisher spends on marketing may be several times what they've already spent on development. If they kill a mediocre product at this point, they save all that marketing money. If they let a mediocre product go forward and it tanks, they've lost much more than just the development costs.

Once a publisher has made the decision to go forward, the game is in alpha-test. This is a period of internal testing by the publisher, developer, or both together. A few weeks before alpha, a testing manager will create a test plan, a master document listing all the tests to be run to check each feature. Testers will be hired, or reassigned from other projects, to execute the test plan. The number varies with the size and importance of the project, but it's not unusual to have 25 or 30 testers working full-time on a single game. The testing manager will also set up a *bug database* to keep track of bugs that the testers have found. Every time a bug is logged, the programmers will have to deal with it, and when done, claim that it has been fixed. The testing manager doesn't take the programmer's word for it, however! The bug remains "open," that is, flagged as a problem, until a tester has re-tested for it and verified that the fix really worked.

Alpha testing can go on for weeks or even months. It's a hard, grueling time. The bugs seem to come in an endless stream, and the programmers develop a secret hatred of the testers and the bug database. In the meantime, the artists, audio people, and other content providers are hurrying to provide the remainder of the data needed to complete the game.

INSIDE
iNFO   If you keep your nose too close to the grindstone, your work gets out of focus. When you are working hard toward a goal, your brain doesn't have time to do any lateral thinking, and you often don't have the ability to step back and clearly evaluate what you've done. Taking a break does more than give your body a rest; it also allows your mind to break out of the rut it gets into during crunch time, permitting you to see your work with a new perspective. Try not to work more than two weeks in a row without a day off.

Localization

If your product is going to be sold in another country, you have to plan for it in advance, as I mentioned in Chapter 2. Localization has an impact across the whole development team, even the programming:

> **Programmers**   Programmers must write the software so that all text is read in from files and none is hardwired into the code. Far Eastern languages require two bytes, rather than one, to store each character of text, so if the game is to be localized for one of those languages, the programmers must allocate additional memory for the text. On console machines, the programmers must make sure the code works on both PAL and NTSC television systems.

> **Artists**   This group must create multiple versions of any art that includes text, and multiple versions of any art that is culturally sensitive. Nazi symbols are forbidden in Germany, for example, so games about World War II require special artwork for the German market.

> **Audio engineers**   Audio engineers have to record separate versions of any voiceover dialog in every language the game will support. The game may even need different music; Japanese and American tastes are somewhat different, for example.

> **Writers**   Writers must get their material translated. In addition to the in-game text, the product will need a new box and manual for each country.

All this work should be completed before the end of alpha, and, of course, it all has to be tested.

Beta Testing

When all the content is ready, all the levels designed, and all the art and audio created—including foreign versions—the game is complete. This point is called *beta*, and for external developers, it's another important milestone. The game's still not ready to be shipped, however—not by a long shot. The internal testers are now working on the beta version and the programmers are still fixing the bugs they find. In fact, the internal testers now have a new set of things to test: they not only have to make sure that each feature works, but that it works on every level, with every team or weapon or airplane that the game contains. All the content must be checked to make sure it works with the game. This process is called *beta-testing*.

Once the game is in beta-test, the publisher can, if they want, do *open* beta testing. In open beta testing, the publisher allows members of the general public to test the game—in effect, a field test. It's only possible with PC games; console games cannot be tested this way because the public doesn't have the specialized development hardware necessary to run the game. In order to prevent piracy, the external beta testers are normally given a copy of the game that only works for a limited time; they also sign an agreement not to make copies of the game. Open beta testing is normally restricted to a fixed period.

Open beta testing is of mixed value. On the one hand, ordinary gamers will think of all kinds of weird things to try on the game that the alpha test plan might not have included. The outside beta testers might have hardware configurations that are different from the ones the internal testers have. In those respects, open beta testing is tougher and potentially covers areas that alpha testing didn't. It also has some marketing value; non-employee beta-testers will talk and raise gamers' enthusiasm about the game (as long as it isn't too buggy when they get it).

On the other hand, however, open beta testing is haphazard. You can't hand external beta testers a checklist and make them complete it; they're not getting paid. You can never be quite sure what they'll cover and what they'll ignore. Also, because they're ordinary gamers and not professional testers, they might not be as observant, or be able to describe the bugs they find in a way that's helpful to the programmers. They might even report things as bugs that are just features they don't like. Open beta testing takes a lot of management, and not all publishers bother with it on all games.

Configuration Testing

Configuration testing applies only to PC games, not to console games. Toward the end of the testing period, when the program is looking pretty stable, the publisher still starts trying it on different combinations of hardware and operating system variants. They'll usually have a *config lab*—a room full of PCs with several combinations of video cards, audio cards, memory, processor speeds, and versions of the target operating system. This lets them discover if the game has problems with a particular manufacturer's hardware, and helps them determine what the minimum acceptable configuration for the machine is. Obviously, they can't test every possible combination of every graphics and audio card; there are just too many. But configuration testing is an essential step before any PC game can be released.

Disney's Christmas Configuration Calamity

In the summer of 1994, Walt Disney Corporation had a mega-hit movie on its hands with *The Lion King*. Seeking to capitalize on this, they brought out a *Lion King* video game for the PC, which they made available in time for Christmas. About that time, a computer industry trade group, hoping to boost sales of CD-ROM drives and sound cards, had the bright idea of defining a standard called the "Multimedia PC"—a PC machine with an 80486 processor, an 8-bit Sound Blaster card or equivalent, and a single-speed CD-ROM drive. Millions of people bought machines marked "Multimedia PC" in the belief that they were the hottest thing going in audio and video for the personal computer.

Unfortunately, someone at Disney had decided *The Lion King* would sound better on a 16-bit sound card … and that was the machine they developed it for. It didn't work, as shipped, on the much-vaunted Multimedia PC.

Christmas morning 1994 was an unmitigated disaster for Disney. Thousands upon thousands of angry parents called Disney's help line to ask why their game wouldn't work on what they believed was the latest and greatest PC. In the end, over half the games were returned for a refund.

If only they had done a configuration test with an 8-bit sound card…

Content Ratings

In many countries in the world, a video game must be submitted to a ratings body to determine how violent, scary, or sexually explicit it is before it may be sold. This is done after the game reaches beta, when all the content is present. The rating institution takes a few days or weeks to examine the game and return a rating, which the publisher is required to print on the game's box and possibly in any future advertising as well.

In America, rating is done by the Entertainment Software Rating Board. This is not required by law (that would be a violation of the First Amendment), but some retailers refuse to carry games that have not been ESRB-rated. Some also refuse to carry games with an AO (Adults Only) or M (Mature) rating. Although many developers object to having their games labeled in this way, the system does help the consumers know what it is they're getting. It is actually superior to the American movie-rating system, because in addition to a letter grade it also supplies "content descriptors"—short phrases that indicate what sorts of things the player will see in the game.

Obtaining the ratings for every country in which the game will be sold is a major job, and most publishers have a special department set up just to handle the paperwork and keep track of the process for each game.

Quality Assurance

Quality assurance sounds like a fancy term for testing, but in fact it refers to a particular aspect of the process. Normally, a game goes to QA when all the bugs in the bug database are fixed and the producer is convinced the game is ready to ship. The QA department tests it for a number of hours, and gives it a simple pass/fail grade. QA doesn't try to determine whether a game is enjoyable or well-balanced; it is concerned only with whether it works as a piece of software. If a game ever crashes, responds inappropriately to a command, or displays something it isn't supposed to display, it fails QA and cannot be shipped. QA also checks to make sure that all the details in the manual are correct:

that the images on the screen match the pictures in the manual, and that the commands are documented correctly and work as described.

The QA department at a publisher is normally separate from, and independent of, the production department that is responsible for the game. That way they can't be pressured into passing the game even if it has problems.

A QA Failure

In January of 1999, Electronic Arts had to recall 100,000 copies of the PlayStation version of their *Tiger Woods 99* game. Someone had (possibly accidentally) included a data file on the disc that didn't belong there, an AVI movie of the highly blasphemous original *South Park* pilot called "The Spirit of Christmas." There was no way to see it accidentally by playing the game, but all the same it was extremely embarrassing—and costly—to EA. The error was made worse by the fact that EA didn't have the rights to *South Park* anyway; they were held by Acclaim. A simple QA check, verifying the identity and purpose of each file, would have saved the company a small fortune.

Licensor and Console Manufacturer Approvals

If a game is based on a licensed property of some kind—*Nancy Drew,* for example, or Major League Baseball—the terms of the license contract will require the publisher to submit a copy of the game to the licensor for their approval. They want to be sure that the publisher isn't misusing their characters, logos, or whatever it is that the license provides. They can be extremely strict about this, insisting that every color be exactly right and that the game include no inappropriate material for their license. Recently, the National Football League has begun cracking down on video games that represent football as more violent than it really is (which is extreme enough in any case!).

In addition to the property licensors, the console manufacturers also have an approvals process. They have both content and quality standards, because the game is going to go out with their logo on it. In addition to performing their own technical tests, the console manufacturer will make sure the subject matter meets their guidelines, and even the package design gets close scrutiny.

If a game is going to be published on more than one console, each version has to be approved by its own console manufacturer. For example, Activision's *Tony Hawk's Pro Skater 4* is available for the Xbox, PlayStation 2, and GameCube all at once, so Activision had to submit it to all three manufacturers, Microsoft, Sony, and Nintendo, for their approval process—in addition to sending it to Tony Hawk himself! This is not a minor moment in the development cycle of the game: If the product fails quality control, the console company (under the terms of the license the publisher signed with them) may be able to require changes or even force the publisher to kill the project.

A Sample Development Schedule

Here's a sample development schedule for a hypothetical 18-month project. Let's say that we're going to make a console game with a license of some kind—*Pro Line-backer Barbie*®, or something of the sort. We'll have to include extra time in the schedule for the license holder and console manufacturer to check over and approve the product. We'll also assume that this is an English-only game, so it doesn't require localization. This example does not include the marketing or sales effort, which is, of course, going on in parallel with development.

Suppose we pick a ship date of November 15, 2005—in other words, in time for the holiday shopping season. We'll want to leave a month of lead time for the console company to manufacture the games for us, because a lot of other publishers are having their games manufactured around then, too. (Cartridge games for machines like the Game Boy Advance actually require longer than this; for disc-based games it's often less, especially at other times of the year). That sets our actual gold master date at October 15, 2005. Therefore, for an 18-month project, we'll need to start on April 15, 2004.

> ❭ *April 15, 2004: Pre-production begins.* A small team is doing concept design, technical research, and prototyping work. They're also building the tools they will use during full production.

> ❭ *July 15, 2004: Conceptual design complete; partially playable prototype.* Three months into the project, the designers will have written a thorough design script. The programmers will use it as a "requirements document" to create a technical design for the final product.

> ❭ *October 15, 2004: Full production begins. Technical design complete; tools complete; playable prototype.* Using the prototype, the designers can see how the game's mechanics are working and fine-tune as necessary. The team staffs up to full strength.

During full production, there will be numerous milestones to make sure the project is on track. Since these vary with the actual nature of the code and content, I haven't included them here.

> ❭ *April 15, 2005: Formal testing begins.* Although the game isn't complete yet, the producers have been testing parts of it all along. Now, a testing manager assembles a test plan and assigns a limited number of testers to begin work on the parts of the game that are finished.

❱ *May 15, 2005: Alpha. All features are present.* All aspects of the game should be playable, though the levels, artwork, and audio may not be complete. Testing staffs up to full strength for alpha test.

❱ *July 15, 2005: Beta. All content is present.* All the creative elements of the game—pictures, sound, and text—should be complete, all the levels built, and the game should not crash. Beta testing begins.

❱ *September 1, 2005: QA. The game appears to be finished and bug-free.* Since this is a console product, no configuration testing is necessary, but the game goes through intensive testing by the Quality Assurance staff to be sure it is ready for the approvals process. Beta isn't formally over until QA says it is; they have the last word.

❱ *September 15, 2005: Approval process begins.* Copies of the game go off to the license holders and to the console manufacturer for their approval; they also go to the appropriate government or industry regulatory bodies for a rating evaluation.

❱ *October 15, 2005: Gold master!* The game goes to the console company for manufacturing. Unless there's going to be a sequel or a version on another platform, this project is officially over.

This makes it all look marvelously simple and easy, but, of course, it isn't. Schedules can slip and projects get behind for an infinite number of reasons, but I won't depress you by listing them here. As in this example, schedules are frequently created backward from the desired ship date (the day when the game is first available to the customer). If the ship date is too near to get all the work done on time, one of three things must happen:

❱ The publisher has to decide to ship it later.

❱ The developer has to add people to the project.

❱ Both publisher and developer have to agree to reduce the scope of the game.

There's also a fourth option: making everybody work harder. This is often tried, but almost never works.

❙TAGE 5: MANUFACTURING

At long, long last—a year or even two years after that initial, brilliant idea—the game is ready to be manufactured and go out to the distributor or retailers. At this point, it has "gone gold" in industry jargon.

In the case of console games, the console manufacturer actually constructs the boxes and presses the discs. Manufacturing console games requires more time than PC games, because the console game companies have to do *every* publisher's games. That means a lot of publishers standing in line, waiting anxiously for their product to come back. Console games also tend to come in standard boxes, so the publisher has little control over what they get back. They design the printing, but the shape of the container is out of their hands.

With PC games, the publisher can shop around to find the best manufacturing deal. Often there are huge economies of scale: a run of 70,000 games can cost exactly as much as a run of 100,000. The manufacturers want large runs so they don't have to reset their equipment for someone else, and they're willing to give discounts to get them.

Pressing a single CD or DVD costs under a dollar in large quantities; the real money goes for the cardboard and those beautiful multicolored sleeves. Box design has a significant effect on the customer's sense of perceived value. A heavy box with a big manual inside feels valuable. A box with a cover flap and more details inside seems nice; there's more to read about the product. A box with very little printing on it is suspect. It gives the impression that there isn't much to the game.

Ultimately, however, manufacturing is one of the places where the publisher wants to keep costs as low as possible, because it's where the rubber meets the road so far as profits are concerned. Every dime they spend on developing and marketing the game, they can consider an investment in its future success; every extra dime they spend on the box comes straight off the bottom line.

WAR STORIES

My first task when I was hired at Electronic Arts was to help reverse-engineer the original Nintendo Entertainment System, or NES. A company named Tengen (part of Atari Games) had announced that they found a way around the Nintendo "lock-out chip" that was in every game cartridge to discourage pirating (and independent publishing). I believe EA thought it would soon be possible to publish their games for the NES, as long as they could legally figure out how the machine worked on their own in order to reverse-engineer it.

EA assigned Jim Nitchals and me to figure out how the NES worked. We didn't even know what microprocessor it used. We desoldered and removed the ROM chips inside a few game cartridges and jury-rigged them up to EPROM burners to read out every byte inside them. There it was, the machine code that we had cut our collective programmer teeth on: MOS Technologies 6502 instructions! (Most of the early personal computers used the 6502 microprocessor, so we weren't that surprised.)

Once we knew what kind of microprocessor was in the machine, everything else fell into place. We could now write programs to try to figure out how the beast worked. Eventually, we were able to discover everything about the machine through looking at what

WAR STORIES CONTINUED

published games did and trying things out with our own programs.

To complicate matters, Jim and I had been working away from all of the other game developers and in fact had been entrusted not to communicate anything about what we were doing to anyone. We had to keep a logbook on how we reverse-engineered the NES, and we had to endure hours of mind-numbing meetings with EA's attorneys to make sure we followed the same "clean room" techniques that Compaq Computer had followed when they reverse-engineered the IBM PC. This wasn't a physical clean room, with bunny suits and air-filters, but a legal clean room, designed to make sure EA couldn't be sued by Nintendo for violating their copyrights.

EA didn't end up supporting the NES, but later on the company used some of the techniques we had learned to reverse-engineer the SEGA Genesis. Jim and I ported Populous, a PC game, to the Genesis. A trade show was coming up in a few months and Trip Hawkins (the CEO of EA at the time) wanted to present a working Genesis game to some SEGA executives at that show. It was a great coup to prove to them that EA could develop games for the Genesis, legally but without their permission, before it was even available in the United States.

Although EA never actually built unlicensed cartridges for sale, they used this knowledge to force SEGA to give them a better license deal than any other publisher had, and to allow EA to manufacture the cartridges themselves at a substantial cost savings. Of all the publishers who produced SEGA Genesis products, only EA was allowed to manufacture its own cartridges. SEGA put up with this rather than fight because they wanted EA's support to help the Genesis beat the Super Nintendo. Both companies profited handsomely from the arrangement.

—Kevin McGrath, Retired Game Programmer

RAP-UP

That's it, beginning to end, soup to nuts. You now know how a game goes from a brilliant idea in one person's mind to shelves and shelves full of shiny boxes. Once you have your job in the game industry, you'll have an idea of what's going on and why. In the next chapter, I'll start talking about how you make yourself ready to *get* that job.

CHAPTER

5

Preparing to Be a Game Developer

NOW we get down to the nitty-gritty, the essential details of preparing to be a game developer. The first part of this chapter is devoted to formal education—getting someone else to teach you in a school of some kind. You have a number of options, especially if you're still young. And if you're older and already have a job in another industry, take heart—your skills and experience may be quite valuable in the game industry.

The second part of the chapter is for those of you who don't have the option of getting formal training, for whatever reason. There are still plenty of things you can do to teach yourself and to form connections with the game industry.

IF YOU'RE STILL IN PUBLIC SCHOOL

If you're still in public school, it's too early to devote all your attention to getting a job in the game industry—you're not ready for that level of specialization, and there are plenty of other interesting careers to consider as well. After you've looked into it, you might find that something else (brain surgeon, supermodel, captain of industry) seems more attractive. But now is a good time to lay the groundwork. It takes a lot of learning to become a game developer, especially if you want to become an expert at either the creative or technical side of things. In this section, I'll talk about some things you can do while you're still in school.

Uncover Your Talents

In order to have a successful creative career, you have to meet two conditions. First, do you *like* doing it? Second, are you *good* at doing it? If you like doing something but you aren't very good at it, you should see if you can get better with practice and the help of a good teacher. On the other hand, if you're good at something creative but you hate doing it (which is unusual), then there's not a lot of point in it—if you dislike the work, you won't really be able to dedicate yourself to it properly.

The only way to know what talents you have is to try them all. For example, when I was a kid I wrote an essay about pollution and entered it in a contest. To my astonishment, it won a $10 prize (this was a long time ago!), and I got my picture in the local newspaper. From this, I concluded that writing—non-fiction, at least—would come fairly easily to me. On the other hand, I tried to learn the viola at about the same time, and it didn't take me long to discover that I have no talent for it. I love listening to music, but I'm hopeless at making it and I hate practicing.

Do you like writing stories or plays? How about designing buildings or vehicles or clothing? Can you draw? What kinds of subjects? Landscapes, objects, people? Ever tried to compose music? Experiment with as many of these things as you can. Talent is one of those hidden qualities that you never really know you have until you suddenly discover it—if you don't try, you'll never find out.

Lay the Foundations

Before you can specialize in the skills you need to be a game developer, you have to lay the foundations. Video games may seem like they're just light entertainment, but there's a surprising amount of knowledge that underlies them. For example, if you try doing graphics programming without knowing the elements of analytical geometry, you will either be very frustrated or (if you're especially smart) you'll waste a lot of time reinventing principles originally discovered by René Descartes 400 years ago.

Here's a list of the things I think a young game-developer-in-training should study in school, no matter what area you decide to specialize in:

> **Using computers and creativity tools**   Obviously, being familiar and comfortable with computers is vitally important if you're going to work with them all day long. You can probably teach yourself this entirely on your own, but there's no harm in taking classes in using a word processor, paint program, spreadsheet, and other typical tools. Even if you are only interested in one field, you should try to get a little experience with as many different computer tools as you can. Flexibility is a terribly valuable asset, and a programmer who *has* used an audio waveform editor is just that little bit more valuable than a programmer who hasn't.

> **Computer programming**   You can't be a programmer without learning programming, and even if you're self-taught (I was), you'll be a better one if you let someone teach you about it. Even if you don't want to be a programmer, you should take some programming classes if they're available. It's very helpful for *everyone* in game development to have a general understanding of what programmers do. If your school doesn't offer programming classes, don't despair; you can teach yourself well enough out of books and then pick up the formal learning in college.

> **English (writing, both composition and creative)**   Absolutely essential for game designers and scriptwriters. Marketing and some production jobs require writing skills as well. Games may be mostly about sound and images these days, but a development team will write a heck of a lot of words on

the way to getting a game on the store shelves. The industry also does a lot of its work by e-mail, especially between publishers, external developers, and subcontractors. E-mail may seem like a trivial reason to study English, but if you can't express yourself quickly and cleanly in print, it's going to slow you down.

❱ **English (literature)** This is where you read the great stories, from *Beowulf* to *Harry Potter* (and if you don't think *Harry Potter* is great storytelling, you've missed something). If you have any interest in being a game designer, you need to read, read, read. Watching TV isn't the same—even with a DVD, you can't conveniently flip back and forth between two sections, or make notes in the margin about how the story is being constructed.

❱ **Mathematics** If you're not good at math, you can still find work in the game industry, but it's essential for a lot of jobs. Algebra, geometry, analytical geometry, and trigonometry are required for anyone who wants to do programming, and very useful to anyone else, too. Probability and statistics are highly valuable for understanding random numbers and natural phenomena, which many games simulate. If you're going to do any physics programming you will definitely need calculus, and you should have a nodding acquaintance with it in any case.

❱ **Art** Critical for artists; almost as critical for anyone else. The look of a game creates a huge part of its atmosphere and emotional tone: cheerful, threatening, funny, mysterious, surreal, and so on. Even if you can't draw a stick-figure, you should take art to learn the uses of line and color, light and shadow, mass and perspective. Anybody can use a 3-D modeling tool to make a world that looks like a bunch of rectangular rooms with cubical crates in them; it takes art to make a real place and populate it with real people and creatures.

❱ **Music** Try watching *Star Wars* with the sound off, and you'll quickly get a lesson in the importance of how music creates mood and enhances storytelling. The screen tells us *what* is happening, but the music tells us how to feel about it. As with art, even if you can't create music, you can still learn to appreciate what it does for a game.

❱ **Science** Most games aren't about science, but many implement scientific principles: gravity, electricity, optics, aerodynamics. Biology and anatomy are both useful for artists. If you ever want to work on a sports game or vehicle simulation, it's imperative you understand Newton's laws of motion, and they turn up in a surprising number of other places as well. To make walking and running animations that look right, you have to have a grasp of the principles of acceleration and momentum.

) **History**   Unfortunately, in my experience, history is not taught very well in public school; it's either a dull series of dates and events or a propaganda exercise. But a lot of games are set in different periods of history, and that affects almost everything you see on the screen: buildings, clothing, vehicles, and personal items, as well as the language and manners of the people. Try to look beyond the raw facts and get an understanding of what it was like to live during a given period in history. If you can tell your Egyptians from your Romans, and you find the names and cultures interesting, that's all to the good.

) **Typing**   It sounds silly, but typing fast and accurately will make your experience of using computers both more pleasant and more productive. You don't want to be hunting-and-pecking your whole life. You don't necessarily have to take typing classes; there are plenty of software packages that can teach it to you.

Almost everything you can learn in school—even P.E.—has applications in video game development somewhere. Soak it all up!

Don't Drop Out!

Suppose you and a few friends have put together a great-looking game in your spare time, managed to get it in front of a publisher, and the publisher has shown some interest in putting it on the market. It's a fantastic opportunity, not to be missed, right?

Well, yes, it is a fantastic opportunity, and if you can do it without having to quit school, you should certainly try. But don't drop out in order to do it. You have to take the longer view, think ahead. You can't establish a game development company on the basis of one single game; you have to be able to crank out new ones year after year. What's going to happen after this game is done? Are all your friends going to want to stick around and keep working with you? Or are you, as is more likely, going to be out hunting for a job … without a diploma?

It *is* possible to get a job in the game industry without having graduated from high school, but it will be a lot easier, and in the long run your career will be a lot more successful, if you have that sheepskin. It's a simple fact of life that the higher you go in a company, the tougher the competition is to get there. If you want to build the games that turn *you* on, then you need to be in a position of authority. The better-educated you are, the better the chances that people will take you seriously enough to give you that chance.

There are always a few high-profile exceptions to these principles—Abraham Lincoln only had one year of formal schooling—but they were usually a matter of luck rather than choice, and you can't count on them working for you as well. Lay the proper foundations for your career by graduating from school.

SELECTING YOUR HIGHER EDUCATION

Your last big decision in high school is, of course, where you're going to go to college. *You should go to college if you can possibly afford to do so.* It's unlikely that your high school classes will have been able to give you the depth of learning or experience that you need to be a professional game developer. Even if you've done a lot of programming or artwork on your own, it will be difficult to compete in the job market with people who have degrees.

In this section, I'm going to give you some pointers on choosing a school or college to attend. Once you've read it, you can turn to Appendix A for a list of educational institutions with game development programs or other forms of training that you might want to explore.

INSIDE **info** Be wary of any program that prides itself on how "intensive" it is, or promises that it delivers a four-year degree in only three years. The quality of a teacher is not measured by how fast he talks. To learn a subject properly, you need time to think about it and time to practice it—*especially* a skill like art, music, or programming. Nobody can turn you from a raw beginner into an advanced 3-D graphics programmer in six months, no matter what they claim. It's *your* education, so choose a school that goes at a pace that suits you.

University or Trade School?

The first question is whether you want to get a bachelor's degree at a four-year university, or an associate degree or other certification at a junior college or trade school. There are significant tradeoffs in both cases.

Four-Year Degrees

If you go to a four-year school you'll get a traditional university education. This will require that you take classes in a variety of areas: the natural and applied sciences, the social sciences, and the humanities. Most schools will also have a basic writing requirement, and some will have a foreign language requirement as well. After a certain amount of general study, you'll declare a major and start concentrating on your particular field of interest.

If you choose to go this route, I would recommend against any university that emphasizes only the liberal arts and does not have any engineering or technical facilities at all. If you're planning to be a composer, you may not care, but ideally you should be working with technological tools throughout your college education.

Pros   The following are some advantages of going the four-year route:

❯ A bachelor's degree is more prestigious than an associate degree, and is often listed as a minimum requirement in job advertisements. The most important practical reason for getting a B.A. or B.S. is simply that it opens doors.

❯ If you aren't absolutely certain you want to be a game developer, you'll have more opportunities to explore a range of subjects at a four-year university. If you change your mind and decide you'd rather be in marketing, or in some other field entirely, a university will have the resources to help you with that—it's less likely that you'll have to transfer and start over somewhere else. If you *do* transfer somewhere else, your credits from a four-year university are more likely to be accepted elsewhere. Your time (and money!) won't have been wasted.

❯ You'll end up a better-educated person, with more exposure to a wide range of ideas, cultures, and issues—at least, if you pay attention and take advantage of the opportunities that a university offers. This is a less tangible, but, in my opinion, very important benefit.

Cons   These are some of the disadvantages of going the four-year route:

❯ A university education takes longer and costs more than a trade-school degree. This can be a serious consideration if money is tight or you need to begin earning an income quickly.

❯ If you're only interested in games, you may feel that a university's distribution requirements are just a boring series of hoops to jump through before you can do what you really want. You may not like having to pay for classes that you feel you don't need.

❯ A four-year university is less likely to have faculty who have worked in the game industry, and to have close ties to it, than a trade school.

❯ An ordinary university's computer science department may not have the specialized gear—special audio hardware, motion capture equipment, and other tools—that the game industry uses.

Trade Schools and Special Programs

Art and music schools have been around for some time, of course, but we're now starting to see the emergence of trade schools dedicated to new media careers. Few are specifically intended for game developers and no one else (DigiPen in Washington state being a notable exception). Most cover such things as graphic design, multimedia, and programming for web sites as well. Full Sail, in Florida, covers game development in addition to film and music industry techniques. A number of traditional art colleges have added game art to their lineup as well. Appendix A contains an extensive list.

Pros These are some of the benefits of attending a trade school rather than a four-year university:

❯ At a trade school you'll be working on exactly the subject that interests you. It's directly intended to help you get a job, rather than a general education. If it's a good school, it will have relationships with major game companies and a track record of placing its graduates at them.

❯ Your teachers may be former members of industry, or taking a break from it between projects. Their real-world experience can be invaluable; you may learn as much from chatting with them informally as you do in class.

❯ A trade school takes less time and costs less money.

WAR STORIES

I graduated a few years back with a degree in Engineering Mathematics and Computer Science from the Speed Engineering School at the University of Louisville. While I was there, I also interned for a company that developed virtual reality arcade games, but, unfortunately, they went bankrupt. Although it was my dream job, I was young and afraid that the game industry was too unstable for me to support myself. After graduating, I took software engineering jobs with higher salaries at larger, more stable companies. I switched companies a few times during the Internet boom, and my salary increased significantly. However, that all changed during 2001–2002. I saw many coworkers lose their positions, and I realized that programming for the game industry is not the only unstable job. I wanted to get back into games, but I needed to catch up with the latest technologies in game development. I decided to enroll in the game design program at Full Sail and I am currently halfway through the curriculum.

I am taking courses at Full Sail geared specifically to the game industry that many four-year colleges do not offer. For example, Full Sail has classes about programming on a console, real time 3-D modeling, and immersive multiplayer gaming, to name a few. However, they also teach the basics, such as object-oriented software design, data structures, and artificial intelligence.

—Lauren Logan, Student, Full Sail

Cons   Here are some of the drawbacks of trade schools:

❯ Trade school degrees are less well-respected than four-year degrees; some will be below the minimum required to apply for a particular job.

❯ Industry experts don't always make the best teachers. It's one thing to know a subject and quite another to teach it to someone else. You may also find that they're not entirely up to speed on the academic niceties like keeping office hours, grading on the curve, or lecturing intelligibly.

❯ If you change your mind and decide to go elsewhere, you may have more difficulty getting your credits transferred from a trade school.

The Two-Year/Four-Year Question: A Personal View

You'll have to consider a great many variables to decide how to manage your post-secondary education: such things as your financial circumstances, how far you're willing to move, your own educational goals, and so on. Without knowing all that, it's impossible for me to give you specific advice. Only you can determine what's best for you.

However, if you have any ambition to *design* games yourself someday (and many game developers do), then I think you should get a four-year degree if you can possibly afford it. Someone with a well-rounded education, who has studied a variety of subjects, has new ideas and knowledge to bring to their job. The game business is full of people who don't have any interests outside our own little high-tech cocoon, and our products suffer for it—the games all start to look alike after a while. If you have studied the writing of Charles Dickens or the history of the Zulu wars, then you know things about character development or infantry tactics that might be useful in a future game.

A trade school teaches you how things *are:* its focus is on learning the skills to do a particular job. There's no question that that is immediately useful in the short term, but if you're young and don't yet have a lot of responsibilities, you have the freedom to plan for the longer term as well. A university, with its wider areas of study and its emphasis on research as well as learning, encourages you to think about how things *might be.* That's a good attitude for someone who wants to design games someday.

How to Evaluate the Programs

There are whole books devoted to choosing a college, and I'm not going to try to duplicate their more general material here. For the basic information, go to the public library and check in the reference section for books like *The Fiske Guide to Colleges* or *The Best 345 Colleges;* or look at some of the many college guides available online. When it comes to deciding which one would be good for game development, though, use some of the following criteria as a guide.

> ❱ *Check out the catalog and course descriptions.* The single most useful thing you can do to evaluate a college's program is study its course catalog and descriptions. To help you determine how thoroughly a program covers the subject, I have included a document in Appendix B called the *IGDA Curriculum Framework.* Read the next section, called "What to Study in College," to learn how it can help you evaluate a college's offerings.

INSIDE INFO   If you want to become a programmer in the PC or console retail game industry, avoid "new media" educational programs that concentrate on development for the Web. The big games that come in shrink-wrapped boxes are written in C++, not JavaScript or perl. Shockwave is OK for prototyping the user interface and even the core mechanics in some cases, but it's not a substitute for the real deal. You will need a more hardcore programming education.

> ❱ *Check out the faculty.* Visit the program's web site to see who it has on staff, then go to the faculty members' web pages to find out their current areas of research. If the whole program seems to consist of one or two people, beware; they may not be able to offer you the breadth or depth of experience they should. Read the professors' curriculum vitae (the academic name for a résumé) to see how long they've been teaching and what subjects. If the faculty's interests don't seem to match any of your own, that's a warning sign.

> ❱ *Visit the campus.* If you live close by, contact the department or program and try to arrange for a tour—most are happy to hear from prospective students. Try to interview a professor or two if any are free while you're there. Tell them what you want to learn and ask for their candid opinion whether this is the right program to learn it in. Also take special note of any computer labs, video edit suites, or audio recording studios. If the gear seems to be old and run-down, or has seen hard use, that tells you that the program doesn't have much money or any ongoing relationships with hardware vendors. It's a sad fact that in high technology, richer is better. The more new equipment and software they have for you to work with, the better prepared you will be to enter the job market. However, don't let yourself be convinced by flashy facilities alone! A great lab won't much help if the faculty is uninterested in games.

❱ *Try to talk to a current student or recent graduate.* This is not an uncommon request, so don't be shy about asking the program admissions office to give you the name of someone. Of course, they'll give you someone who has a positive opinion of them, but all the same you can learn a lot about the culture of the program, the workload, the faculty, facilities, and student life in general. A student will also be able to tell you whether the teaching was primarily theoretical, or had real practical value, which can be hard to determine from the course catalog alone.

❱ *See what job placement facilities they have.* A trade school or other training program is more likely to emphasize this than a university program, but every school should have a means of getting students connected up with employers. See what kinds of things they offer: on-campus interviews, career counselors on staff, files on employers, and so on. Also ask if they have any statistics on their graduates' careers, or experience with placing their students into internship programs. A good program will be proud of its graduates' success and anxious to let you know about it. If a lot of students are ending up working for publishers or developers you've heard of, that's a very good sign. If they all seem to end up in some other industry, that suggests that the school's claim to turn out game developers is a bit shaky.

❱ *Make sure the school is accredited.* Unfortunately, anybody can rent some office space, put in a few tables and chairs, and start taking money from students under a fancy name like The Academy of Innovative Media for the New Millennium—but their degrees are worthless if they're not accredited. This won't be an issue with a major university, but if you're planning to attend a trade school, art college, or other training program, particularly one that's new, check to make sure it is accredited. This means an accrediting agency will keep an eye on the school to make sure the quality of its teaching is up to snuff, its professors meet certain academic standards, and so on. The school should list the accrediting agency on its web site, and the agency itself should be recognized by the United States Department of Education. DigiPen, for example, is accredited by the Accrediting Commission of Career Schools and Colleges of Technology.

How Do They Feel about Games?

It's a fact: video games are not yet respectable. We may be a multibillion dollar business that employs hundreds of thousands of people worldwide, and be the fastest-growing (and by some measures, the most enjoyable) entertainment medium in America, but to a lot of people we're still just kid's stuff. The game industry is full of young people, most of whom grew up playing video games and loving them. The academic community, especially at the big universities, is older and more conservative. A sizable chunk of that group doesn't think video games are a legitimate subject of scholarship, because games are (they believe) nothing but light popular entertainment. The same people, or their academic forebears, thought in the 1980s that TV wasn't worth studying, and in the 1960s that film wasn't worth studying. *You need to avoid these people!*

In your research, when talking to professors at schools you're interested in, ask them flat-out what they think of video games. If they're enthusiastic and they can see the latent potential in the medium, you've hit the jackpot: you found a person who will support your dream of becoming a game developer. If they're neutral, then use other criteria to judge: they might still be excellent people to learn programming or art from. If they're disdainful, dismissive, or openly hostile, stay away. It's hard to establish a good rapport with a teacher who disapproves of what you're trying to achieve, and you won't be able to count on their wholehearted support and interest in your projects. Remember, part of what you're doing in college is working on your portfolio. You can't do that effectively if your professor has no respect for your work.

WHAT TO STUDY IN COLLEGE

By the time you reach college, whether it's a four-year university or a trade school, you should have a pretty good idea of where your strengths and weaknesses are, and be ready to start specializing in the areas that interest you most. A few people will have the talent and energy to double-major in art and computer science at the same time, but for most of us mortals, it's time to start studying your particular craft intensively.

I spent a long time trying to define all the things that you could study in college to help you become a game developer, and then I realized someone else had done it much better than I could. Appendix B of this book contains a document written by the IGDA's Education Committee called the *IGDA Curriculum Framework*. It includes a list of a large number of *core topics* that could be helpful to a student who wants to become a game developer. Note that I said "could be helpful." That doesn't mean you have to study every single one! It also shows how these topics relate to particular careers in the game industry. Since the Education Committee did such an excellent job, I thought it would be better to reprint their work than try to duplicate it myself.

This section doesn't list the specific software and hardware tools used by the game industry; they're covered in Chapter 6.

How to Use the Curriculum Framework

For our purposes, the Framework is divided into three key sections: an overview of the core topics; a detailed breakdown of the core topics; and a section relating the core topics to actual careers in the industry. There are two useful things you can do with it: use it to decide what you need or want to study in order to attain your educational goals, and use it to determine whether a given academic program seems likely to meet your needs.

Deciding What to Study

Here's how to use the Framework to help you decide what you want to study:

1. To start with, you have to know what careers you're interested in, based on your experience so far. To find out more about them, read Chapter 6.

2. Next, turn to the Framework in Appendix B, and find the section named "Overview of Core Topics." Read the whole section. This will give you a good introduction to all the general areas that might be useful to a game developer, or anyone in any part of the game industry.

3. Now go to the section named "Tying Core Topics to Career Options." In this section, look at the careers listed. Find the career option that most closely resembles what you want to do, and see which core topics the Education Committee suggests for that career. In some cases, they will recommend only part of a core topic, not all of it.

4. Turn to the section named "Core Topics Breakdown." Using the list of core topics that you found in step 3, read the detailed breakdown of each core topic. These are the particular subjects that the IGDA Education Committee suggests would be relevant: the ones that would be most useful for you to study for that career. Go through and highlight the ones from your list. If you're interested in more than one career, use different colored highlighters for each one (but note that some will overlap!).

Remember, the Framework is not a curriculum or a course of study, it is simply a list of useful topics. Don't assume you *must* study everything in it, or even everything it recommends for a given career.

Determining Whether an Academic Program Has What You Need

Now you have a list of subjects that it would be good to study for the career you want. At this point, you can begin evaluating the programs at different academic institutions to see if they will meet your needs. Get hold of the college's course catalog (they're often online, or in the reference section at public libraries). Compare the courses offered by the school's program with the subjects that you highlighted in the Framework. You can't simply compare course titles, however, you'll have to read the descriptions as well. A good many professors put the syllabus for their courses on their university web sites. See if the course descriptions and the syllabi look as if they're addressing the topics you marked. The more they overlap, the more useful their teaching will probably be to you.

Because game development is so multi-disciplinary, chances are you won't find all this material located in the same part of the course catalog. You may need to check the College of Art, the College of Engineering, and the College of Humanities and Sciences (for example) to find out if they have courses that include the material you want. Bear in mind that different institutions will be organized in different ways, too.

As you do this, here are a few more things to remember as well:

> *Size isn't the same as quality.* If you find a program that seems to cover a lot of the material on your list, so much the better. However, that doesn't guarantee that the teaching or facilities are any good. Be sure to check out other aspects of the school as well, using the suggestions I gave you earlier, in the section called "How to Evaluate the Programs."

> *No educational institution will implement all the material in the Framework.* Don't expect that you will find a college that does; there's just too much there. The fact that a program doesn't have something you want doesn't mean it's a bad program; it just means that it might not be suitable for you.

> *A good education is not just about game development.* Choosing a college involves a lot more than ticking boxes. Don't follow this process too slavishly. Remember, a well-rounded education at a good school will serve you better in the long run, even if the school doesn't offer every little thing on your list.

Some Important Disclaimers

The IGDA has kindly allowed me to reprint the Curriculum Framework, but they're not responsible for the rest of this book, nor for the advice I'm giving you. Here are two things to keep in mind as you use the Framework:

> *It was originally designed for educators, not for students.* I think the Framework will be extremely valuable to you, but they didn't actually intend for it to be used this way. If you find that it doesn't really help you, blame me, not the IGDA!

> *The Framework is not perfect or finished.* It is an ongoing work in progress, which will be revised and refined continually. The version I have printed is the most recent public draft (February, 2003). As new versions become available, you can find them on the IGDA's web site, at http://www.igda.org/academia.

Color Outside the Lines!

The game industry has not yet specialized to the point that a developer can know exactly one subject and remain utterly ignorant of the others, and because of the swiftly evolving nature of our medium, it probably won't. We don't have rigidly defined, union-mandated job descriptions like the film and theater business, and I hope we never get them. Please don't consider the core topics in the Curriculum Framework to be bounded regions that you shouldn't stray out of. Every programmer should know something about art and music and writing; every artist should know something about programming and writing and music; and so on. In addition to your own specialty, try to take at least one or two of the introductory classes in each of the others as well.

In my time as a programmer I designed menu layouts, touched up pictures, reprocessed audio, edited movies, and did a hundred and one other little tasks that had nothing to do with writing code. If I had to wait for someone else every time I needed to correct a minor error in the content, I'd be waiting still. On a busy project, sometimes there just isn't anybody else. Cultivate flexibility and self-reliance, and they will serve you well.

Learn about Particular Areas

The Curriculum Framework is a great way to identify what you might want to study, and to figure out if a given institution will be able to teach it to you. In this section, I'm going to give you a few hints about getting an education in some of the key areas of game development.

Game Design

Relatively few traditional liberal arts universities teach game design principles as part of an undergraduate major, because it's just too new a field and not yet established. It's coming, but you'll have to look around. However, you should find courses on game design at both trade schools and in postgraduate programs dedicated specifically to the game and new media industries. You can also read a number of books on the subject, among them one called *Andrew Rollings and Ernest Adams on Game Design,* which I have a particular reason for recommending!

INSIDE iNFO Game design is highly interdisciplinary. You have to be the kind of person who goes on *Jeopardy*. And you have to know what makes games work, what makes them fun. Plus, you have to know the difference between what *you* think is fun and what the players do. That's a rare talent.
—Patricia Pizer, Massively-Multiplayer Online Design Specialist, ubi.com

Writing

Writing is the practice of using language to convey ideas, whether they're instructions for repairing an automobile engine or an entire fictitious world populated with fictitious characters. Writing for computer games draws upon many of the same storytelling techniques that the world has used since the time of Homer, and you will need to learn those techniques. Every four-year university will have a writing program, both for ordinary composition as well as fiction writing. Many junior colleges also teach fiction writing of various kinds. However, writing for interactive entertainment adds a twist that Homer never dreamed of: a player who enters the story and acts as both audience and participant; someone entirely outside the writer's control, who has the power—and the right—to change the direction of the story. This requires a new way of thinking about writing, one that is (as yet) unfamiliar to most professors of composition and creative writing. Once you have mastered the basics, you may have to strike out on your own.

INSIDE iNFO Interactive writing is an odd skill, one that's hard to teach. Frankly, an experienced gamer qualifies better than, say, a published novelist. That said, writing ability counts. Can this person tell a story in a compelling way? Can he/she make me laugh, charm me, amaze me with their use of words? I also look for their interpersonal skills. Good writers create believable characters; I think that requires an ability to connect with people, to understand them and empathize with them.
—Susan O'Connor, Freelance Interactive Scriptwriter

Art and Animation

Don't make the mistake of thinking that because game artists use computerized tools all day, there's no need to learn traditional art techniques. For one thing, the computerized tools are themselves analogs of real-world tools: paintbrushes, pencils, airbrushes, and so on. But more importantly, art is about seeing, not merely representing. The graphics in a video game are far more than a set of iconic symbols like *Monopoly* pieces; they create a world for the player to immerse himself in. As an artist you construct the most obvious manifestation of that world, its appearance, and to do that you need to understand the principles of visual creation.

There's a trade-off here: a trade school is more likely to have the high-end graphics tools, both hardware and software, than a traditional university art department. On the other hand, a trade school is also likely to concentrate simply on learning the tools, rather than teaching you the fundamental techniques of art: color, perspective, mass, motion, and so on. Nor is a trade school likely to address art history in any depth. Try to find an institution that covers both the aesthetic and cultural as well as the technical aspects of art.

WAR STORIES

I got my bachelor's degree in illustration at a traditional art college. Some of the professors gave me funny looks when I told them I planned to create art for "computer games." I had to jump through hoops in order to take 3-D classes with the animation department, and then the animation teachers were baffled as to why I would want to make still images from 3-D work. And none of my 3-D teachers placed any importance on texturing!

In quite a few ways, I had to gain an understanding of what it was to be a game artist on my own; then I had to use that knowledge to teach my teachers, so that they could help me to get what I wanted. But despite this, I think the fine-arts route is one of the better ways to become a game artist. Being able to use color, being able to draw an imaginary object in a 2-D space so that it looks 3-D, and quickly; understanding anatomy, and the materials in the world around us,

how things are created and how they decay; these are vital things for any artist wanting to create a character or a world from nothing, in any medium.

As a student taking the fine-arts route, you will have to be motivated to learn the technical side of things on your own. As a student taking the technical route, it is the art you will have to learn on your own. Either way requires ambition and research and a love of the work you are doing.

—Michelle Sullivan, Production Artist, Turbine Entertainment

Audio and Music

If you're good enough to get into Julliard, your talents will probably be wasted in game development (but you never know). Game audio is one of those areas that it's tricky to get an education for, because music schools aren't used to thinking about video games (and especially not things like interactive scoring), while audio engineering tends to be taught in training programs and trade schools rather than a university setting. Your best bet is probably to decide whether you're primarily a musician who needs to pick up some audio engineering techniques, or primarily an audio engineer who needs to be able to understand and record music. If you really are a musician first and foremost, you should develop that talent if you possibly can. Audio engineering is more of a learned skill—highly developed at times, but not as unpredictable as musicianship.

INSIDE INFO There are some schools that offer courses specifically in game audio development, but these courses are almost identical to what you could take à la carte from any university or community college, perhaps with the exception of courses like project management, asset management, and game development scheduling.
—Darryl Duncan, President and Chief Composer, GameBeat Studios

Programming

The programming section of the Curriculum Framework is somewhat larger than the others. That's not because programming is "more important" or "more complicated," but because the variety of techniques employed is greater. A 2-D turn-based strategy game may use the exact same animation and audio techniques as a frenetic 2-D shooter, but under the hood it will be completely different. *But keep calm: nobody is going to expect you to understand it all.* Some of the advanced topics are whole fields of study unto themselves, with their own buildings and faculty! Once you have learned the fundamental techniques, discuss the next step with your advisor and other professors. Obviously, the more you know, the more career options you will have, but it's better to be a real expert in one area than to be a Jack-of-all-trades and master of none.

Because the game programming technology is always changing, you should also be ready to prove to a prospective employer that you have learned how to learn—in other words, that you'll always be able to learn new technologies. You should never stop learning as a programmer. There are, for example, many unemployed COBOL programmers who never learned to program in any other languages. Don't ever let yourself become a technology dinosaur!

INSIDE iNFO *Specialize and gain as much experience in that specialty as you can.* By specialize I mean become a great 3-D graphics programmer, an expert at DirectSound, very well-rounded in developing artificial intelligence, or a programmer that knows all of the ins and outs of game networking—that is, something that will convince a manager that he/she needs you for this project, because they are lacking experience in your particular specialty.
—Kevin McGrath, Retired Game Programmer

Production and Project Management

As with game design, you may not find production and project management classes aimed specifically at the game industry in many four-year universities, but more will start appearing soon. At the moment, most training for production still happens on the job. However, if you're particularly interested in production and you *can* find a school that teaches these things, so much the better.

Project management, as a general topic, is likely to be taught in a business school. Software engineering project management, on the other hand, is more likely to be found in the engineering or computer science departments. Remember, game development is multidisciplinary, and no aspect of it is *more* multidisciplinary than production! Don't be afraid to sign up for courses in parts of the university that you wouldn't otherwise set foot in. Ultimately, you're responsible for your own education, even if the school you're in wants to put you on some kind of "track" and keep you there. A wise student seeks out the knowledge she needs wherever it may be found.

INSIDE iNFO   Audit your opinions with the help of your peers, and never assume that you know the exact way something should be done, as there is always a person who has the better answer.

—Jake Neri, Founder and Partner, Blaze Games

Other Useful Subjects

If you're at a four-year university or some other institution with a broad educational basis, there will be a great many other resources you can take advantage of and subjects you can study. Some, of course, will be mandated by the school's distribution requirements. The following sections contain a list of subjects that I think are particularly valuable for incipient game developers, in addition to the ones described in the previous section.

The Humanities

The humanities are the branches of knowledge concerned with the liberal arts, and since the arts are closely related to entertainment, this area is of the most value. They include

❯ English (and other) literature

❯ Drama

❯ Comparative religion

❯ History

❯ Foreign languages

❯ Photography

The Social Sciences

The social sciences are the study of how people behave in groups. This material makes an invaluable background for many kinds of simulated processes. *Sim City*, one of the greatest games of all time, was inspired in part by research into urban planning.

The following topics fall into the category of social sciences:

❯ Sociology

❯ Anthropology

❯ Psychology

❯ Economics

❯ Political science

❯ Linguistics

The Hard Sciences and Engineering

A great many games use principles from physics, and others make at least passing references to other sciences and engineering. *The Incredible Machine,* although it was mostly a lighthearted puzzle game, incorporated elements of mechanical engineering. *Mind Rover* from CogniToy allows players to wire up sensors and weapons on robots of their own design. The following subjects fall under the heading of science and engineering:

❯ Physics

❯ Chemistry

❯ Biology

❯ Genetics

❯ Geology and earth sciences

❯ Astronomy

❯ Mechanical engineering

❯ Electrical engineering

POSTGRADUATE PROGRAMS

A number of universities are starting to set up master's degree programs in interactive entertainment and other new media studies. They typically require two years to complete. In some respects, they're like the trade schools, because they enable you to concentrate on game development without having to work on anything else; but unlike them, you can't take classes piecemeal. They also tend to have a somewhat broader curriculum, and, of course, you get an advanced degree at the end. Although they are by no means required to get a job, they make you stand out from the competition and they're a good way to carry on your specialized studies intensively after college. Attending one of these programs gives you more time (and facilities) to build up a portfolio.

WAR STORIES

When I graduated from Sarah Lawrence College in 1995, I became a software engineer in a non-game field. I promised my parents that I would return to school when universities offered a master's degree in "something that really interested me." At the time, that seemed like a safe thing to say. Little did I know that several years later I'd be packing up all of my things, selling my house in Denver, and leaving a successful career to go back to school to get a graduate degree in a field that I really love.

My friends who were already in the game industry thought I was crazy to go to school to learn how to make games. My friends outside of the industry thought I was a crazy to leave the life I had worked so hard to create. But my intuition told me it was the right thing for me to do. I wanted to study the medium. I wanted to understand games on all levels. I also wanted to learn how to collaborate with programmers, artists, audio experts, other designers, and everyone else involved in the process.

It was this last desire that led me to the Entertainment Technology Center at Carnegie Mellon University and not to one of the trade schools that specialize in preparing people for a career in the game industry. The ETC doesn't try to teach their students one specific skill. Instead, the focus is on learning how to collaboratively apply your existing skill set to other disciplines. In effect, the ETC is a place to refine what you already know and focus it more closely on gaming or other new media, not a place to learn how to use Maya.

The ETC is also a great place to make contacts and get a surprising amount of "real-world" experience. Most of the curriculum is based around a series of projects, many of which are sponsored by leading technology and entertainment companies. There is also an optional internship between the first and second years of the program. I was lucky enough to work as a Game Design Intern at Maxis on The Sims Unleashed. Not only did I get to learn from some of the most talented developers in the world, but I also got a real "game credit" for my résumé.

I graduated in May 2003 with a Masters of Entertainment Technology degree and was able to go back to Maxis, entering as an Assistant Producer with a lot of game design responsibilities. Will the degree mean anything to my employers? I hope so, but what is more important to me is all that I have learned over the past two years. It has been an invaluable growth opportunity.

—Amy Kalson, Assistant Producer, Maxis

IF YOU'VE ALREADY GOT A JOB IN FILM, TV, OR OTHER ENTERTAINMENT MEDIA

A few years back there was a great deal of talk about "convergence" between various forms of media, including video games. This convergence didn't take place nearly as quickly as everyone expected, mostly because the production methods of software engineering and those of recording film or television are different and not always compatible. (Nobody has to hire 30 people to labor for months testing a TV show to make sure that it works properly in the TV!) However, the areas of overlap between the two industries are growing all the time, especially in the fields of content creation and digital effects. If your current job is based on those kinds of skills, your chances of being able to switch over to the game industry are pretty good. But you need to be aware that the game industry has grown out of a different tradition and its workplace culture is not the same as that of the older media.

Your Head Start and Your Handicap

If you've got a job in film, television, or some other form of entertainment, you have a head start in some respects and a handicap in others. Your head start arises from the fact that you already have a career and you understand some of the basic principles of entertaining people: pictures, sound, character, story, and so on. Unless you're a carpenter or an electrician, you've probably got some skills—creative, administrative, business—that will be of use in the game industry, and a portfolio of work that you can show people. Film production companies, for example, are used to scheduling large, multifaceted projects. Game development companies need those skills as well, although the parameters are different. Both industries do a certain amount of creative writing; both require music and audio production; both license intellectual properties and have relationships with other merchandising businesses. Read the next chapter on skills required by the game industry and look for areas of overlap between your industry and the game industry to decide where your skills could best be put to use.

Your handicap comes from the fact that almost all forms of media *other* than video games are not interactive and are not presented by computer software. Game developers have a different kind of relationship with their audience. Because each player interacts personally with our games, we can't treat them as a mass; we have to think of them as individuals and put ourselves in their shoes. And because games require engineering, the working style of the game industry is very different from that of film and television. Programming is not remotely like scriptwriting; we can't solve problems with a blue pencil. What may seem like a simple creative suggestion can have profound technical implications. As a result, many of the rules that you know about "the way things are done" are different in game development.

INSIDE iNFO   A note to Hollywood folks: game developers do things via e-mail, not the phone. If you're used to getting two dozen phone calls in a morning, and making two dozen more, forget it! Programming in particular requires careful, uninterrupted thought, and you can't do that if the phone is ringing all the time. E-mail lets people defer minor issues until they have a block of time to deal with them, and it creates a useful paper trail of decisions made. Get used to e-mail. Learn to like it.

Learn about the Differences

If you want to get into the game industry, be humble about what you don't know. Even if you've worked on some blockbuster projects that would earn you instant respect in your own business, it won't cut much ice with a game producer unless you can clearly demonstrate how that experience benefits his company. Do the research to learn about how things are different in game development, then be prepared to explain why your skills translate well. The next chapter discusses job roles in the game industry, and you compare them with your own job. If you're approaching a company that has little experience dealing with people in your current line of work, you may want to address this in your cover letter. You should also be ready to discuss it in an interview. Among the first things a potential employer will ask you are, "Why are you changing industries?" and "What makes you think you can do games?" *Don't* say, "'Cause games are the next big thing." Instead, say, "I see this as the natural next step in my career. Here's what I learned in my current job and how it applies to what you're looking for."

If you're not in a high-tech job already, you should definitely consider either taking a few classes in game development and production, or even going the whole hog and getting a master's degree from one of the programs I described in the previous section.

Breaking in: From Television to Games

At the time I was first hired to design and write games for Sierra On-Line (now Sierra Entertainment), I knew nothing about computer games. I had been writing for TV, animation, and comic books for many years, but games were an unknown to me. What sold Sierra on me was my Hollywood writing background, my willingness to move to the obscure mountain town where Sierra was located, and the handy fact that I came with an artist attached (my late husband, a well-known illustrator). My key advantage was that I had already established myself as a writer in other media, especially television. This meant that I didn't have to prove my credibility. In fact, it made me a good catch.

Luckily (for both them and me) I was one of the rare writers at the time who was used to working on computers and wasn't intimidated by having to figure out how to design a game from scratch. I have a natural tendency to embrace new formats and the challenge of a new technology, and I have the kind of technically-oriented mind that lets me pick it up quickly. That remains important to this day when I'm often expected to use a piece of proprietary software to write dialogue. I found many similarities between game writing and TV/animation/comic book writing. All three formats require the writing skill to pack a maximum effect into the least amount of words. What I had the most difficulty with in the beginning was breaking free of linear thought. I have a logical mind and I expected other people to approach things using the same logical series of steps I would take. It wasn't until I finally saw some off-the-street gamers pounding away in chaotic randomness on an early build of my first game that I finally, truly *got* the reality of non-linear thinking. To write effectively for this non-linear medium, a writer must be able to look at any piece of story or dialogue from a hundred different directions, constantly asking the prime question, "What if?"

—*Christy Marx, Freelance Writer*

If You're in High-Tech Hollywood

If you're already in a high-tech part of the film or television industry (digital effects, audio recording and engineering, video editing, or similar), you'll probably find that your skills transfer pretty easily. As the power of video game machines grows, the game industry is making more and more use of these facilities all the time. Of all the people who might come into game development from another industry, you have the best chance of making a smooth transition.

One important difference to keep in mind is that games have to deliver their experience in real time. If you've been involved with digital effects production for the movies, for example, you've probably had big iron to work with: banks of high-end Silicon Graphics workstations taking hours or days to create the visual appearance of a single frame of film. Compare that with a video game console: it has one or two small and comparatively slow graphics processors with which to compute and display 30 frames every second!

IF YOU'VE GOT A JOB ELSEWHERE IN HIGH TECHNOLOGY

What if you're in a different line of high technology? Suppose you've got a job building consumer, business, industrial, or even defense software. Is there a place for you in the game industry? Fortunately, the answer is yes. Like the film or TV people I talked about in the previous section, you've got both a head start and a handicap, but yours are different from theirs.

Your Head Start and Your Handicap

The game industry used to be notoriously ignorant of serious software engineering disciplines: coding standards, version control, that kind of thing. Many programmers were cowboys, used to working all alone and programming "on the bare metal" in assembly language. That's no longer true, and although game coding is seldom pursued with the rigor required of, say, defense contractors, it's far more professional than it used to be. You have a head start over someone fresh out of school, or someone coming in from filmmaking: you already know about software development—usability standards, quality assurance, engineering management—and you've worked in a high-tech production environment.

Your handicap is that you don't know much about entertainment. Games aren't optimized for productivity, they're optimized for fun. You're not used to intentionally challenging your customer; rather the opposite! Nor are you used to creating characters, telling stories, devising puzzles, or simulating the behavior of aliens. And whereas industrial software really has to deliver what it says it will do, games fake it a lot of the time. Just as everything that appears on a movie screen is fake, so is everything that appears in a game. The physics are less accurate. The AI is done with smoke and mirrors, not heavy-duty research. If we need to know how many acres of barley a peasant in the Roman Empire could sow in a week, we don't look it up, we make it up. We're counting on players to suspend their disbelief, enter the fantasy world, and pretend that things are real when they obviously are not. It's a very different mindset. Games are trying to achieve something that traditional software products do not: excitement.

The Legend of Army Battlezone

The details of this story are almost certainly wrong, but even so it's worth re-telling just for the principle; that's what makes it a legend. As the story goes, after Atari produced the coin-op game *Battlezone* in 1980, the U.S. Army paid them a visit. They wanted to find out how Atari was able to make a tank simulator for only a few thousand dollars when the Army was having to pay hundreds of thousands for theirs. The Army was hoping that Atari had invented some amazing new system that could save them millions.

Everyone sat down at a meeting: Army brass on one side of the table; scruffy, long-haired programmers on the other. The Army guys asked, "How do you make sure your physics computations are accurate with such slow, cheap hardware?"

"We don't," said the programmers. "We can't."

"But what if that means you don't compute the trajectory of the shot correctly, and the player's tank gets hit when it's supposed to survive?"

The programmers shrugged. "The player loses his quarter. So what? As long as he can't tell, it doesn't matter."

The Army brass looked baffled. They had never encountered a programmer with such a cavalier attitude toward accuracy. They commissioned a prototype called *Army Battlezone*, but that was as far as it ever got. In the end, the Army decided to keep their own simulators, because when lives are at stake, accuracy counts. Games are just for fun. They don't have to be "right," they only have to be enjoyable.

Learn about the Differences

The biggest difference that you'll notice is all the emphasis on content. Games present more content, and more *kinds* of content, than any other kind of software: still images, 2-D and 3-D animations, video, music, sound effects, dialog, narration, and text, not to mention buttons, menus, cursors, highlights, and other user interface elements. You'll be working with some kinds of people you've probably never even met before, much less thought of as colleagues. After a high-tech engineering company, being surrounded by all these artists and musicians will feel like you're working in Hollywood, or in a Broadway show.

The other big difference you'll notice has to do with the fact that the product you're working on is an inexpensive, consumer retail item rather than, say, a half-million-dollar medical instrument or an embedded guidance system for a torpedo. A video game probably has more code in it than an MRI machine, but it still sells for only $50. In order for a video game to turn a profit, it has to sell hundreds of thousands of units to the general public, and the competition is fierce. Since video games are for pleasure rather than utility, the customer makes her purchasing decision on feel, not features. Tuning and polishing are critical, and missing the Christmas retail season can be disastrous if the publisher was counting on it.

You'll also discover that the game industry is considerably less buttoned-up than other high-tech businesses. T-shirts and flip-flops are common (but don't wear them to an interview). Nerf ball fights help to ease tensions, and people's cubicles are likely to be decorated with all kinds of outrageous things. The flip side of this is that nobody except parents with kids in day care goes home at five. The standard work week is closer to 50 hours than 40, and this can rise to 80 during crunch periods.

INSIDE iNFO Work hard, play hard, learn hard. In spite of its cool atmosphere (casual clothing, flexible hours, game environment), the video game industry is not an easygoing place. To thrive and survive in it, you have to be very good. And the key to achieving this goal is the same as in any other industry: success comes through hard work and dedication to perfection.
—Pascal Luban, General Manager/Lead Game Designer, The Game Design Studio

In order to get a job in the game industry, think about the ways your technical experience applies to game development. Do you know a lot about engineering management? Have you been programming artificial intelligence, simulation, or graphics routines? What about animation or audio and video codecs? Networking and data security are major growth areas in interactive entertainment, as online games become more popular.

As with the people from other creative industries, you should consider going back to school for some retraining if your circumstances permit it. It's probably not necessary if you're hoping to switch from programming network tools for business software to programming network tools for games. But if you're planning a more radical move—from programming into sound engineering, for example—your existing experience is of little value, and retraining can help.

Breaking in: From Silicon Valley to Games

I had wanted to make computer games ever since I was ten, but when I graduated from college in the early 1980s, the console machines and the PC were still too weak to let me do the kinds of big projects I was interested in. Instead, I got a job as a software engineer at a company that built computer-aided design and simulation tools for the electronics industry. It paid well and the work was interesting, but I knew it wasn't going to be my career for life. A few years later, the VGA video card arrived for the PC, which raised the number of colors it could display from 16 to 256, and the Sound Blaster card enabled it to play recorded sound. I figured my time had come, and I began looking for programming jobs in the game industry.

Here's how I went about it. My résumé was quite ordinary, describing my software engineering and management experience. To this I added a short, punchy cover letter with bulleted items that explained how my time in the CAD industry had taught me software engineering discipline and teamwork skills (both of which were rare at that time in the game industry). This was enough to get me an interview at a small developer called Interactive Productions, later known as PF Magic. When I went to the interview I brought along a demo for the IBM PC. I had written a game at home for the fun of it, and had even won a small programming prize for it. The company needed a PC programmer, and the boss was willing to take the gamble. He hired me to write the PC client for one of America Online's early games, *RabbitJack's Casino*.

I put my success down to a combination of luck, experience, and preparation. The luck consisted of discovering a company that happened to need my skills right then (I had not had to search long); the experience was my seven years of programming and management, even if it was for a different industry; and the preparation was my cover letter and demo. The demo was not spectacular, but it was a completed, fully functional game, and I think that made a difference.

OTHER WAYS TO PREPARE YOURSELF

What if you're just not in a position to get a formal education as a game developer? Well, there's a heck of a lot you can do to get an informal one. One of the best things about video games is that there's a huge network of people all talking about games, sharing code and ideas, working together in large groups and small. Here are some ideas for other things you can do to learn about games and get involved with the game industry.

Play the Games

One of the most useful things you can do is to study existing games. If you want to get a feeling for how games work, you should play as many of them as you can afford. If you don't have the money to buy a lot of games, play the demo versions download-able from the publishers' web sites, or form a collective with your friends to buy them and swap them around. Rent video games and play them over a weekend or so. Don't feel you have to finish every game unless you're enjoying it so much that you really want to. Many game developers start a lot of games to see what the content is like and how the gameplay is designed, but don't play past a few levels.

Try Different Genres

Be sure that you study a variety of games. This helps you not only to understand how different kinds of games work, but also to know what kinds you might prefer to work on. The gameplay varies from one genre to another, but so do the art style, the music, the user interface, and many other details. Notice how some games are more suited to the close-in, mouse-and-keyboard interface of the personal computer, and others are better on console machines. Try to play at least one each of these types: a fighting game, a first-person and a third-person shooter, a strategy game, a sports game, a construction/management simulation, a role-playing game, a vehicle simulation, a puzzle game, a children's game, an adventure game, and a web-based game. Be sure to play the single-player, multiplayer local, and multiplayer online versions of these games to get a feeling for the way these variations change the play dynamics.

Look at the Way Games Are Designed

When you're playing, try to think seriously about the game works. Most video games entertain by providing a series of increasingly more difficult challenges, which you learn to solve one by one. They start off beating you, and after a certain amount of practice and familiarization, you can usually beat them pretty easily. Then they notch up the difficulty level, and you start again. Learn to analyze their strengths and weak-nesses. *Why* does a game beat you at first? Most video games aren't smart enough to win through artificial intelligence alone. Is it because it has superior numbers? Or be-cause the odds are deliberately stacked against you? Or because the game has access to information you don't? All these are tricks game designers use to give the machine an advantage. With time and practice, most people learn the tricks and find the weak-nesses in the game's intelligence. When you know those tricks, you'll be able to incor-porate them into your own game designs. (Of course, there are games where this just isn't possible—chess, for example. Chess programs have to win on sheer smarts; they can't use any of these tricks.)

Preparing to Be a Game Developer

Most games have an internal economy—some value changes over time, and without it, you lose (or die). In *Monopoly,* for example, it's money. In a game like *Quake,* it's ammunition, armor points, and hit points. How do resources flow into the game? How do they flow out? How much is luck and how much is skill? How is the game balanced? If they have "easy" and "hard" modes, play the game in both modes and take careful note of what changed.

Examine the User Interface

As you play, notice the way the keyboard, mouse, and joystick are used; the way the screen is laid out; the progression of menus. Are they logical and convenient? Do you find yourself wishing for a special key or button that the game doesn't supply? What is the game's visual perspective: first person, like *Doom* or *Quake?* Observer from behind, like in *Tomb Raider?* A freely moving aerial perspective, as in *Dungeon Keeper?* An isometric perspective, as in *Starcraft?* Can you change camera angles (as in *Madden NFL Football*) and if so, how does the game's playability change when you do? All these things go into the analysis of a game's user interface design.

Take Notes

As you play games, keep a notebook of things you liked and things you didn't. If something stood out as particularly well done, write it down. This may seem silly to your friends, but you're learning from the masters, professional game developers. Years later, that notebook could turn out to be very useful. I've had many a conversation with a colleague in which I said, "You know, I remember a game that tried something like that. Darn! I can't think of the name of it." If I had only kept a notebook back then, I'd have a record of those interesting features and where I saw them.

Breaking in: Playing and Persistence Pay Off

I was working the counter at the Pacific Athletic Club, getting up at 3:45 A.M. to let members in the door. At night, I would play video games. One morning, I let a member in, and found out he worked at EA Sports as a high marketing dude. Of course, I wanted to work there, but what did I have to offer? I didn't know a thing about how games were made, but I was excellent at *Madden.* My EA Marketing guy asked me to write up a résumé, and a list of all the games I had played, and he would get it to the test manager. Sure enough he came through, delivered my résumé, and gave me the number to call to see if I could get an interview. Did I know anything about testing? No, but I called every day for a month and a half till I finally got an interview to work on the *NHL Hockey* test team. Mortified, I went to the interview, and met with a group of producers. I knew nothing about hockey, but gave it my best shot. Somehow in the interview, I got the point across that I was a football guy, and the producers were kind enough to pass me over to the *Madden* people rather than just tell me I wasn't a fit. I phone interviewed with the two APs on *Madden*, and I was sure that it wasn't going well as the two were laughing through the entire thing! Later, when I told them about this, they said that they were just joking around and had known from early on they wanted to bring me in.

—*Jake Neri, Founder and Partner, Blaze Games*

Develop Your Own Games or Game Elements

Nowadays, it's imperative that you have a demo or portfolio when you go to a job interview for a creative position. Experienced developers have published games they can refer to, but as a newcomer, you need to take something along to show you've got what it takes. I'll discuss portfolios in more detail in Chapter 7, but for the time being what matters is that you create material, both to practice your skills and to show off to others.

You can do this any time and at any age. If you're lucky, you can do it in conjunction with courses you're taking, so the work earns you credit and has a longer-term value as well. Write, compose, program, model, paint, animate, record—whatever you enjoy. Never throw anything away; you never know when it might turn out to be useful later. If you're developing with a group of friends you can even get some experience with project management by planning who's going to do what and figuring out where the dependencies are among the various chores.

There's a staggering amount of material available to help "garage developers" or "bedroom coders," as they're sometimes called. The best web site for this kind of thing is GameDev (www.gamedev.net), which has over a thousand articles on game development and a special page just for beginners. You should also check out the Yahoo! directory's page under Recreation > Games > Computer Games > Programming for an extensive list of web sites with resources.

Best of all, it doesn't have to cost you a lot of money. If you've got a computer, you can make a video game. Thanks to the open source movement, and the fact that programmers love to share their work, you can find all the tools you need available for download on the Web, either completely free or as inexpensive shareware. They won't have all the power and flexibility of professional tools, of course; they may occasionally be buggy and not very well supported. But your goal is to make a demo that'll get you a job, and you can certainly do that with the resources available. Appendix C contains a list of free tools you can use for game development.

Attend Industry Events

There's no better way to learn about games and meet game developers than by hanging out where they hang out. Definitely join the IGDA. There are no entrance require-

iNTERVIEW WITH DAVE BRYSON

The Value of a Demo

I actually got into the game industry by browsing inside a computer shop, where I bumped into Dave Jones of Lemmings fame (he owned the shop). I asked him to look at an Amiga "megademo" I was working on at the time. When he later saw the demo, he was so impressed he hired me on the spot, so if you want a programming job, it really helps to develop a demo of what you can achieve in your own time, and show that.

—Dave Bryson, Engine Programmer, Electronic Arts UK

ments, and a student membership is only $35. If there's a local chapter, attend its meetings; you'll make a lot of great contacts, and even if they're not hiring, they can answer questions about the industry. Go to the Game Developers' Conference, the Electronic Entertainment Expo (E3), or if you're in Britain, the GDC-Europe and the European Computer Trade Show (ECTS). I discuss these and other events in more detail in Appendix C.

iNSIDE iNFO If I were starting out, I'd try to meet as many people in the industry as I could. Not through job interviews, but through industry events and meetings and happy hours. And I'd write, every day, as much as possible. One day, someone is going to ask you the magic question, "Can I see some of your work?" All you'll want to say is "Yes."
—Susan O'Connor, Freelance Interactive Scriptwriter

Follow the Press

The game industry has spawned a huge publishing industry as well. You should subscribe to at least one gamer's magazine and read it religiously. This will enable you to keep up on trends in the industry, know who's doing well and who's doing badly, and so on. And in addition to the consumer press, you should also read the trade magazines. Although there aren't a lot of journals devoted specifically to game development, you should read the ones that exist, and also other sources devoted to high technology and new media in general. That way, when you're in an interview, you'll be able to discuss industry events and issues intelligently.

Be Your Own Press

If you're in school, and your school has a newspaper or a web site, take your experience playing games and turn it into something of value for your classmates. Write reviews of the latest video games. Study trends in the industry and write about them for composition assignments. Learn about some of the famous game designers and write about their careers. Write about censorship, ratings systems, and violence in the media. If you have access to some web space (and most big Internet service providers now offer a little web space free along with their other account services), create a fan web site about some of your favorite games, or a review web site. Although the computer game industry is nowhere near as big as, say, the film industry, there's still plenty to say about it.

If your work is really good, see if your local newspaper has anybody who routinely reviews video games. If they don't, they might be interested in publishing what you've written. It can't hurt to ask.

Although none of this is going to immediately get you a job in the industry, doing it shows that you're serious. Look at it this way: suppose you're a hiring manager, and you've got two nearly identical résumés from entry-level people. One person has been playing, thinking, and writing about games in his spare time, while the other has been hanging out at the mall. Which one are *you* going to ask in for an interview?

Take Part in Beta Tests

If you visit a lot of publishers' web sites, you'll have seen sign-up pages for external beta testers. External beta testing takes two forms: *open,* meaning that anyone is allowed to download and play the game; and *closed,* meaning that the company chooses a specific group of people from a pool of applicants. Open beta testing allows the company to try the game on a wide range of hardware configurations, but since they don't have any control over who signs up, the quality of the bug reports tends to be rather uneven. With closed beta testing, the company hopes to find people who are serious and dedicated to helping them make a better game.

Beta testing is a great way to get to know someone inside a game company: the testing manager. Try to get accepted for closed betas if you can: instead of being one name out of hundreds participating, you'll be one name out of 40 or 50.

One of the advantages of beta testing is that you don't have to live near the company to do it. Here's what you need to be a beta tester:

> **A good PC** Unless they're making products for children, most publishers design their games for a fairly high-end PC. If your graphics hardware is more than two years old, or your CPU runs at less than half the speed of the current top-of-the-line product, it's probably too slow to run the latest games.

> **A decent Internet connection** A 56K modem is the absolute minimum; a cable modem or ADSL connection is much preferable. Many beta tests require that you download huge files, 100MB and more. If you're testing an online game, you may also be at a significant gameplay disadvantage with a slower connection.

> **Time** In order to be of real use as a beta tester, you have to be willing to devote some time to it—several hours a week. For online testing, you may

need to make yourself available at specific times. The company will probably also ask you to fill out surveys or provide written feedback about the game.

> **A minimum age** Many beta tests require that participants sign a non-disclosure agreement or some other kind of contract that prohibits participants from making copies of the game or even talking about it with friends. In order for these contracts to be binding, the player must be over 18. In cases where there is no contract, publishers may still set an age limit of 13, because the Children's Online Privacy Protection Act (COPPA) prohibits the collection of personal data on anyone younger than that.

Here are some tips on being a good beta tester—the kind that makes the manager sit up and pay attention:

> *Take careful notes.* A bug report that says "game crashed" is worthless. When a problem occurs, write down exactly what you were doing and what you saw on the screen at the time. Don't write a novel, but try to cover thoroughly everything that could have a bearing on the situation. If you have the ability to capture screen shots, definitely do so if they help to illustrate the bug.

> *Take ownership of problems.* You can simply report bugs as they occur, but your reports will have more value if you try to get some understanding of *why* they occurred, especially if you're having configuration problems. Try to track down the source of the problem. Turn off some features of the game and see if it still happens. Get involved!

> *Be patient.* Remember, you're playing with unfinished software; it's going to have bugs in it. If you get 90 percent of the way through a brutally hard level and the game crashes, well, that's why you're testing it. Take a deep breath, count to ten, then report the bug accurately and try again.

> *Be courteous and constructive.* Don't send reports saying, "This is the lamest piece of junk I ever played," even if it's true. First, that isn't helpful; second, it's bound to annoy whoever's reading it and make her discount whatever else you have to say. The company will look more kindly on useful suggestions for improvement, although you have to realize that by the time a game reaches beta, it's too late for any substantial changes.

If you can develop a positive, constructive relationship with the testing manager, establishing your intelligence and dedication, then you can open up a dialog about working for the company. Don't rush this, however. Beta test is a rough time, and everyone is extremely busy trying to get the product out; they don't have much time to think about hiring. Demonstrate your usefulness first and make your pitch later, after the beta test period has ended.

Think of beta testing not just as a hoop to jump through on the way to a job, but a means of building up experience. That's what it really is.

Attend Focus Groups

When companies want to get some feedback from their customers about a product they're working on, they often hold a *focus group*. This is a gathering of anywhere from 4 to 20 or 30 people whom the company believes are representative of their target market for the product. They get you together for three or four hours, usually at their facility, show you the product, and ask for your reactions. Then they take the results back and make adjustments to the product accordingly.

If there's a game development or publishing company in your area, find out what they make and try to get in on a focus group or two. Call the company, ask for the marketing department, and let them know you're interested. If you have any credentials—like having done beta tests, or reviewed games for a school newspaper, say—be sure to mention them. Participating in focus groups isn't doing game development, but it will enable you to meet some of the people in the company, and get an idea of what a work-in-progress is really like.

WRAP-UP

There's no denying it: the better your education, the farther up the ladder you can start. In a competitive job market for game developers, a formal education is extremely valuable, but it isn't absolutely required if you're willing to work hard and prove yourself. Whether formal or informal, though, remember that education only really works when the student has a blazing drive to learn. To become a game developer, it's up to you to supply the energy and the direction. Armed with the advice I've given you, go out and actively seek the knowledge you need.

INTERVIEW WITH JAKE NERI

Passion

When I am looking for candidates, what I am searching for is that spark—that undefined nugget of life in the candidate that says this person has heart, soul, and creativity. There are many people who know how to program, or do art, but I am looking for people who do their job with passion and don't just punch the clock. I will accept anyone's shortcomings as long as there is the passionate upside. People who have passion for their work will do whatever it takes to overcome their limitations, and that's exactly the candidate I want.

—Jake Neri, Founder and Partner, Blaze Games

Skills and Careers in the Game Industry

IN this chapter, I'll discuss the different jobs you can get as a game developer, and the skills they require. At the end, I'll also cover various entry-level jobs not directly associated with building games, which may help you if you want to get your foot in the door. I'll also talk about a few jobs that don't directly involve game development but still allow you to exercise your creativity in the game business.

One thing I *won't* do is try to spell out exact requirements and responsibilities for each type of job I discuss. The game industry is much too flexible for that, and no two companies have exactly the same needs. This is entertainment, not making widgets on an assembly line. If I were to tell you that a user interface designer must have a bachelor's degree in human-computer interaction and two years' experience, the very next job ad you see for a user interface designer would contradict me. Worse yet, if you took me at my word, and you didn't have the exact experience that I listed, you might not even read the ad, and thereby miss a great opportunity. It's more important for you to understand what *kind* of work is involved in each position, and what *kind* of skills you need, rather than to have a bullet-list of artificial requirements.

Before I get down to the nitty-gritty, I'm going to discuss the two primary regions of the business: *production* and *development*.

PRODUCTION VERSUS DEVELOPMENT

The distinction between production and development arose back when publishers first started doing external development. The development company would consist of a small number of people, seldom more than ten and often only one or two. They would create all the software, art, and music for the game—thus, this group naturally came to be known as *development*. At the same time, the publishing company would have a producer (normally just one) who was their liaison with the development company.

As products got larger and began to be designed for multiple platforms, or as part of entire product lines, it became evident that a single producer could no longer handle the work alone. The publishers created additional job titles: executive producers to oversee product lines, and associate producers and others to help the primary producer. This group of people was collectively known as *production*. They don't actually build the game, but they have a tremendous amount of influence over it. Development companies grew as well, of course, and formed fairly flat hierarchies based around each project they were working on.

INSIDE inFO The two words *production* and *development* are used somewhat differently depending on whether they're referring to a *group of people* or a *process*. When we speak of the group of people collectively called "production," we mean the producers and associated employees at the publisher. When we speak of the group called "development," we mean the programmers and other developers, either at a development company (external development) or at the publisher (internal development). However, when we speak of the *process,* the two terms are fairly interchangeable. "The game is in production" and "the game is in development" mean the same thing.

Two Different Mindsets

Apart from actual job responsibilities, the differences between production and development are largely attitudinal, and have to do with who it is they're working for and why. Production must always think of the game as a *product,* a consumer item to be sold at retail. They're concerned with being sure it gets done on time and under budget, and above all that it meets the publisher's needs. The producer is ultimately responsible to the publisher for the quality and enjoyability of the product, but also for its salability. A good producer always has her company's financial interests at heart.

Development, on the other hand, sees the game more as a *creative work*. Obviously, they want it to sell well and make a lot of money, but actually selling it is the publisher's problem. The developer's day-to-day concern is making the game fun, exciting, challenging, and attractive, and his reward is the opportunity to express his creativity. The work becomes an end in itself.

INSIDE inFO The suits may call it "product," but the process of making a really *good* game is about finding some way of transferring your joy, pride, and love of your creation to the end user.
—Robin Green, R&D Programmer, Sony Computer Entertainment of America

This isn't a rigid division, of course: developers also care about getting the game done on time, and producers care about making it wonderful. But the distinction is still there, generating a gentle (and sometimes not-so-gentle) tug of war between creative perfectionism on one side and business pragmatism on the other. (While Michelangelo was painting the Sistine Chapel, Pope Julius II, who was paying for it, asked him repeatedly, "When will you make an end?!" Michelangelo's reply: "When it's finished.")

What about Internal Development?

When development takes place inside a publishing company, these divisions are smoothed over a little. Everyone's working under one roof, and they're all depending on the same outfit for their paycheck. How strongly they feel the distinction between production and development depends on how the company is organized. For example, the development team could be independent of the production team, reporting to a development manager. That's how it was when I first got a job as a programmer at Electronic Arts (EA). I had a producer, but he was actually on another floor of the building, and I felt my primary responsibility was to my development manager. On the other hand, the developers could be directly under the producer, so they're all part of the same team. In that case, the tug-of-war between creativity and pragmatism (or between art and business, if you like) is more likely to be a matter of individual viewpoints than part of a collective attitude.

Internal and External Producers: Still More Confusion!

Originally, the title of "producer" was only used for an employee at a publishing company. Development companies were so small that they didn't have much management apart from a lead programmer. In time, however, as development companies grew, they began to get full-time development managers, and just to complicate matters further, the development companies began to call these people "producers" as well. So now an externally developed game might have *two* producers: one at the publisher, looking out for its interests; and one at the development company, overseeing the actual construction of the game.

As a result, the concept of "internal" and "external" producers has arisen—*but it doesn't mean internal and external to the publisher* as it does with internal and external development. Instead, it refers to the location of the producer with respect to the development team. Ellen Beeman, whose story you'll read a little later in this chapter, is an *internal* producer working at Monolith, a development company, on an *externally developed* product for their publisher, Sierra Entertainment. That is, she has a development team working for her inside her company, so she is an internal producer. In the meantime, Sierra Entertainment also has a producer responsible for the product at their end. Because development is taking place *outside* Sierra, this person is an *external* producer.

In order to avoid further confusion, in this chapter I'll pretend that all producers work for publishers. If I need to talk about the person overseeing development at a development company, I'll call that person the *development manager*.

A Warning about Job Titles, Responsibilities, and Org Charts

As I've said before, the game industry isn't as old as other entertainment media, and it hasn't had time to settle into standard ways of working. As a result, the job titles and responsibilities vary considerably from one company to another. For example, testing might also be known as playtesting, quality assurance, or quality control. Likewise, no two companies are likely to organize their reporting structure in quite the same way.

The testers at a publishing company may report to the producer or an associate producer, or they may be part of an entirely separate department. And just to make matters worse, it's not uncommon for companies to reorganize every year or two.

For our purposes, I'm going to discuss the job titles and responsibilities most consistently used in the industry, and invent a hypothetical organization chart for them to belong to. But as I'm discussing each title in detail, I'll also give you synonyms, other names that may be used for the position.

Here are a few tips for dealing with this situation when job-hunting:

❯ *The same title will mean different things at different companies, and even in different departments in the same company!* The only way to be sure exactly what your responsibilities will be is to ask during the interview. Talk to whomever your boss is going to be, and get him to spell out his expectations for the role in as much detail as possible. Especially on the production side, tasks tend to be assigned on an ad-hoc basis depending on the talents, skills, and interests of the individuals who make up the team.

❯ *You can't tell from the title whether a job is a management position or not.* When I worked at EA, the position of Technical Director (TD), although it sounded grand, was actually an advisory one. TDs didn't have anyone reporting to them. Again, you will simply have to ask.

❯ *In reading job ads, don't worry too much about "junior" or "senior." Look at the experience and education requirements instead.* To some people, senior means 15 years' experience; to others it means five. If you think you can do the job, apply for the job.

❯ *Don't be impressed by a fancy title.* Even if your business card says "Director of Technology Design," you'll still have to put in 15-hour days fixing bugs during crunch time. The company will also be more than happy to give you an impressive title if you'll cut your salary requirements by $10,000 a year. Fancy titles cost nothing—and get you nothing, either.

The Two (Well, Three) Types of Career Ladders

This distinction between production and development creates two different kinds of career ladder, one kind for production and another kind for development. As I'm describing them, you'll find it helpful to refer to Figure 6-1, which shows their relative degrees of authority in a project or company. You'll notice there's also a third kind in between production and development, for game design. It's something of a special case, and I'll discuss it separately.

A career ladder is not the same as an organization chart. A career ladder shows you how you are likely to be promoted as you gain skill and experience in the job, not

FIGURE 6-1

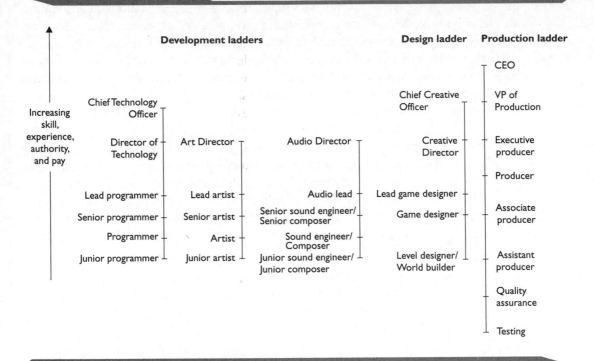

Typical career ladders for game developers

who you report to. An artist will be promoted to senior artist, but doesn't necessarily report to one; it's more likely that they both report to the lead artist. As I warned earlier, not every company will have all these positions, and not all of them will call them by the same name.

The Development Ladders

As you can see from the figure, development comprises multiple ladders of the same type, all defined by skills in a particular technical or creative area. To move up the ladder you're on, you need to improve your proficiency in that area. You do this primarily through experience on the job, but you can also get professional education as you go along—for example, by taking courses and reading articles to keep up-to-speed on the latest tools and technologies.

On the development ladders, the actual nature of the work doesn't tend to change much as you get promoted; you simply get more responsibility and more critical (and harder!) tasks to do. A junior programmer and senior programmer both spend most of their time programming. Only when you get to be a lead programmer do responsibilities start to shift: you take on administrative, management, and leadership tasks and have to give up some of the actual coding.

Notice that, compared to the production ladder, the development ladders start high up in terms of responsibility, authority, and pay. Programming, art, and audio design require more skills and training than testing or customer service, so you come in at a better rate of pay. On the other hand, the development ladders are also shorter. At the upper echelons of company management, you have to stop writing code and start concentrating on other things: leading people and making money. If you're a great programmer, the company will want to keep you doing programming. You can only continue moving upward if you can persuade the company that you're actually a better manager than you are a programmer. If you want to continue to be promoted, you'll have to shift to a different ladder.

The Production Ladder

Advancement up the production ladder is based not on your mastery of a particular technical or creative skill, but on more intangible qualities: leadership, organization, flexibility, attention to detail, and, above all, a peculiar characteristic called *product sense*. Product sense is the ability to tell whether a half-finished game, or even just a game idea, is going to be fun or not, if it's going to sell well, and, most importantly, what's needed to fix it if these things are lacking. You can have no technical or artistic skill at all, and be completely unable to build a game, and yet still have brilliant product sense. The people who have a high degree of product sense can make millions for their company.

The first thing you'll notice about the production ladder in Figure 6-1 is that it goes from the very bottom of the company to the very top. If you can demonstrate excellent product sense and management capability, you can just keep moving up, producing first individual games, then whole product lines, and finally being in charge of all of production. At this level, your work will consist almost entirely of financial and product planning, and all the creativity will have gone out of it—but the option is open to you if you have what it takes. Publishers tend to promote people who make money for them. It's that simple.

The entry level on the production ladder is very low. If you don't have any development experience or special training, you can still get a job in the business, but it will be poorly-paid donkey-work at the start. There's not a lot of creativity or self-expression in testing video games, and not a lot of money either. However, if you're passionate enough about games to take any job that's going, then grab that bottom rung and start hauling yourself up.

The Game Design Ladder

I've put the design ladder in between production and development because game design can belong to either organization. Sometimes the development team designs the game; other times the production team does. At some companies, design may actually be folded into the production ladder so that level designer is the next step up from tester. Unlike programming, for example, the nature of a game designer's work changes somewhat as she gets promoted.

How Do I Change from One Ladder to Another?

Moving *up* a career ladder is largely based on demonstrated proficiency in your existing specialty. If you're ambitious, hardworking, competent, and the job opportunities arise, you should move up naturally with time and experience. Moving from one ladder to another, however, is a different story. Since different ladders require different skill sets, you have to learn whatever is needed in the new ladder. This may require dropping back down a rung or two, also.

It's really just like getting a job in the first place: you have to prove you can do the work. If you want to stop being an animator and become a musician, then compose some music in your spare time, put together a demo CD, and look out for opportunities. It's not as easy as getting promoted in your existing field, though. Many managers tend to put people in pigeonholes: if your boss has been thinking of you as an animator, she may require some convincing that you're a composer as well.

Finally, it's important to realize that you won't be able to do this on a whim. For one thing, the company may not need you in the position that you want, and may prefer that you remain where you are. Why should they let you stop being an animator with three years' experience on the job in order to be a composer with none? You can't expect them to transfer you just to make *you* happy; if you want your employer to do it, you need to persuade them that it's in *their* best interests. If they refuse, then you'll have to decide if it's important enough to you to leave your job over. You can always go out and look for another job in your new profession, but of course your current job doesn't count as experience toward it. (It does count as time spent in the game industry, however, which is definitely meaningful.)

It can be done, with time and preparation; and sometimes the chance just comes along, too. If it's what you want to do, then get the training you need, build up a portfolio or at least a solid argument why you should move, and keep on the lookout for opportunities.

Project Organization

Just as no two companies use exactly the same titles, no two projects are organized in exactly the same way. However, there are some commonly used organizational structures, and I'll describe some of them here.

Production

At the publisher, the production teams are normally organized around related product lines: all the sports games will be handled by one executive producer, all the RPGs by another, and so on. The hierarchy subdivides the work accordingly: under the executive producer, one producer will be responsible for a particular game, and his associate producers will each take responsibility for one machine that the game is released on, assuming it's going to be developed for multiple machines. Alternatively, each associate may oversee a different aspect of the production process: obtaining data from licensors, working with marketing, and so on.

Figure 6-2 shows one possible structure. This is one executive producer's production teams (the publisher's other functions, such as marketing and sales, are not shown). The figure also assumes that all the development is external, so there are no developers shown.

In this particular case, there is an independent testing group which serves all the different products the executive producer is responsible for. This approach is efficient because it enables the testing manager to pull the testers off one project and move them to another without changing who they report to. If the testers worked for the individual producers, they would constantly be moving around from boss to boss as the projects' testing requirements changed. The downside of this arrangement is that each producer has to go to the testing manager to request testers, and has no direct control over them. If two projects both need testers at the same time, the testing manager has to resolve the conflict.

FIGURE 6-2

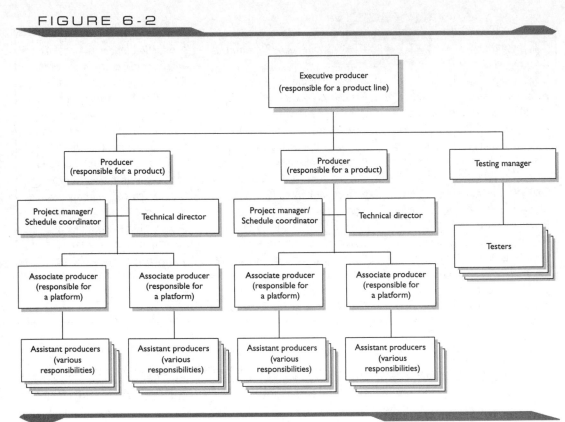

A production department with independent testing

Associate and assistant producers report to each producer. In addition, project managers and technical directors report to their producer in an independent capacity. All these positions are described later in the chapter.

Development

Development companies are far smaller than publishers. Because they don't need a sales or marketing department, almost all their staff work directly on games. (Independent developers that self-publish are an exception, but they, too, tend to be small due to the nature of the business.)

Figure 6-3 illustrates one possible structure for a development team. You'll notice that the primary division of the hierarchy is by type of skill. In this example, I have included an incorporated audio team, but on smaller projects it's quite common to find

FIGURE 6-3

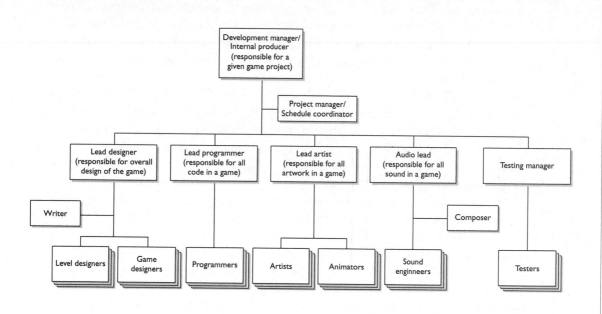

A development team with incorporated testing

that the audio department is independent, like the testing department in Figure 6-2. Small projects don't always need a full-time audio staff. When that is the case, the development company sets up a central audio department and assigns individual engineers to different projects on an as-needed basis.

(Another reason for having a separate audio department is the amount of special equipment they require and the amount of noise they make—literally. In a company that mostly has cubicles for its employees, audio people will still have offices so their work doesn't distract their coworkers. They also usually have big speakers, mixer boards, and similar gear that other people don't need, so they require extra space.)

In Figure 6-3, the lead designer has a writer working directly for her, and the audio lead has a composer. It's rare for a game to need more than one of these people unless the project includes an unusual amount of text or music. In addition, many designers double as writers. Music and writing are also the two professions most commonly outsourced to freelancers or independent houses.

Matrix Management

Matrix management refers to a situation in which you report to two bosses at once: one up the hierarchy, and one sideways across it. The idea is to organize the company in two different ways simultaneously based on different criteria. For example, the boss up the ladder is responsible for the project you're on, and all the other people on the same project report to her. The boss to the side oversees all the people with the same kind of job, no matter what project they're on—in other words, all the artists in the company report sideways to an art director. (See Figure 6-4 for an example.) The purpose of this is usually to create and enforce certain standards across projects: if all the artists are required by their art director (sideways) to use a particular style or particular methods, the company's products will be more uniform and development times more predictable. That's the theory, at least.

In practice, this can cause problems, for two reasons. First, what happens when your two bosses disagree with one another over how to do something? Even with clearly defined areas of authority there are often exceptions, for pragmatic reasons—for example, perhaps the development manager (upward) will ask you to use a technique or tool that the art director (sideways) doesn't approve of, because the development manager thinks it will help the game get finished sooner. The art director, who has no loyalty to any given project, stands on principle and complains that the development manager is undermining his authority. Confusion ensues and time is wasted.

The other reason matrix management can cause problems is that employees are like cats: they really only love whoever feeds them. When there are conflicting orders, or

FIGURE 6-4

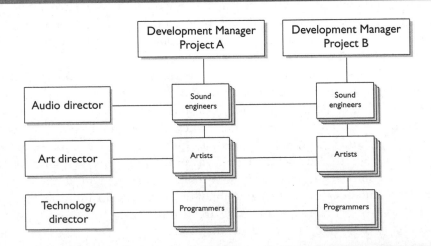

Matrix management

even just perspectives, the employees will give their loyalty to whoever writes their annual review at the end of the year—the person who determines their salary and bonus.

Just because a company implements matrix management, that doesn't mean you should avoid it; Microsoft has done so for years with considerable success. But it's something to know about going in. During your interviewing, if your prospective boss starts talking about how you'll have a "dotted line" reporting relationship to someone else, you're probably seeing matrix management at work. Find out who will actually be writing your review.

PROGRAMMING

Programming is the hub around which everything revolves, or, to mix metaphors, it's the projector that produces the pictures and sounds that the players interact with. The software *is* the game; the pictures and sound are its visible manifestation. If you took away the art and the audio, you would still have a video game running inside the machine, you just couldn't see or hear it.

Because the software is the hub into which all the other assets fit—art, animation, video, audio, text, and so on—programmers spend only part of their time writing code. In addition to writing, testing, and debugging software, you'll also be sitting in meetings designing new objects and routines with other programmers, and hashing out details with the designers, artists, and audio people.

A Day in the Life of an Engine Programmer

Typically, I tend to get into work just before 10 A.M. Electronic Arts is quite flexible about working hours; as long as you put in about eight working hours and get the job done, you're not frowned upon. I start the day by reading my e-mail, catching up on any interesting technical information the studios across the water have posted, and replying to any queries about the graphics engine.

At the moment, I am working out the requirements for our next iteration of the engine, so I spend some time speaking to all the designers and artists and getting an idea of what fancy-pants capabilities they want.

At about 12:30, it's time for lunch at our in-studio restaurant, where I sit down to a nice hot meal and check out the latest music videos on MTV. After a quick post-lunch session of *Command & Conquer: Generals* (although most people in the studio seem to be playing *Battlefield 1942*, I'm personally more of a Real Time–Strategy fan), it's back to work!

Most of the time, when I'm not in a meeting, I am sitting at my computer, either writing new code or modifying/debugging existing code. (Yes, my code has bugs like everyone else's.)

> On Mondays, we have a programmers' team meeting where we usually discuss what everyone has been doing for the last week and tackle any hot issues. This is our chance to let off steam about any systems that need to be changed or ask any general questions about how all our work fits together. Friday is beer day. At around 5 P.M., we all go down to the in-studio bar, knock back a beer, and eat some cake! A nice finish to a hard-working week.
>
> —*Dave Bryson, Engine Programmer, Electronic Arts UK*

Talents and Skills

Although it sounds like an oxymoron, programming is a creative activity. It depends more on the creativity of the engineer, who tries to construct something robust and useful, than the creativity of the artist, who tries to make something aesthetically meaningful. Programming requires a degree of something we might call *technical imagination:* the ability to envision in your mind how a task can be accomplished.

A programmer also requires a logical and painstaking mind. Computers execute instructions; as a programmer, it's up to you to give them instructions that make sense. You must be the sort of person who can work with minute technical details. A single misplaced keystroke—typing >= instead of <=, for example—can have catastrophic consequences.

INSIDE INFO In doing engine programming, it's essential to think in a logical and structured way. When working with systems that could potentially be used on multiple game projects, they *need* to be designed in a logical way. Otherwise, you can end up making people jump through more hoops than necessary.
—Dave Bryson, Engine Programmer, Electronic Arts UK

Some of the necessary requirements for the job are

❯ **Game programming experience** Testing and producing are professions that you can learn on the job by working your way up, but a programmer is expected to know her stuff already; that's why you can come in at a higher rate of pay. Although you may not able to get experience programming a console, you should already have programmed a game, or parts of a game, before you go job-hunting as a programmer. I'll discuss this more in the section "Building Your Portfolio or Demo" in Chapter 7.

❯ **Mathematics** Different specialties need different amounts of math (addressed in the "Specializations" section that follows), but every programmer must be happy and comfortable with mathematical concepts. All video games are, at one level or another, mathematical models.

The key skills you should have include

➤ **Object-oriented software design** Object-oriented programming has gone from being an academic curiosity to the game industry's standard way of working in ten years flat. "You're still thinking procedurally" is a programmer's most cutting put-down.

➤ **Code documentation** There was a time when game programmers didn't bother to document their code because there was usually only one programmer on the project (although it was still bad practice not to) and they didn't expect to ever use the code again. Now it's normal for several programmers to work on the same piece of software, and for the same software to be used in three or four different products. You must be able to write code that other people can understand, adapt, and maintain, and that means documenting it properly.

➤ **Debugging** This onerous, but necessary, task requires both an analytical mind and the tenaciousness of a detective or scientist. As in the case of a scientist, it's a mistake to jump to conclusions too early about what's going on. Gather the data, sift the facts, then form a hypothesis about the situation and test it. Once your hypothesis has been proven, *then* you can fix the bug.

Tools

In programming, it's less important to know a specific tool vendor's software than it is to be familiar with the machine you're going to program for. No matter who actually sells them, the fundamental tools of a programmer are

➤ **A text editor—preferably one designed for editing program code** Many such editors contain built-in features to help prevent you from creating syntax errors in the code and to keep it looking neat.

➤ **A compiler and linker** The compiler converts program code in a high-level language like C++ into the machine code used by the microprocessor. The linker binds the different modules of a program together into a single executable file.

➤ **A debugger** This is a tool that allows you to watch the internals of a program while it is running, and to step through the program code one line at a time. It's essential for tracking down problems.

To get a job as a programmer you must be thoroughly familiar with using all of the foregoing. In addition to these, there are other tools it's useful to know about:

> **An assembler** The assembler does for assembly-language code what the compiler does for high-level language code, converting it into machine code.

> **A profiler or performance analyzer** This tool enables you to find out where your program is spending its time, so that you can identify and (you hope) optimize slow routines. SN Systems' *TUNER* is a performance analyzer that allows you to monitor all the different microprocessors in the console (see Figure 6-5).

FIGURE 6-5

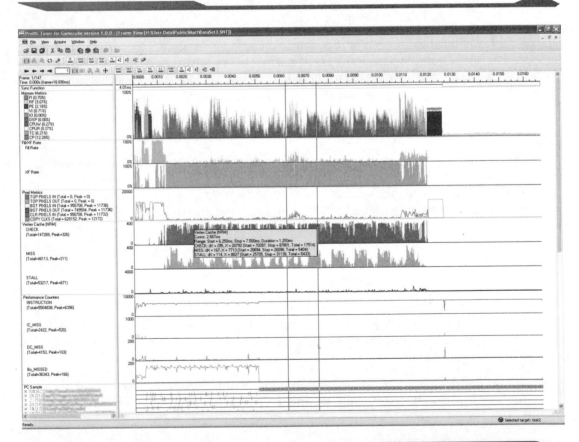

SN Systems' TUNER performance analyzer *(Image courtesy of SN Systems)*

❭ **An integrated development environment, sometimes called an IDE**   An application program that combines the elements of an editor, compiler, linker, and debugger, as well as everything else you'll need, into a single tool, meaning you don't have to keep going out of one application and into another as you work. Metrowerks' *CodeWarrior* is an IDE (see Figure 6-6).

❭ **A console development station**   Unlike the PC, game consoles can't be programmed just by themselves; they require a specially modified console plus a cable for connecting it to a PC. A development station normally

FIGURE 6-6

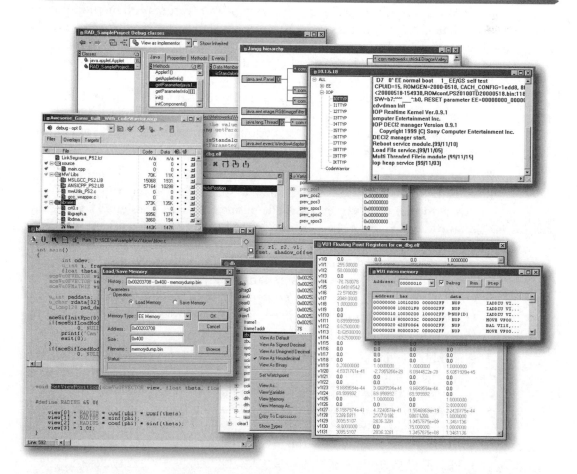

The Metrowerks' *CodeWarrior* integrated development environment *(Image courtesy of Metrowerks)*

consists of a PC, the special console, and a suite of programming tools (compiler, debugger, and so on) designed to create software for the console. You use the tools on the PC, but download the program they produce into the console to run it. You won't be able to get your hands on a console development station by yourself because you have to have a development license from a publisher. Don't worry about this too much, however; employers know that entry-level programmers won't have had access to one and won't expect it.

Programming Languages

Talk to a bunch of programmers about programming languages, and in five minutes you'll find yourself embroiled in a religious war over features and methodologies. C is faster than C++. Python makes the best scripting language. No, Python is too slow, use Lua instead, and so on. Forget all that theorizing. The right programming language for a developer looking for a job is the language that most employers use.

) **C++ and C**   C++ is now *the* language of retail game development, bar none, though some people still do things in pure C, its procedurally-oriented predecessor. If you're going to get a job as a programmer of PC or console games, you *must* learn C++.

) **Java**   You won't find Java much in use for building large PC games or console products, but it turns up in Web-based games and all kinds of other, smaller devices—even mobile phones. Java was designed specifically to allow the same program to run on a wide variety of machines, which makes it ideal for devices like personal digital assistants. Like C++, it's an object-oriented language. Some university computer science programs are starting to teach Java as their standard programming language, because it enforces better software engineering habits than C++ or C. However, Java is missing some important features that C++ includes, so it's not a substitute for learning C++.

) **Assembly language**   You should learn at least one machine's assembly language as a training exercise, but you won't ever be required to program a whole game in it unless you're developing for something truly tiny like a Tamagotchi. The days when games were coded "down on the bare metal" are long gone. However, unless you're developing device-independent software, you should know the instruction set of any machine that you're programming, and be able to understand what the code is doing as you single-step through it in the debugger.

INSIDE info Microsoft has recently introduced a new language called C#, which is their answer to Java. C# allows you to use DirectX (described next) very conveniently, but don't learn it instead of C++. Since C# programs require Microsoft's .NET system, the language is unlikely to become standard on console machines.

Application Programming Interfaces (APIs)

An application programming interface (API) is a pre-written set of software routines that you can build into your program to accomplish certain tasks for you. In some cases, an API is a product your company must purchase a license to use; other APIs are free. Certain APIs are so commonly used by the game industry that it's smart to know them before hunting for a programming job:

> **DirectX** This is a large API, provided free by Microsoft, that is designed to simplify programming the PC in a variety of ways. It provides a standard set of routines for doing graphics, audio, and other tasks, so the programmer can work in the abstract and doesn't have to think about the actual hardware. DirectX is only available for the Microsoft Windows operating system. If you want to become a Windows PC programmer, especially a graphics programmer, then DirectX experience is essential.

> **OpenGL** Like DirectX, OpenGL is a software interface to graphics hardware that enables developers to create hardware-independent graphics programs. The major differences are that OpenGL only provides graphics tools, while DirectX includes support for audio, input devices, networking, and other features; and OpenGL is available for other operating systems besides Windows. If you want to port a program from Windows to Linux, for example, it will require less modification if it is written using OpenGL.

Specializations

Because game programming is so diverse—game software does more kinds of things than any other kind of software, even high-end military simulations—there are many ways to specialize. Among them are

> **Graphics** Probably the most common specialization, and the most in demand. The appearance of graphics engines has not lessened the need for great graphics programmers. Graphics is so large a field that it has its own subcategories. The key ones required for games are

>> **3-D graphics** Without a doubt, the most technically prestigious area of graphics programming. It requires a great deal of math. This is just about the only area in which publishers and developers are willing to

fund pure research without tying it to a specific product, because they know it will pay off in the long run. As a 3-D graphics programmer you will probably have little to do with the actual game; you may be developing an engine that will be used by several different games.

> **Video compression and playback**   Although pre-rendered movies are not as fashionable as they once were, games still use them, and game developers still try to find ever more efficient ways of compressing and playing them.

> **Animation**   Pre-rendered animation is one thing; animation on-the-fly, with constantly changing conditions, is quite another. Considerable research has gone into making creatures and people walk realistically under all circumstances: fast and slow, up hills and down, and so on.

> **Audio**   Console machines contain special-purpose audio processors that must be programmed close to the bare metal; this is the job of the audio programmer. Although you may not have access to a console development station before you get a job, if you want to be an audio programmer you should try to get some experience working with digital signal processors (DSPs) in school. On the PC, audio device control is normally handled by the operating system, but there are many other audio tasks as well: streaming and mixing sounds on-the-fly in response to game events, for example. Interactive music also requires audio programmers.

> **Physics**   To be a physics programmer you must be entirely comfortable with both trigonometry and calculus. Without trigonometry, you can't understand the formulas needed for measuring distance, and you can program only the most trivial of movement algorithms without calculus. The field is even more mathematical than 3-D graphics programming. Physics programming is used most heavily in vehicle simulators and sports games, although it has applications in any game that tries to make the movement of solid bodies look realistic.

> **Artificial intelligence**   Another large and important specialty. Game AI is a combination of real artificial intelligence, as studied in university research programs, and a lot of clever smoke and mirrors to make a game *seem* intelligent. But a game can't rely only on smoke and mirrors, especially a game of perfect information like chess. AI programming doesn't require that much math, although it helps. It's more about finding ways to make appropriate decisions in a given situation.

> **Simulation**   Not the simulation of vehicles, but the simulation of complex processes. In many popular games, the player is trying to manage a set of complex interactions among interrelated systems. *Sim City* is the classic

example. Simulation programming is the skill that creates those systems, and it should be a required subject of study for any game programmer.

❭ **User interface programming**   User interfaces in environments like the Windows or Macintosh desktop are pretty straightforward: menus and dialog boxes, mostly supplied by operating system commands. User interfaces in video games are a much greater challenge. Unlike ordinary software, games have to map a fantasy situation (flying a starship, exploring a dungeon) onto a limited input device, and they must respond quickly, smoothly, accurately, and predictably at all times, despite highly variable loads on the CPU. A bad user interface can destroy an otherwise good game, so this is a valuable skill.

❭ **Utilities (editors, graphic conversion tools, level builders)**   Games are becoming increasingly *data-driven;* that is, instead of having the level design hard-coded into the software, it is read in from data files. To build those data files, the level designers need tools: utilities that let them create game settings and fill them with challenges. Tools programming is an unglamorous but vital part of this process.

❭ **Scripting languages**   In addition to being data-driven, games are also increasingly *programmable,* that is, they can execute instructions given to them in a scripting language. A scripting language is a miniature programming language that lets the designers program in features themselves. To program scripting languages you must be familiar with parsing and compiler design, both subjects you can study as part of a computer science degree.

❭ **Network and server programming**   This is a new specialty for the game industry, and one of rapidly growing importance. With a significant amount of revenue coming from online games, the industry needs network programmers in a way that it never did before. With thousands of players all logged on at once, MMORPGs are a severe test of the server programmer's skill.

❭ **Porting**   Also called "converting," porting means taking a game that works on one machine and making it work on another. This is a somewhat specialized skill, because it requires an intimate knowledge of both machines—not only how they work, but how to make a game that was optimized for play on one machine just as enjoyable on another one. Port programmers don't get the chance to work on entirely new games, but it can be a lucrative business for those who are good at it. Porting is normally done through work-for-hire contracts rather than advances against royalties.

❭ **Cryptography and security**   Piracy is a multibillion-dollar problem, and one that the industry has so far been unable to defeat. Data security is a growth business, not only to discourage piracy, but also to prevent hacking and cheating in multiplayer games. There are not a great many jobs available in the game industry yet for someone who *only* knows this field—you would be better off in commercial or defense applications—but it's a useful second string to your bow, especially if you're interested in online games. This tends to be a strongly mathematical field.

Inside the Job of a Port Programmer

Westlake Interactive is primarily a PC-to-Macintosh conversion house. As such, we generally hire programmers rather than artists and designers. Mac experience is obviously a must, but along with that we look for coders who are comfortable with having 500,000+ lines of unfamiliar C++ source dumped in their laps every five or six months. Being able to quickly understand and work with very large systems is critical for porters.

Port programmers also must be "jacks of all trades." From a programming standpoint they need to be able to understand and write 3-D graphics, sound, networking, I/O, and assembly code. They have to know (and be comfortable programming with) APIs for multiple operating systems. They must know the technical differences between various C++ compilers such as Microsoft Visual Studio, Metrowerks' *CodeWarrior*, and GNU C++. Finally, they also need to have a bit of an artistic flair in the event that certain pieces of game art or sound have to be tweaked for the new platform. Experience with tools such as Photoshop and Sound Forge comes in very handy.

Most of a typical day is spent debugging. In fact, port programmers spend their lives in the debugger. We do write a fair amount of original code during the course of porting a game, but the vast majority of our time is spent tracing through someone else's code finding data that needs to be byte-swapped or determining how to make various game systems work on the new platform.

—*Phil Sulak, Vice President, Westlake Interactive, Inc.*

ART AND ANIMATION

Art and animation work is the largest part of game development, whether you measure it by the number of people the project employs, megabytes of content produced, or size of the budget. It's the part of the project that brings the game to the player, that makes an abstract design concrete and visible. Art production creates thousands of files of all different kinds: still images, 3-D models, and both 2-D and 3-D animations. A 3-D animation is seldom one file; it often requires several, all storing different data about the thing being animated. As an artist, you'll be building all this material using the tools I described earlier. You'll also be working with the designers, to turn their ideas into visible objects, and with programmers, to incorporate the results of your work into the game. Sound engineers, too, play a role in your job: they must synchronize their sound effects to the animations you create so that the footstep or gunshot occurs in conjunction with its visible cause on the screen.

Art creation requires many steps to bring a game to life: from the initial concept, to 3-D modeling, motion-capture, animation, texturing, and generating the final files that the program will actually use. This process is called the *production pipeline*. Furthermore, because no two games are quite the same, the production pipeline isn't the same on any two projects. When you're interviewing, you can ask for details about the production pipeline to learn more about where your potential job will fit into it.

A big part of art production, especially for the lead artist, is asset management. As a new developer, you probably haven't yet needed serious asset management tools. The kinds of projects you do on your own or in college are seldom large enough to require anything more than a well-organized directory structure. Once you start work on a big project for a company, though, matters are different: with a dozen or more people working on thousands of assets, some kind of management and revision control is required to make sure things don't get lost or accidentally changed. *Alienbrain*, from NXN Software, is one example of an asset management system. An employer probably won't expect you to have used these tools already, but it's helpful to know that they exist and what they're for.

A Day in the Life of a Production Artist

I'm a bit of a night-owl, so I tend to get in to work around 10 A.M. Usually, I will be in the middle of a project that takes a week or three, so I'll fire up *Maya* and *Photoshop*. In *Maya*, I'll have, say, a bunch of buildings that I've built and that I'm texturing. In *Photoshop*, I'll have a stack of half-finished textures, along with reference materials. I'll hop back and forth between programs, adjusting UVs and trying out new colors. Periodically, I'll dash over to other people to ask them about what I'm making, or what they've made that I'll want to be sure my buildings match for consistency purposes. I'll load previously made art into both programs for size and color comparison, and then every so often I'll grab my art director to get his feedback and guidance—if he hasn't wandered by already.

My work is punctuated by program crashes, by people wanting feedback on their own work, by e-mail from friends, by the sudden crowd that has grown around someone's computer as they elicit oohs and ahs, quick teaching sessions (in which I'm both the teacher and the student, on different occasions), Nerf skirmishes, meetings about design issues, amusing web sites, interviews with potential new artists, trips to other desks to see my own work in the game engine, and our monthly company meeting/ice-cream-social/pep-rally.

—*Michelle Sullivan, Production Artist, Turbine Entertainment*

Talents and Skills

Art and animation work obviously requires a strong visual sense; an understanding of design color and movement, as well as the imagination and skill to turn descriptions and ideas into actual drawings and models.

 **A key thing to know about this job is … it is important to be an artist who just happens to be using the medium of computers.**
—Michelle Sullivan, Production Artist, Turbine Entertainment

An artist should be able to draw. That may sound obvious, but in fact a good many people try to get into game art having learned to use the software tools, but without actually knowing much about converting an imaginary, or even a real, object into an image. *Adobe Photoshop* may let you create all sorts of interesting visual effects, but that doesn't make you an artist. Learn the traditional skills first. They're mostly available in art classes: drawing, painting, sculpting, traditional animation. After that—once you know that you are, by instinct, ability, and inclination, an artist—then move on to the technical tools listed in the next section. Read through the "Specializations" section as well for more details about the skills required.

Game artists must be reasonably comfortable with mathematical concepts. Although the nature of the work is primarily creative and aesthetic, you often have to adjust your creations to account for the technical limitations imposed by the hardware. When the programmers tell you that you only have so many polygons or so much memory available, it'll be up to you to decide how to allocate them to different parts of the artwork most effectively.

As for talent … well, that's one of the great indefinables. We all recognize artistic talent when we see it, and nobody knows where it comes from. Either you have it or you don't. But the process of trying to learn the skills will tell you for sure, if you look at your work critically and listen to your heart.

Tools

Open a magazine dedicated to computer graphics and you'll find yourself confronted by a bewildering array of products for sale. Computer graphic artists and animators have more tools to choose from than just about any other development profession. That's because art tools are used by other industries as well—film, video production, advertising, and so on—so there's a great deal of demand for them.

3-D Tools

These are the leading 3-D modeling and animation tools used by the game industry, with *3ds max* and *Maya* well in front of the others. If you're planning to get a job doing

3-D modeling, you should definitely try to get some experience in one or the other of them. *Maya* has a free tutorial version that will let you become familiar with the features and user interface, although you won't be able to use the resulting files in a game.

The various tools available include

❭ *3ds max* from Discreet (shown in Figure 6-7)

❭ *Maya* from Alias|Wavefront

❭ *LightWave 3-D* from NewTek

❭ *Softimage|3D* from Softimage

FIGURE 6-7

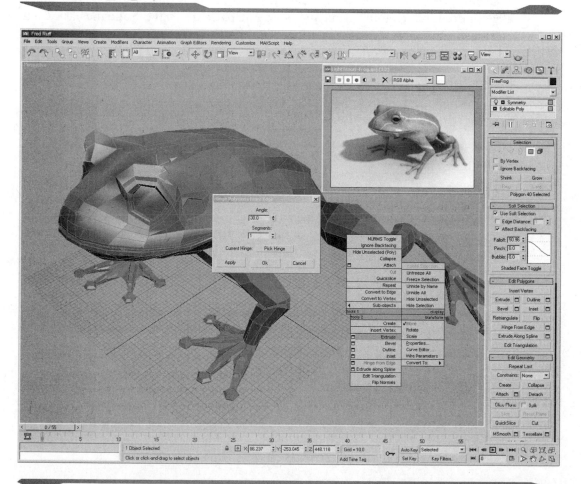

3ds max from Discreet *(Image courtesy of Discreet)*

2-D Tools

2-D tools are used for creating textures, backgrounds, user interface elements, and many other items that appear in a game but don't require a 3-D model. The following are among the most commonly used, but if you can't get your hands on one of these, there are plenty of free painting tools available.

> *Photoshop* from Adobe

> *Illustrator* from Adobe

> *Graphics Suite* from Corel

In addition to the drawing and painting programs previously listed, there are literally hundreds of "plug-in" elements—software packages that expand the basic capabilities of these programs. They allow you to take ordinary photographs or other images and add visual effects to them for a variety of stylized looks.

Hardware Tools

The words "artist" and "hardware" don't really sound as if they go together, but—surprisingly—artists actually use more kinds of outboard equipment in their day-to-day jobs than programmers do. The more experience you can grab with the following, the better:

> **Scanners (both flatbed and slide or film)**   Like laser printers, scanners have gone from being rare and expensive to cheap and ubiquitous in the last few years. They let you digitize graphic scrap from printed sources, and scan pencil or marker drawings for computerized reproduction.

> **Drawing tablets, also sometimes called Wacom tablets (the Wacom company makes them)**   These let you draw with a pen instead of a mouse, which is a more natural motion; they're also pressure-sensitive, unlike a mouse, so you can really "paint" with them.

> **Digital cameras (both still and video)**   Although the pictures you'll take probably won't end up in the game as finished artwork, digital cameras are invaluable for grabbing reference material. If you're the kind of artist who's always on the lookout for visually interesting material, keep a small digital camera with you wherever you go. You never know when an interesting building, plant, or person might turn up. Digital cameras are also useful when creating photo-realistic textures for 3-D objects.

❭ **Motion capture gear**   These tools are more the province of specialists, but if you get the chance to see some in use or, even better, work with some, take it. It's great experience to have in your arsenal.

Specializations

As with programming, there are numerous subcategories of artwork jobs that require their own skills. Furthermore, video game art is subject to numerous technical limitations based on the graphics processing power and memory available in the target machine. The artists must work closely with the programmers to ensure the assets they create will actually work in the game, and they often have to revise their creations to change the amount of memory they consume. These are considerations they seldom tell you about in art school!

❭ **3-D modeling**   Modelers sculpt the objects, characters, buildings, and everything else that is going to appear in a modern 3-D game. These assets comprise just about everything the player will see in the game, apart from user interface elements like menus. The modeler starts with a concept sketch and builds a three-dimensional wireframe model of the object in question, to which a texture can be applied to give it a surface. If the object isn't going to move, then the work is done once it looks right from all angles, but if it's actually a vehicle, creature, or stationary machine, it must also be animated— the next specialty.

❭ **3-D animation**   Modeling is challenging enough, but animating things to look right when they move is far more complicated. In the case of machinery, the motion tends to be predictable, but the real challenge is people or creatures that walk, jump, dance or fly. The 3-D animator must build up a jointed bone structure, called an armature, which is, in effect, the skeleton of the creature. The armature includes data that defines at what angles each joint may move, and for what distance. The animator then creates a 3-D model of the creature's surface and attaches it to the armature, showing how the outside of the leg, for example, relates to the bone inside, and how the skin stretches and compresses in the region of the joints as they bend. If the creature is flexible rather than rigid like a machine, its weight causes the skin to sway as it walks, and it gets even more complicated if it is wearing hanging clothing like a skirt or cloak—the material must move correctly in response to the creature's actions. Defining these details, and creating and testing animation cycles for walking, running, climbing, and all the other actions that the creature can take, is the job of the 3-D animator.

❱ **Texturing**   The surface appearance of an object in a 3-D game is created by applying a 2-D drawing to the wireframe model that describes the object. This drawing is called a texture, and creating that drawing is the role of a texture artist. It requires a peculiar ability to mentally "unwrap" the surface from an object and paint it flat. For example, when you're creating the texture for a person's head, the texture has to include the face (front and center), as well as the ears (*as seen from the side,* not from the front).

❱ **2-D art work (pixel painting) and 2-D animation**   Not all games are 3-D, and even those that are still require traditional 2-D artwork in addition to textures. 2-D images are used for user interface items such as menus, buttons, and icons; they're also used as backgrounds in static screens like mission briefings and recaps, transitions between gameplay modes, maps, inventories, dashboard instruments, and so on.

❱ **Storyboarding**   A storyboard is a series of sketches used to plan the progression of some action or event that will appear on the screen. Film directors use storyboards to plan shots; game artists use storyboards in the same way, as well as to lay out user interfaces, map the branching flow of a game, and even specify the behavior of a computer-controlled character. A game storyboard is really a cross between a film-style storyboard and a programmer's flowchart.

❱ **Concept sketching**   When a designer comes up with a written description of a character, object, creature, vehicle, or anything else that will be an important feature of a game, somebody needs to make a concept sketch of it. Concept sketches sell game ideas to producers and executives by turning abstract concepts into concrete images. Most are done in pencil or marker, although a good many are also made directly on the computer. As with storyboarding, a game company seldom needs anyone to do concept sketches full-time, but it's a valuable skill to have just the same.

▲UDIO AND MUSIC

Play a game with the speakers turned off, and you'll quickly realize how important sound is. The pictures tell you *what* is happening, but the sound tells you how it feels and even what it means. Even *Pong* benefited from its cheerful "blip" sound when you hit the ball and its sad "bwonk" sound when you missed it. Nowadays, games can have hundreds of different effects and ambient noises, as well as a full orchestral musical score.

As I said earlier in this chapter, the audio engineers are the ones most likely to be organized into a separate department of their own, partly because their work is noisy and can distract their colleagues, and partly because they're not always needed full-time on a project.

A Day in the Life of an Audio Lead

One of the major things about my job is that no day is ever the same, because there are so many different aspects to it: sound effects design, tracklaying, music briefs, music editing, voice casting/recording/directing/editing, game mixing, location recording, scheduling, and implementing audio into the game. The majority of the time I work in either the sound studio or my office (a mini sound studio itself) but occasionally I might be on location recording sound for a game (for example, rally cars, Formula One cars, crowds, roller coasters, ambiences for *Harry Potter*).

The day I'm going to describe is from the heat of the project.

First thing in the morning, I'd catch up with e-mail and then check the list of what has to be done today that I had written before going home the previous day. (I'm a great list writer.) After checking mail, I'd inform the rest of the audio team about any updates or changes. The audio team is scheduled alongside the game team so I'd pop in and see that everyone is OK, have a listen to some of the things they were doing, talk with them about it, and exchange ideas. I love sound design. It's what I've always wanted to do so I'll also be designing the sfx. Exchanging ideas is good, as the sfx have to work together. Listening to other sounds from the same level of the game can have a direct influence on the ones I'm working on, or other members of the audio team and vice versa. I'd then go back to my room and work on some of the sfx I'm designing. When I'm happy with these, I'll author them to the game through EA's own sound tools so I can listen to them as they're played back in the game. I have to make sure they work with the visuals, music, and overall style we're trying to achieve in the soundtrack.

If there's a recording session the following day, I'd confirm the talent for this session. I usually have a hand in casting the voice talent, and if a director is not hired for the session, I'll direct this the next day. Before lunch, I'd also check to see if the new music assets had arrived (from an outside composer) and review these so another guy or girl on the team can edit them and get them working in the game.

Then I'd probably have lunch for around half an hour.

In the afternoon, I may have to catch up with the artists to see how the cut-scenes are progressing so I can work out what sounds are needed for them. If some are ready, I will go down to the studio and start working on a tracklay for them.

This work would probably be ongoing. On a normal day, I'd hope to leave the office around 6:30 and on a hectic day carry on till late in the evening. Throughout the day, I'd be checking e-mail to see if there were any changes in the game, or if any urgent matters needed addressing. There would probably be a few meetings on some days, too.

—*Adele Kellett, Audio Lead and Sound Effects Designer, Electronic Arts UK*

Talents and Skills

Audio work requires good ears. This doesn't just mean the ability to hear quiet or distant sounds, but the ability to mix sounds together and make them sound right. A great deal of audio engineering consists of matching different sounds to achieve a correct overall experience. You must design the game's effects so they correspond with what the player is seeing. Two pro linemen colliding sound different from a wide receiver colliding with a cornerback, and so on. A sound engineer has to imagine an event or scene in his head (if it isn't yet visible in the game), then create the right combination of sounds to bring life to that scene.

Technical Audio Skills

In addition to the many aesthetic considerations, there are technical skills to think about:

> ❯ **Recording**   Setting up and "dialing-in" (tweaking) audio recording equipment for the purposes required, then actually capturing the material. Recording ambient sounds in an open place requires different gear and different settings than when recording an actor in a sound booth or a band in a studio.

> ❯ **Mixing**   Combining sounds to create an integrated audio experience, and applying digital effects, such as echoes, to change the way the results are interpreted by the ear.

> ❯ **Editing**   Cutting and pasting sound effects, music, and dialog. Editing dialog together out of individual words or phrases so that it sounds natural is particularly tricky. It requires a close working relationship between the writer or designer, who creates the recording script, and the sound engineer, who cuts up and reassembles the sounds.

Composing

Composing and editing music is a distinct specialty of audio skill. It used to be thought of as a purely artistic talent, but with modern synthesized music it involves considerable technical ability as well. Obviously, as a composer you must understand music in all its aspects: how it creates rhythm and pace and sets an emotional tone, and how it works with what you see on the screen. You must also be able to play an instrument, preferably the piano, since synthesizers are all keyboard-based.

INSIDE info I believe that a natural musical ability is an absolute must for a game composer. School can teach the important technical aspects of digital audio production and sound design, but nothing can replace the musical skill to make things sounds good! There is no substitute for a high level of natural-born musical ability.
—Darryl Duncan, President and Chief Composer, GameBeat Studios

Tools

A surprising number of audio tools are created for the Macintosh. Apple Computer created good graphics and audio hardware for the Mac before IBM did for the PC, so that's the machine that many tool vendors chose to support, and because of their momentum, they still do.

Waveform Editors

A waveform editor lets you edit and manipulate recorded sound. You can cut and paste dialogue, mix ambient noises and music, add echoes and other effects, and create sound effects to be associated with particular events in the game. Most sound cards come with a simple waveform editor and there are several inexpensive shareware ones as well, so you shouldn't have any trouble getting experience using one.

When you move up to a professional audio suite, these are some of the tools you will encounter:

> *Pro Tools* from Digidesign

> *Sound Forge* from Sonic Foundry (shown in Figure 6-8)

> *Peak* from Bias, Inc.

Music Tools and MIDI Sequencers

Music appears in games in two forms: as compressed wave files (MP3s) and as MIDI files. It gets there in one of two ways, either from live recordings of actual musicians, or as synthesized music made with a MIDI sequencer. A MIDI sequencer is a piece of software that takes information about the notes you want to play and the instruments you want to play them on, and combines it together to drive a synthesizer to produce music. It can do all kinds of other things as well, changing the dynamics and the quality of the artificial "room" the music is being played in (from a shower stall to a concert hall). If you're composing and synthesizing your own music, these are some of the tools you're likely to use in a professional suite.

> *Cubasis* from Steinberg

> *Digital Performer* from Mark of the Unicorn

> *SONAR* from Cakewalk

FIGURE 6-8

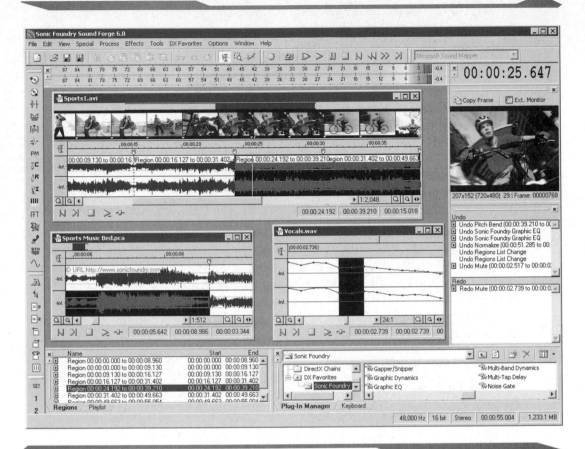

Sound Forge 6.0 from Sonic Foundry *(Image courtesy of Sonic Foundry)*

INSIDE iNFO You can learn a surprising amount about audio by being in a band or, even better, doing the sound work for a band. You'll become familiar with all the outboard gear (microphones, mixers, equalizers, and so on) as well as the principles of recording. It won't address the more obscure aspects of game audio, but the hands-on experience is useful.

Specializations

Just as with programming and art, audio production jobs break down into several specialties:

❭ Sound effects creation and Foley editing   In the movies, the sound you hear is a mixture of real sound recorded on the set (mostly dialog, though ambient sounds are also recorded where suitable), plus effects that are added afterward. In games, there is no set, so all sounds are necessarily added afterward. Audio engineers spend a lot of time trying to find or create effects that sound appropriate for the scene in the game. Foley editing is a film industry term for the process of synchronizing sounds to events on the screen.

❭ Studio recording of talent   All the dialog in a game has to be recorded somewhere, and this happens in a studio, specifically in a place called the "voice booth." The actor sits in the booth with a script, away from any other sounds, and the engineer and others sit outside. The task requires some specific technical knowledge not needed elsewhere. When you are recording a voice actor on two different days, for example, you have to make sure that the recording levels and other conditions are set so that his voice sounds the same on both days—otherwise, when the sound recording is played back in the game, the players will notice an odd variation that (to them) occurs for no reason. Directing an actor requires people-skills: you have to convey the mood you want to the actor in order to get the right emotional tone in the material.

Live recording of music is yet another story and is, of course, a career unto itself in the film, television, and music industries. In the game industry, we don't often record music live, but it does happen occasionally in games that want to cash in on a hot band's name-recognition. It can be very cool to claim your game has new, exclusive material from a hit group. More frequently, however, the games use tracks from commercially released albums.

❭ Music composition, including adaptive music   Composing isn't a required skill for all audio engineers, but it's certainly a valuable one. Game composers are somewhere between classical composers and composers for film. Unlike with film, they can't be entirely sure what's happening on the screen at any given time, unless they're composing for a cut-scene or other non-interactive sequence. That means the music must be general enough to work with whatever is happening. Unlike classical composing, however, it can't be abstract: it must support the game experience.

Adaptive music, sometimes called interactive music, is a somewhat experimental field which involves creating music that changes automatically in response to circumstances in the game. It's exciting and has tremendous potential, but despite several years of effort is still in its infancy.

INSIDE INFO There have been people going around lately saying that there's lots of money in audio for games. Hmmm. You know, they're right, in a way. When I went to my first Amway meeting, they told me that I could make millions of dollars, and that I could work part-time. They didn't tell me that I couldn't do both. There is lots of money in audio for games, but you *have* to be lucky, you *have* to work your butt off, and it's all a totally unreasonable risk of your lifetime. So you'd damn well better love making audio and love games. And you have to love the other self-important geeks who make games. I have no problem with that: I'm the Patron Saint of the Nerds.
—George Alistair Sanger, Legendary Audio Guy, The Fat Man

WRITING

Writing is a part of many different jobs in the game industry: game design, marketing, and public relations to name only three. Until recently, the industry hasn't made much use of full-time professional writers, and unfortunately, it shows! Too many games in the past had two-dimensional characters, lame plots, and atrocious dialog. This is finally starting to change as we get properly-skilled writers in the industry. However, it's still rare for a writer to have a full-time job at a publisher or developer doing nothing but writing; they tend either to be freelance, or to occupy other jobs in which their writing skills are useful.

A Day in the Life of a Writer

I can sum up my daily life in three words: reading, writing, and meeting. As an offsite writer, I have to be sure that I'm connected to the project; otherwise, I could spend days writing material that the team can't use. (Ouch.) So I spend part of my day reviewing design documents, level flowcharts, client e-mail—you name it. I go in to the developer's office a few times a week, so I can ask questions, review the most recent build, and basically goof off with the team/client. Friendly relations make the work easier.

I also try to put all of my initial design assumptions in writing. Things like, "The target audience is this … they like this …" If I'm working with branded characters, I'll provide a brief brand analysis as well. If the developers like what they see, then I can get down to business.

The reason they hire me, of course, is to write. I take the game designer's initial structure and run with it. I'll create character studies, a back story or two, and a story synopsis. I also create descriptions of the player's experience, and I also simply tell the story, start to finish.

This all overlaps with design. That's why it's so important to have a close working relationship with the designer; that way, we can build on each other's work. Some designers are more visual than verbal, and they count on me to translate their images into words. Other designers are captivated by the storyline, and we can have a great time hashing out the details.

Once I get signoff on all of that material, I can actually write lines of dialog! I used to think that scriptwriting would be the core function of my job; more often, it's just icing on the cake. Story design and story structure—that's where the real work lies.

I'm afraid I've given you more than a day-in-the-life; I've given you a project synopsis! On a daily basis, I'd have to say that what I do is daydream. After I've absorbed all of the design documentation, I imagine the game … I imagine the characters in the game … I imagine the people who will be playing the game … and I play around with different scenarios in my head, adding and subtracting until I've created an experience in my head that feels right. If anyone wants to see the creative experience in action, watch *Adaptation*! It's like that, minus the self-hatred (most of the time).

—*Susan O'Connor, Interactive Scriptwriter*

Talents and Skills

Writers obviously have to be able to write! They need a good grasp of English, or whatever the language of the product will be. And—I can't emphasize this enough—it has to be proper English. If you can't spell, punctuate, and form coherent sentences, you aren't a writer no matter how articulate you may be in person. You also have to be able to create structured, intelligently organized documents that explain, that flow naturally from topic to topic, and that hang together and make sense.

Game writing naturally falls into two categories:

> **Fiction writing**   Games are fiction, and they require a fiction writer's skills. This means the ability to create plots, characters, scenes, and dialog; to build dramatic tension and set pace; to evoke emotion; to narrate events. In a game, of course, most of the events are created by the player, but it's still up to the writer to make them make sense within the context of the game's plot, if it has one.

> **Technical writing**   Whether the writer is creating manuals, design documents, help screens, or similar material, she needs the skills of a technical writer: clarity, conciseness, organization, and precision.

Your high school composition and freshman English classes will have shown you whether you have what it takes to write general nonfiction. If you flunked them, or hated them, or never even took them, then forget it. But if you loved them—as I did—then that's a good sign. You should also have taken a course in, or tried, some forms of fiction writing as well: short stories and drama, preferably. Opportunities to learn writing techniques, both fiction and non-fiction, abound. There are all kinds of classes and books to help out, and groups of writers often get together to read each others' work and share ideas in many communities. Because so many people want to write, and because all you need is pen and paper, it's one of the least expensive things to learn how to do.

Tools

In terms of software tools, the standard office suite is about all you need. A word processor alone is not enough, however. Although you may not generate spreadsheets or PowerPoint presentations yourself, you will probably be given some to look at, so you'll need to be able to open and modify those files.

You must also keep your computer up-to-date. Although, in principle, a writer could use a ten-year-old machine (English hasn't gotten any harder to type!), in practice you need to be able to play the games to know what the current hot products are like. It doesn't have to be the top of the line, but it shouldn't be more than three or four years old. For the same reason, you should own at least one console machine, and the more you can afford, the better.

Apart from the technical tools, you need a decent writer's library. A good dictionary and thesaurus are essential, not for looking up spellings (the word processor can take care of that) but for finding the right word for the job. The *Chicago Manual of Style* is one of the standard reference works on punctuation, usage, and document design.

You can, of course, choose from a vast number of books on fiction writing and storytelling, and you'll have to decide which ones best meet your needs. One of the most popular in Hollywood writing circles is *The Writer's Journey: Mythic Structure for Writers,* by Christopher Vogler.

In addition to the general reference material, you should also have books relating to the subject you're writing about. Since I'm particularly interested in mythology, for example, I make a lot of use of *Brewer's Dictionary of Phrase and Fable,* and the works of Roberto Calasso.

Specializations

A writer in the game industry needs to be a generalist, not a specialist; there isn't enough demand for them to be able to specialize in just one area. However, these are some of the various things you might be asked to create as a writer:

> **Game design documents**   The game designers normally document the design of the game, but occasionally the designers are too busy to cast their work into prose form, and they hire a writer to do it for them. The writer must attend design meetings, take copious notes, ask numerous questions, and then go away and organize it all into a document. Design documentation is a form of technical writing with a creative side, since it often includes fiction elements as well: backstory, character definitions, plot outlines, and so on.

❱ **Audio/video recording scripts**   Every word that is spoken in a game must be recorded in a sound studio, which means there has to be a script. Game scripts are not like film or radio scripts, however. They often have six or seven different lines of dialog to cover the same situation, so the player won't get sick of hearing the same phrase over and over. As a writer, it's up to you to create all those variants. In addition, game dialog is often cut up into pieces, and the pieces played back in a different order when the game is played. This allows the game to "mix and match" different bits of dialog to correspond to the situation in the game. It takes a fair amount of skill to write this kind of dialog in such a way that it always makes sense no matter what order it is played in.

❱ **Text that appears in the game**   Although all-text games are long gone, there's still a surprising amount of text in games. You find it in mission or level briefings, journals, background information, introductory narrative, and other areas.

❱ **Manuals**   Game manuals have gotten smaller and smaller over the years, as game genres have begun to evolve somewhat standardized user interfaces. It's no longer necessary to explain every menu in detail, because the players already know what to expect. Games still need manuals, however— especially highly technical games like flight simulators.

❱ **Ad copy**   Marketing departments need writers to create ad copy, box copy, and other promotional material to help sell the games.

GAME DESIGN

Game design is one of the most highly sought-after roles in the industry, and one of the least understood. As a game designer, you *don't* spend all day thinking up fun ideas for games; that aspect takes up 20 percent of your time or even less. Game design consists of four steps:

❱ Imagining a game

❱ Defining the way the game works, as a system of rules

❱ Describing the elements that make it up

❱ Transmitting this information to the other members of the team

The last three of these steps take up most of your time and can be surprisingly hard work. They're also tremendous fun if you have the right skills and attitude, and a great team to work with. Game design is a highly collaborative process, more so, in fact, than just about any other job in development or production. A designer seldom has ultimate authority over his game, even if he's the lead designer. Everyone on the project wants to make a creative contribution, and that means that ideas and suggestions will be coming in all the time. Part of the designer's job is to take this material and decide which of it is genuinely useful and which won't work, then integrate the best parts into the game. This often means compromise—and a certain amount of ego-management as well. Because the job is so collaborative, game design requires people skills and leadership ability in addition to the other qualities needed.

As you might expect, a game designer's work is heavily loaded toward the beginning of the project. They work all the way through, but the most intense and creative period occurs during pre-production and prototyping, because that's when decisions are made that become expensive to change later on.

Design Jobs

Because game designers' work changes significantly as they move up, I will describe each job in the career ladder separately, starting at the bottom.

Level Designer

Level designers build the individual levels or missions that make up the game. They're the ones who decide what the player will be trying to achieve at any given moment during the game. They take the game elements and mechanics that the designers have created, and use a level editor to create the challenges that the player will face. Level designers are a strange contradiction: although they have the least amount of design authority over the interior mechanics of the game, they have the greatest effect on the player's actual experience of it. If the company were designing *Monopoly,* it would be a level designer who decides how the properties are distributed around the board, where all the Chance and Community Chest squares are, and how much rent each property charges.

A level designer is also partly a tester: is up to him not only to create the level, but also to playtest and balance it. The level designer reports back to the designers if he finds that there are certain strategies that always win, or certain units or elements of the game that don't have any practical use.

Level design is a job that's easy to get experience in before you start job-hunting, because so many games now ship with level editors built in. You can create your own levels for *Warcraft III* and similar games and add them to your portfolio.

Game Designer

Game designers are more senior than level designers, and their job is radically different. They take the overall vision of the game and make it real by fleshing out the details of how it actually works. They devise the core mechanics of the game and they create the world in which it will take place. They describe the key characters and determine how those characters will behave and (generally) how they will look. Game designers define the rules that the player plays by, and all the sights and sounds the player will experience, although actually creating those sights and sounds is the job of the artists and audio people. If the company were designing *Monopoly,* it would be the game designer who says, "The board is going to be a circle that the players go around and around, with properties distributed around it. When a player stops on a property, he has to pay rent to the owner, or he can buy the property from the bank if it's not yet owned by someone."

Game designer is seldom an entry-level position because it's so highly sought-after, but if you have done game design in college or on your own, and you have a strong portfolio of documents that you have created and demos of games you were involved with designing, you may be able to land a job as game designer. Making levels for existing games probably won't do it, though, because that seldom involves modifying the core mechanics. If that is where your experience lies you're more likely to get a job as a level designer.

Lead Designer

If a project is big enough to need one, a lead designer will manage the design process. The lead designer's role is to set the large-scale vision of the game and establish the reasons that someone would want to play it in the first place. He blocks out the major areas that need work, and then hands them off to the game designers for refinement. If the company were designing *Monopoly,* it would be the lead designer who says, "We're going to make a board game about buying and selling real estate. The object of the game is to accumulate as much money as possible and bankrupt all the other players."

As the name implies, part of the lead designer's job is managerial; he's responsible for making sure the rest of the design team gets their work done as well as doing his own.

Lead designer is not an entry-level position   Unless you go to work for a company so small that it doesn't have any other designers. At publishers and other larger companies, most people have to pay their dues for several years before they can be lead designers.

A Day in the Life of a Game Designer

So I wake up and turn off the alarm. Then I go back to sleep for a couple of hours. Eventually, I make my way to the office, with or without breakfast. Once I reach my desk (after being stopped to answer at least six questions on my way, or possibly being pulled into a meeting), I look at my e-mail. This can take very little time or a great deal. I look at the developer mailing lists I subscribe to and see if anything useful has come up.

The danger in looking at my e-mail is that I may then get pulled into conversations, post-fests and more meetings. Of course, the alternative is that I have no idea what's going on and I look silly. Difficult choice, really.

After the e-mail (which, of course, streams in all day creating a constant distraction), I generally check the web sites that pertain to the game or genre I'm working on. After that, I try to do actual work.

As a designer, I do spend a lot of time in meetings. I spend time there recording and sorting out suggestions, issues, and questions about the game design. I frequently spend a good part of my day synthesizing all this information into usable plans. I also spend time meeting with artists, programmers, QA, and so on.

In addition, I do a lot of writing. Design specs need to be maintained and reviewed constantly so testers are working from accurate descriptions of what they should be seeing in-game. Sometimes, I'm working on proposals. In my current position, I'm relating game analysis information to the developer.

Did I mention research? Aside from playing games and generally surfing and calling it research, I really do a great deal of research. This can be anything from reading texts about user interface design or anthropology to scanning the web for information pertinent to a problem I'm trying to solve.

Playing games. My game, other people's games, new games, classic games. It is, honestly, research. I learn a great deal from what other people have done and are doing. Sometimes it's something to steal, sometimes it's something to avoid.

If I'm lucky, I've remembered to go eat lunch, but not often. Usually, I remember to have dinner. Of course, the length of my day depends tremendously on the stage the game is at currently. For instance, when a title is in its pre-production phase, I leave at a reasonable hour. When we're about to launch, well, I don't have a life.

Regardless, I have fun. I love what I do and enjoy doing it. During a crunch period, at 3:00 in the morning, I'm still happier to be there than at any other job at 2:00 in the afternoon. And it's about fun; you can't make good games if you're not having fun.

—*Patricia Pizer, Massively-Multiplayer Online Design Specialist, ubi.com*

Talents and Skills

To be a game designer at any level, you need to have the following qualities and abilities:

> **Imagination**   Imagination comes in many forms. Visual and auditory imagination is the ability to invent new objects and think about how they look and sound. Dramatic imagination involves creating characters, plots, scenes, and relationships. Conceptual imagination enables you to think about ideas and the relationships between them. Lateral thinking is among the most useful forms of imagination: it's the ability to create unexpected angles and twists on familiar material. Imagination requires exercise to keep it strong and fresh; constant use will keep your imaginative mind vigorous.

❯ **Writing skills**   Except for level designers, writing is the game designer's core task, the thing that she spends most of her time doing. A designer has to document her ideas, both so that the other members of the team know how the game is going to work, and also so that she has a record of the decisions she has made and those that she still has to make. Design documents must be clear, concise but thorough, well-organized, unambiguous, and above all readable. To be a designer, you *must* know the rules of spelling, grammar, and punctuation. You *must* have a good vocabulary and the ability to write a clean sentence. If you've learned a lot of shortcuts and funny spellings chatting online, unlearn them now. Cute abbreviations may look cool in a chat room, but they just make you look like a fanboy in a business document.

❯ **Technical awareness**   A game designer who doesn't understand what computers can do, and more importantly, what they can't do, is going to create designs that no one can build—and won't stay employed for long. You don't have to be a programmer by profession, but it helps greatly to have done some programming, even if only in a scripting language.

❯ **Analytical competence**   A game is a system, a set of rules governing the relations between things like hit points, armor, strength, and so on. In order to devise and, above all, tune and balance such systems, you must be able to think logically about cause and effect. Game design is far more than "wouldn't it be fun if …" It's actually much closer to, "OK, so what's going to happen when …" To answer that question, you need analytical competence.

❯ **Comfort with mathematics**   I'm not talking about calculus or even trigonometry, but a game designer who has trouble with simple arithmetic will be constrained to developing nothing but adventure games. When 300 archers shoot at 500 charging knights at a distance of 200 yards, you must be able to devise a formula that determines how many knights will still be alive by the time they get to the archers.

❯ **Aesthetic competence**   Devising the visual appearance of a game world is a collaboration between game designers and artists, but it's not going to be helped if you don't have any taste. Lazy designers copy what other games do; good designers create worlds with a fresh new look that impresses everyone.

❯ **Research and study**   Designing a flight simulator? Do you know the maximum level-flight speed, climb rate, and service ceiling of each of your aircraft? If not, then where do you go to find out? Designers must be able to do research, which includes using the public library as well as surfing the Web. Then they have to make notes about what they've learned, and write it all down. Yes, that's right—just like in school. But this time you get paid for it!

> **Storyboarding and concept sketching** It's an enormous time-saver to be able to make your own concept sketches and storyboards: you can draw what you're thinking of, rather than trying to describe it to someone else. These aren't required skills, but they're valuable ones. For more details, see the "Specializations" section under "Art and Animation" earlier in this chapter.

Tools

Game designers do a little bit of everything. They use word processors, spreadsheets, databases, paint programs, audio waveform editors, and sometimes they even do a little programming. Some companies want designers to be able to use 3-D modeling and animation tools, too. Except for the word processor, they seldom need high-end versions of these tools, but they should know the basic principles behind all of them.

Level designers also use a tool called a level editor. This used to be a quick-and-dirty piece of software hacked together in-house to help the level designer build the levels in the game, but now many PC games are starting to be sold with the level editor included, so they're more professionally built. The level editor allows you to define the landscape that makes up the level, construct buildings, place enemies, and set triggers which will cause certain events to take place when they're tripped in various ways.

So far as hardware is concerned, a game designer should have a reasonably up-to-date workstation, no more than three years old, and as many different types of console machines as the company can afford. Designers need to be able to play recent games to find out what the competition has been doing.

Specializations

Like writers, game designers tend to be generalists: they do a little of everything and there's seldom a need for them to concentrate on one task exclusively. However, there are two areas that do require additional knowledge:

> **User interface design** No matter how fascinating the game concept, spectacular the artwork, or evocative the audio, if the user interface is badly designed, the game will flop. User interface designers create the conduit between the player and the game world; they allow the player to project his will into it. In order to do this, they have to establish a relationship between a set of buttons and analog controls, and a fictional person, vehicle, city, or whatever in the game world. This must be smooth and natural to use, so that after a while the player forgets that he's using a game machine at all, and feels truly immersed in the world.

> **AI design** Designing artificial intelligence isn't programming, but it comes as close as any area of game design ever does. An AI designer works closely with an AI programmer to specify how people or creatures will behave in a

game, and how the game as a whole will react, both strategically and tactically, to the player's actions. An AI designer will often write pseudo-code for a programmer to implement, and will help to define the states of a software construct called a finite state machine.

PRODUCING AND PROJECT MANAGEMENT

Producing normally belongs on the production side of the business, although as projects grow in size, many development companies are starting to hire producers of their own to help run the team. Traditionally, however, a producer works for a publisher, and has a publisher's mindset.

Production Jobs

As with game design, production jobs tend to change in nature as you rise up the ranks, so I'm going to describe them separately.

Assistant Producer

Assistant producer is the bottom rung of the production ladder, the first level at which you begin to get involved with building games as opposed to simply testing them, for example. As such, assistant producers do a tremendous amount of donkey-work of all kinds—some of it creative, much of it not. Here's a list of some of the things that assistant producers tend to do:

❭ Ship and receive documents, equipment, and CDs to developers.

❭ Make backups of all the project material.

❭ Purchase and play competing products to help the team determine how to surpass them.

❭ Test milestone deliveries to see if they meet requirements, and report back to the producer.

❭ Assist with testing the game and maintaining the bug database during testing phases.

❭ Assemble data needed by the game and convert them into a form usable by the programmers, such as athlete photographs for a sports game.

❭ Level design work if time and requirements permit.

Apart from these specific items, it's the assistant producer's job to support the producer and associate producers with their own tasks, which is how you learn the business.

Associate Producer

Associate producers are the heart of the production team, helping the producer, overseeing everything, and solving all sorts of problems. If the game will be released on more than one platform, each associate producer may take responsibility for one machine: one handles the Xbox version, one the PS2 version, and so on. The work can be divided up in other ways as well. The organization of a production team really depends on the skills and interests of the people involved.

Here are just some of the things associate producers do:

❯ Assist the producer in budgeting and scheduling the project in pre-production.

❯ Confer with the design team about the design of the game and the publisher's requirements.

❯ Keep continuous track of the development team's progress in the associate producer's designated areas of responsibility, and report back to the producer.

❯ Help the producer to maintain the project documentation, especially schedules.

❯ Oversee the work of assistant producers and/or testers.

❯ Assist the testing manager in developing a test plan for the game.

❯ Make arrangements with licensors (such as sports leagues, movie companies, and so on) to obtain photographs, logos, and other licensed intellectual property that the game will use.

❯ Supply material (such as screenshots) from the game to the publisher's marketing department, for use in advertising and other promotions.

❯ Research and recommend outside suppliers of services such as music composition or writing.

❯ Assemble the package of materials needed to send a game off for approvals by the licensors and the console manufacturer (if necessary), and for a rating by the rating board.

❯ Attend trade shows and other events, demonstrating the product to potential buyers.

❯ Run focus tests, usually in concert with the marketing department.

Producer

A producer looks after the development of one or more games—preferably just one, but it depends on how big the games are. Whether at a publisher or developer, the producer is responsible for getting the game done, and he oversees everything about the production process. If development is being done internally, he may also be the head of the development process as well, with the various leads reporting to him.

The producer is usually the final authority regarding creative decisions on a given game. This doesn't mean he can act dictatorially, and if he tries, the result is frequently a disaster. A few producers work as game designers at the same time, but most are so busy with administrative details that they delegate that responsibility to a lead designer who reports to them.

These are some of the things producers do:

- Find game ideas, products, and talent for the publisher to develop. Listen to pitches from development companies.

- Determine the size and scale of a project, assess the risks involved, and build its budget, schedule, and task list.

- Promote the product to the rest of the publishing company: sales, marketing, and executive staff, to keep them enthusiastic.

- Work with the lead game designer to define the broad outlines of the game.

- Verify (with the help of the production team) that each milestone delivery meets the requirements in the contract, and sign off on milestone payments.

- Make sure that the game meets the company's standards and requirements, and is fun to play.

- Negotiate contracts with outside suppliers, based on recommendations from research done by the associate producers.

- Oversee the work of the rest of the production team, and hire and promote people as appropriate.

- In cases where development is under the producer, work directly with the various leads (art, audio, and so on) to ensure that the project is on schedule and the teams have the resources they need. Where development is external, work with the development manager at the development company. Maintain constant vigilance to ensure that the game is on track, creatively, technically, and as a commercial product.

- Keep track of project spending to be sure it remains within budget; when cost overruns do occur, seek ways to minimize them.

- Identify tasks and issues that require coordination with the marketing, sales, legal, public relations, QA, and other departments of the publisher, and perform or delegate them as appropriate.

> Assist the marketing department in designing their sales campaign for the product. Attend trade shows and other events; meet with important clients if requested.

> Verify that all necessary legal rights have been obtained for materials used in the game before it ships.

> Make progress reports to the executive producer and senior executive staff.

> Resolve creative or other conflicts within the team, with the assistance of HR when necessary.

> Chair team meetings and schedule team events. Take responsibility for morale and productivity.

Producer is not ordinarily an entry-level position   On smaller projects such as Web-based games, it may be possible to become a producer if you can demonstrate you had some production experience in college or elsewhere.

INSIDE iNFO   A surprising amount of a producer's job is "selling" the game *inside* the publisher. At a big publisher, with numerous projects going on at once, it can be hard to attract the attention of senior executives or a busy marketing department. To get these people excited about a prospective game, the producer and designers will create documents, presentations, and even short films—like TV advertisements for the product—that the marketing and sales people will find enjoyable and memorable. Using my experience as a video producer, I made several of these at Electronic Arts, which helped to secure funding for such products as *Michelle Kwan Figure Skating*.

Executive Producer

An executive producer is typically responsible for an entire line of products. Apart from playing the games that she is responsible for from time to time, and conveying her impressions back down the line, she has very little direct creative involvement with an individual game. Executive producers handle the highest-level relationships in production: they maintain connections with marketing, public relations, sales, the legal department, and anyone else in other areas who might have any impact on the product. Executive producers negotiate development contracts and license agreements, and they work with senior management to create the company's product plan.

Executive producer is not an entry-level position   The only way to obtain it is by shipping successful products. Even if you have already shipped other kinds of software, or made other entertainment products such as music or television shows, you are unlikely to be hired as an executive producer in the game industry; the nature of the work is just too different. (Several early efforts to import executive producers from other creative industries were expensive disasters.)

A Day in the Life of a Producer

I've been in the game industry for over a dozen years. I'm now working at Monolith Productions, a development studio in Kirkland, Washington, where I'm currently managing a 25-person team working on three different first-person shooter (FPS) projects.

Most of my day is spent checking with my leads on various topics, writing e-mail or talking on the phone, reviewing design documents and writing management documentation for our publisher, and being immersed in that essential producer tool, *Microsoft Project*. This particular day started with me sending an update to our terrific Sierra marketing and PR people about the upcoming milestone for one of our projects. Then I talked with my QA lead and the programmers to make sure they're on schedule for our milestone to be delivered tomorrow.

A little later, it was time for some testing on the multiplayer FPS project. While I love FPS games, I'm actually not very good at them, so I'm mostly cannon fodder for the rest of the team. But it's important for me to participate, for many reasons.

Next up was working with our Lead Audio guy to fix a problem that was preventing me from recording audio in a training video we're making for our artists. As I have some digital video experience, I've taken over the task of recording our 3-D art training sessions. After that, a brief moment to mourn my ripped pants leg, which I tore while crawling under the desk to set up the video recording equipment. Oh well! After the recording session, I spent some time digitizing and editing the training video.

Then I worked on the Pre-Production milestone descriptions document for our next major project. This was mostly revisions, since our schedule and budget had changed this week. I reviewed a consulting contract for an artist we're going to hire next week. Then I met with my database programmer for an update on our custom art asset tracking database project.

Next I reviewed the latest version of the design document for our newest project, with the design and art Leads. I had some concerns that we wouldn't have time for all of the world art and level maps, so we talked about structuring the project in a more prioritized, flexible way. Then I dealt with a small crisis, talking to our publisher about localization problems in Asia for the most recently shipped game. This turned out to be a false alarm, just an installation error during localization testing. Lastly, I spent some time updating my *Microsoft Project* files, checking for tasks that the team had completed and synchronizing that information back into *Project*.

At the end of the day, I had one last cup of coffee, said goodnight to the team, and headed home to my husband and daughters. Another day closer to gold master!

—*Ellen Guon Beeman, Producer, Monolith Productions Inc.*

Talents and Skills

The talents and skills required by a producer are many and varied, and the most important of them cannot be learned in school. Producers are generalists. Unlike programmers, sound engineers, artists, or writers, their job is not based on exercising a particular creative skill, but on working with a creative team to ensure that everything comes together as a fun, salable, and profitable product. Producers seldom build parts of the game themselves (although assistant and associate producers often contribute various elements); instead, they work to keep everything else moving smoothly, and in crunch time they lend a hand anywhere they can.

Abstract Talents and Skills

Because so much of production work is administrative, producers require more abstract skills than most other game professions:

‣ **"Product sense"** As I've already described, the most critical talent of all is a mysterious ability called "product sense"—the capacity to tell if a partially completed game is going to be fun and to sell well, and especially, how to fix it if it won't. Nobody is quite sure where product sense comes from. It's partly based on a deep understanding of the game player and the game market, but it's also based on a love of games just for themselves. Many people think they have good product sense, but only a few really reach the stratospheric heights at which they make tens of millions of dollars for their company. Product sense isn't purely innate, though, because the longer you work in the game industry, the better you get at it.

‣ **Leadership** This quality is less important at the assistant and associate levels, but it's critical if you ever want to rise above those levels. A producer is the head of a team of people, and that means you have to lead: inspire, encourage, render judgment, and when necessary, enforce discipline. Producers must also find workable compromises between people with different ideas of how things should be, and that, too, is a leadership skill. Leadership is partly a talent, an innate capacity for inspiring enthusiasm and commitment, but it's also a learned skill, which is why there are so many courses in it. Poor leadership has killed untold numbers of otherwise good game projects.

‣ **Communication** You see the phrase "excellent oral and written communication skills" listed as a requirement so often in job ads that it has become a cliché. Nevertheless, for producers, communication skills are essential. Producers write documents and memos; they run meetings; they give presentations to senior executives; they attend trade shows and talk to potential customers.

If you feel confident about those tasks, then you might be a candidate for a producer's job; on the other hand, if you prefer computer languages to human ones, look elsewhere.

❭ Negotiation   More than simply bargaining, negotiation is a process of finding a way to make both sides happy with a deal. Producers are usually the point people in negotiations between developers and publishers. The publisher wants the best deal they can get—but "best" doesn't always mean "cheapest." A developer who has been pressured into a bad deal is unlikely to be motivated to do quality work, and a good producer knows this.

❭ Organizational ability   Modern game projects are huge, with dozens of people, hundreds of tasks, and literally thousands of files. All this is ultimately the producer's responsibility. Even with external development, where the producer doesn't directly oversee the work, she still has to know what is supposed to happen when and what should be delivered at each milestone—and why. To be a producer you must be able to plan, organize, and keep track of a great many things at once. Don't forget, in addition to the development work itself, producers also have to do liaison work with the marketing, PR, legal and other departments at the publisher.

❭ Attention to detail   Another vital requirement at all levels of production is attention to detail. Assistant and associate producers deal with the thousands of necessary details to make sure the game is constructed properly, that it's fun, and that it's bug-free when it ships. Computers are notoriously unforgiving of errors, and a tiny mistake can turn into an expensive and embarrassing debacle for the publisher. At the upper levels, producers and executive producers must be able to delegate authority appropriately to the people under them. For them, attention to detail doesn't mean handling every detail personally; it means making sure everyone else is doing so properly. Game projects often fail because they're run by a person who only sees the "big picture" and can't be bothered to look after the details. (The opposite extreme, trying to handle everything yourself, is called "micro-management" and is usually a disaster because there's too much for one person to handle.)

INSIDE iNFO   Good communications are the alpha and omega of production. Treat your team with respect if you expect the same back. Make a point of going to the pub (or whatever) with your team every now and then: no matter how approachable you make yourself at work, there are always important things that you will only be told after a couple of pints.
—Kim Blake, Producer, Particle Systems

Concrete Skills

In addition to all the abstract qualities I described earlier, there are also a few specific skills you can learn in school or elsewhere:

) **Project management techniques**   Project management is the delicate art of balancing the tasks that you have to do, the resources (both staff and technical resources) that you have to do them with, and the amount of time that you have. Risk assessment and contingency planning are also vital parts of project management. This skill is commonly taught in business school and in some software engineering programs, and there are many, many books on the subject. Be aware, however, that every field is different and project management for games differs from project management for other software because of all the different types of assets and creative people involved.

) **Budgeting and scheduling**   As with project management, you can learn how to make budgets and schedules through books and classes. Until you've been in the game industry a while you won't know the rules of thumb to do it for game development, but you probably won't be asked to in an entry-level position.

) **All other game development skills**   No, I'm not kidding. As I said, a producer is a generalist. You should certainly be able to play and test games. It also helps to know how to use 3-D modeling and animation tools a little; edit audio and video a little; even program a little. A key element of overseeing other people's work is understanding what those jobs entail. In addition, producers often pitch in wherever they can be of help; the more you know how to do, the more useful you can be, especially at the assistant and associate levels.

 Rob Fulop, a former boss of mine, used to say this about creating any kind of product: "You can have it fast, good, or cheap: pick any two." That about sums it up.

Tools

At a bare minimum, producers need to be familiar and comfortable with word processors and spreadsheet programs. You can build a reasonable schedule for a project using *Excel* if there aren't too many people and tasks involved. Beyond that, you will need to learn formal project management techniques and learn to use the software that supports them, such as *Microsoft Project*. These tools have features that identify dependencies among tasks, compute staffing requirements, and help you keep track of progress. After e-mail, *Microsoft Project* is the producer's #1 tool.

Specializations

Producers tend to be generalists, because their work isn't based on a technical or creative skill, but on the ability to oversee a process and help it along in whatever way necessary. However, there are a couple of specialized jobs on the production side of things.

Technical Director (TD)

Producers seldom have the technical experience to judge the quality of computer programming, or a programming team, by themselves. When a product is being developed out-of-house, someone at the publisher needs to be able to check the development company's code to make sure it meets software engineering standards, and to advise the producer on technical issues. This person is a technical director—sometimes called a technical producer or technical advisor.

A TD is usually a senior software engineer with a broad range of experience, possibly including some management. However, within a publisher, on an external development project, a TD is not a managerial position. It's primarily advisory, although it does come with some authority. One of the TD's tasks is to check each milestone delivery to make sure that the code is up to snuff. If it isn't, the TD can advise the producer not to authorize the next milestone payment.

In addition to examining the code and advising the producer, the TD also serves as an emergency resource for the developers. With his experience, he can lend a hand where needed, helping to track down particularly difficult bugs and solving other technical problems. He also recommends particular technical approaches or libraries of routines, and helps to get the developers coding resources and tools they may need.

Finally, a TD plays an important role in checking out new development teams that the publisher is considering working with. He'll read the programmers' résumés, talk to them about their experience, and look over their gear and facilities. He'll also examine the proposed technical design of a product that the developer is pitching to the publisher to see if it's really feasible or just pie-in-the-sky. All this is critically important to a publisher who's considering investing millions of dollars in a group of people.

Technical director is not an entry-level position   It's theoretically possible to get a TD position from outside the industry, but you would have to have a heck of a lot of experience programming the target hardware—and particularly game programming—already, presumably on your own or as part of a group. Be prepared to demonstrate detailed technical knowledge of the machine and experience at working with software development teams.

Project Manager

On large projects, the producer may be too busy to keep track of the progress of all the tasks by herself. If this happens, she may get a project manager to help out. Although it sounds like one, this is not a leadership position. Rather, the purpose of the job is to manage information—specifically, the information about who's doing what, what has been done, what is left to do, and how long it's all taking. Other titles for this position are Scheduler, Project Planner, Production Manager, and Project Coordinator.

INSIDE INFO   One thing to be wary of about the project manager position: If it's your job to go around with a checklist and make sure everyone is doing what they're supposed to, and is meeting their schedules, you can quickly come to be perceived as the "group nag," especially if you don't have any actual management authority. If you are disliked by many of your group, you are unlikely to be promoted into a leadership position even if your project management skills are excellent. In order to prevent this, you must cultivate a cheerful, outgoing disposition, and *never betray emotion* or make it personal when someone tells you they're behind with their work. If it's a discipline problem, it's up to their boss to solve it, not you. All you're supposed to do is gather data. When you start passing judgment or leveling criticism, people will begin to lie to you, and then the data you gather will be worthless—which will make your own job impossible.

Project management skills from non-software industries don't translate well to software development, and game software is pretty different from other kinds of software as well, because of all the art and audio assets involved. Your best bet is to show that you've done project management of some kind of game development, perhaps in college.

Don't confuse the term "project manager" with "*product* manager." Product manager is a marketing position.

TESTING AND QUALITY ASSURANCE

Testing is a crucial part of game development. The rule of thumb is that fully a third of the development process should be given over to testing. Despite years of research to try to create bugproof programming languages and software engineering methods, games are still prone to errors.

Testing falls into several categories:

❭ **Bug testing**   This is quite simply looking for software errors: crash bugs, game misbehavior, or cosmetic defects. When you find a bug, you try to reproduce it, then log the conditions under which it occurred in a bug database and move on to the next item on the test plan. When the programmers claim to have fixed it, you go back and try to reproduce it again to verify the fix.

) **Gameplay testing and tuning**   This is the most enjoyable part of testing. The object here is to be sure the game is enjoyable and well-balanced.

) **Configuration testing**   More important on the PC than on consoles, config testing means trying the game out on a variety of types of hardware to be sure it works properly with all of them.

) **Quality assurance**   The final checks before the product goes out the door. (It's listed as a specialization next.)

Testing video games isn't as much fun as it sounds. You don't play the game in order to win it, or even for enjoyment; you play it according to a strict plan that lays out what features you are testing. It goes on for weeks and months, and after a while you can get sick of the sight of the game.

Testing *is* fun, though. Testers get an up-close-and-personal look at the development process because they interact with everyone: audio, artists, and programmers. As the project proceeds, you get to watch a raw, unfinished piece of software turn into an actual game, a product that thousands of people will buy and play. If it's a multiplayer game, a lot of testers like to hang around after hours just to play against each other for fun, rather than as part of the plan. There's a certain camaraderie that grows up during those final crazy weeks of a project.

Testing belongs to both production and development: both the publisher and the developer will have testers. Other job titles for testers include Game Analyst and Quality Assurance Analyst.

Breaking in: All Experience Is Good Experience

My entry into the games business was somewhat of an accident. I had recently completed my A.A.S. degree in computer science from the local community college, and was looking for a programming job. Most of the companies I interviewed with were in very conservative and established industries, such as banks and insurance companies. I wasn't thrilled about working for any of them, and they all wanted more experience than I had to offer. After several months of this, I resorted to sending résumés to almost any ad in the paper that mentioned computer knowledge at all!

Eventually I accepted an interview with GT Interactive without even realizing that it was a computer game company. The job description was rather vague and mentioned nothing about PC games, so you can probably imagine my surprise when I saw the posters for *Wolfenstein 3-D* and *Doom II* on the walls!

After speaking with my soon-to-be-boss for only a few minutes, I realized that he was primarily interested in my own computer experience, especially in the area of Bulletin Board Systems. He told me he was looking for someone who could set up a large BBS for technical support and other customer service inquiries. I had been running one of these from my home for years, but only added it to my résumé as an afterthought. It paid off though, since he offered me the job on the spot, and informed me that a large portion of my time would be spent on testing new games before they were released. Needless to say, I accepted the position and have been in the industry ever since.

—Jon Gramlich, QA Analyst, Monolith Productions

Talents and Skills

To be a good tester, you need to be a keen-eyed, analytical observer. You can't just watch the action; you have to look at the whole screen to make sure everything is happening the way it's supposed to.

 Attention to detail   This lies at the heart of game testing. What *exactly* were you doing when things went wrong? What *exactly* happened on the screen when it happened? If you weren't paying attention, your bug report isn't going to be any use.

 Good communication skills   Not only do you have to notice what went wrong, you also have to explain it, accurately and unambiguously, to the programmer who's going to try and fix it. A bug report that says "Game locked up" tells them nothing. A little *diplomacy* wouldn't be wasted, either. Remember, programmers have pride in their work; every bug is an embarrassing error. Keep the bug reports factual and polite!

 Gaming ability   You need to be a pretty decent gamer, because you won't get much done if you aren't one. You don't have to be Thresh, though: if you're *too* good you won't be able to tell if a game is too hard for an ordinary person.

 Patience   This is a key virtue in a tester—and it's one of the reasons why customer service is good training for testing. If you get frustrated because a game crashes 15 times in a row, you're missing the point: those crashes are data. They are what you're there for in the first place.

 Programming   It really helps to have some programming skills, too, in order to understand the way that software works and the ways in which it can break. It's not a requirement necessarily, but it *is* a distinct advantage.

Tools

Testing (as opposed to debugging) doesn't use a lot of technical tools. You should be playing the game on a machine that closely resembles the user's machine, because the idea is to test the game in "field conditions," as much as possible.

❱ **The bug database**   The testing manager (your boss) will have set up a database for recording bugs in the product you're testing. When you find a bug, you create a new entry for it and enter the details. You won't have to know anything about database programming or management to use it. It's seldom any more complicated than filling in a form or using a search facility on a web site. The most commonly used database programs are *FileMaker Pro* and *Microsoft Access,* if you want to get some experience working with them ahead of time.

❱ **A VCR**   It's very hard to remember exactly what you were doing when a bug occurs, especially if the program crashes and the screen goes blank. Most testing nowadays is done with a VCR attached to the video output of the machine so you can record what you're doing as you go. In addition to allowing you to retrace your steps, the VCR enables you to show the bug to one of the programmers if it's an intermittent problem that is not easily reproducible.

Specializations

Testing games is a fairly uniform activity, and the nature of the work doesn't change that much from day to day. But there are a few specializations in the field.

Testing Manager

I list testing manager as a specialization, rather than a promotion up from tester, because it usually isn't available as a promotion from tester. Most often, testers go on to become assistant and associate producers first. Testers don't have enough administrative experience to move directly to testing manager. Once they have gained the necessary management skills in production, then they can move sideways to be a testing manager.

Testing managers do a little testing themselves to help out during crunch time, but their real job consists of four key tasks:

❱ **Defining the test plan for a game**   This is an enormous and extremely intricate problem that requires a thorough understanding of how software works and how it can be proven to work correctly. The testing manager consults with the designers and programmers to document every function and aspect of the game that is subject to observational analysis (stepping through the code in a debugger doesn't count!), then builds a plan for actually performing that analysis.

❭ **Building and maintaining a bug database** This task requires database skills, usually with *Microsoft Access* or *Filemaker Pro*. It's not the same as database programming, however; you don't have to write code. The bug database provides a means of uniquely recording each bug found, who found it, under what circumstances, and any other useful observations that may help solve the bug, as well as a status flag to indicate whether it is unfixed, claimed fixed, or verified fixed.

❭ **Implementing the test plan** In practice, this means overseeing the work of the testers: assigning parts of the test plan to them to perform, checking their progress, and generally acting as their boss.

❭ **Maintaining relations with the development team** Every bug the testers find, someone on the development team has to fix. This means that testing results data is constantly flowing to the developers, and new, corrected, builds of the software are constantly flowing back to the testers for verification. The testing manager oversees this process, making sure the testers are working on the current version. It also requires a little diplomacy: testers sometimes take a little too much glee in reporting a bug, and programmers can suffer from injured pride. Part of the testing manager's job is to prevent this, and to make sure everyone realizes they're all on the same side.

Testing manager is not an entry-level position However, if you have experience managing software tests in other industries, you may be a good candidate for a testing manager in the game industry. There are differences, but they are not insurmountable.

Formal software testing methods are now the subject of courses at colleges and trade schools.

Configuration Tester

Configuration testing, as I mentioned earlier in this chapter, involves checking to see whether the game works with various combinations of hardware, usually on PCs rather than consoles (although console games that use special input devices also require configuration testing). Config testing also requires a test plan, to determine what features and what hardware will be tested—it isn't possible to test all combinations. Config testers need to be particularly familiar with PC hardware, because they spend a lot of time installing and removing audio and video cards, as well as trying out different joysticks and controllers.

Config tester could be an entry-level position for someone who has experience working in an IT department or even building computers.

Quality Assurance

As I explained in Chapter 4, QA isn't quite the same as regular testing. Testing is concerned with improving playability and finding bugs, QA is more concerned with appearances and "correctness." The object of quality assurance is to verify that a product meets certain standards, does not contain any flagrant errors, and—in the case of console games—is ready to go off to the manufacturer for their approval. There's no such thing as "good enough" in QA; a product either passes, or it fails.

QA is exacting work. It doesn't require any particular training, but it does require a rigorous approach to the job. You need to be supremely detail-oriented, a perfectionist. You also need to be hard-nosed. Toward the end of a project, when everyone has been killing themselves for the last six weeks straight, they're not going to want to hear that there's a minor misspelling deep in a third-level menu that hardly anybody will see. Producers have been known to rant and rave about "QA bureaucrats" holding up a product through sheer petty-mindedness. It's the job of the QA analyst to stick to his guns: he's the last line of defense against the game going out the door with a mistake in it.

NON-DEVELOPMENT JOBS

In this section, I'm going to mention a couple of jobs that don't directly involve game development, but are still close to the process. If you don't necessarily want to build games, but you think you'd like to work at a game company, you might consider one of them. Even though you won't be making the games themselves, these fields still require you to exercise some creativity.

Marketing

Suppose you love games and everything about them, you could talk about them all day, you're brimful of enthusiasm for them … but you just don't like the finicky, technical business of *making* the darn things?! Well, if you're imaginative, organized, and you feel you understand the game customer and game markets extremely well, then marketing might be for you.

Marketing isn't about actually selling the product—getting on the phone, or going to a meeting, and persuading a retailer to buy it. Rather, it's about selling it on the large scale: advertising it, promoting it, making sure other people hear about it. Marketing is the art of attracting attention, of making a product look beautiful and sound wonderful, of persuading people to spend their money on something. It isn't the same as advertising, but they are closely related fields. Advertising is specifically about people via the media; marketing includes a number of other activities as well.

INSIDE iNFO Marketing isn't always as well-respected by game developers as it could be. Marketing people get to meet the celebrities who endorse the games; they throw big launch parties; they set up (and accompany) press junkets. Game developers don't get all these perks, and they can be a little resentful of the fact that they're the ones who actually build the game while other people seem to get all the fun. What they don't realize is that marketing is also very hard work. It takes weeks of planning to set up one of these events, and I never heard of one of the organizers enjoying them very much; they're too busy making sure everything goes smoothly. OK, you get to meet Tony Hawk or Pierce Brosnan for five minutes, but for that privilege you do weeks of preparation. Don't be put off by the occasional snide comment you'll hear about marketing. Marketing and production have to work closely together, and at a successful company, they respect each other's contribution.

Here are some things marketers work on:

❯ **Ad campaigns**   Obviously a game needs attractive ads to go in magazines, on posters, and (occasionally) on TV to sell the game. Sometimes these are made through an advertising agency, but they're often designed by the marketing department directly.

❯ **Product design**   The publisher's marketing department, not the producers or developers, decides how the box is going to look. The box plays an important role in selling the product: it has to say "pick me up!" to a browsing consumer. Marketing usually has artists, or product designers, of its own to design the box. They also write the text that appears there. They work with the game designers to decide which are the key features they want to mention, and they get screen shots and other material from the game's artists.

❯ **Store displays**   When you visit the software store, you'll see a lot of posters, cardboard cut-outs, flyers, shelf-markers, and other items helping to sell particular games. The retailers themselves don't make them; they come from the publishers. Someone has to design all these things, and that's the marketing department.

❯ **Licenses**   Negotiating new licenses for intellectual property like *Harry Potter* is a business and legal function that often takes place at the highest levels of the publisher, but once the contract has been agreed upon, there is a tremendous amount of work in coordinating the marketing.

The license-holder will have all kinds of images and other data to give the publisher's marketing and development groups for use in building and selling the game. The publisher may also make joint marketing plans with other licensees of the same property, such as movie studios or book publishers. That way they can take advantage of the public's interest in the property to sell several different items at once.

▶ **Trade shows and special events**   At a trade show like E3, a publisher shows off its forthcoming games to the retailers and takes advance orders for copies. It requires a huge amount of work just to attend such a show; the publisher has to design and build a booth to display their games, then purchase the booth space from the show's sponsors and ship all the materials there and set them up. Since the purpose is to sell the games to retailers, this work is normally done in conjunction with the sales staff, who will also be attending. Similarly, if there are big public events, such as the Super Bowl or the Indianapolis 500, that a lot of the game's potential customers are likely to be watching or attending, the marketing department will throw a party or set up a special event nearby to publicize the game. Organizing one of these involves: finding a venue; hiring entertainers, catering, and security; inviting celebrities who are known to like the game; informing the press, and, of course, shipping all the games, gear, and decorations needed. Planning trade shows and special events is a tremendous amount of work, but it does involve some creativity of its own to make sure everything is attractive and enjoyable.

A Day in the Life of a Marketing Director

A day in the life of a marketing director at Sierra Entertainment usually involves working not only on titles that are shipping in the near term, but also on what we plan to do as a company three to five years in the future. We work on marketing plans, packaging, promotions, and advertisements for games that are about to launch. However, we also spend a good amount of time every day working on products that will be launched a year or more in the future. This involves working with our development teams to put the right game concept in place for its target audience, as well as on our overall plan for what we hope to ship three years or more down the road. And if we are lucky, we end the day with a game or two. I thought that getting a job in the game industry would be Nirvana, simply because I would get a good amount of time to play games. In truth, you do get a bunch of games to play, but the curse is that you don't have nearly enough time to play them.

—*Lee Rossini, Director of Marketing, Sierra Entertainment*

Public Relations

Public relations is that branch of publishing that specifically involves dealing with the press, in their editorial rather than their advertising capacity. PR people write press releases to announce new games and other events associated with them; they assemble "press kits"—documents and CDs containing demos and images—to teach journalists about a product; they send out copies of games to magazines for review; they invite the press to attend parties and other special events to show off games that are soon to be released. The purpose of all this is to generate "buzz"—customer interest and excitement in the months before the product actually comes out. After all, as long as a press article about a game is positive, it's free advertising! The PR department also responds to inquiries and requests for interviews with key people, and responds to any negative publicity that may arise. When promotional events involve both consumers and the press, PR works together with marketing. If you're particularly skilled in English and are good at putting a "spin" on things, PR could be the job for you.

OTHER ENTRY-LEVEL JOBS

What if you don't have the education or experience to get into the game industry in one of the development positions—programmer, artist, musician, and so on? Well, don't despair. Development companies and publishers need a lot of other people as well. If you're willing to start right at the bottom and take any job that's going just for a chance to be around games and game development, then there are several options open to you.

Customer Service

Customer service means talking on the phone to players and helping them solve technical problems with their games. It requires great familiarity with the games, considerable technical competence, and unbelievable patience. As with warranty returns, it's a good way to get your foot in the door while you're hoping to get the attention of someone in testing or production.

Customer service is actually pretty good training for testing. Not only do you have to try to figure out what's wrong with some software, you have to do it long distance, without seeing the screen in front of you! It takes a fair amount of imagination and analytical skill to diagnose a software problem over the phone.

Information Technology

The IT department in a company purchases, installs, backs up, maintains, upgrades, and repairs the company's computers and software. Since the computers are at the core of what every game developer and publisher does, it's an extremely important responsibility.

IT isn't exactly an entry-level position in the sense that you don't have to have any experience: obviously you have to know a lot about computer hardware and software, and especially networking, to work in the IT department. But it's one way to get your foot in the door if you don't have any game development experience. From IT, you might be able to move on to customer service, a natural jump, and then to testing or configuration testing, where your familiarity with hardware will serve you in good stead.

Warranty Returns

This is the department of the publisher that receives faulty products from the customers and sends out new replacements. It doesn't require any special skills at all, apart from a basic familiarity with games and computers. You have to log everything correctly so the company can keep track of problems; if a whole lot of games of one particular title are coming in, there's probably a problem at the manufacturing plant. It's a long way from warranty returns to actually making video games, but it does get you in the door. Once you've got a job with the company, you can meet the people doing the job you *really* want, and maybe get noticed.

Reception

Are you cheerful, personable, professional, and a careful dresser? Maybe reception is for you. The reception department is the public face of the company. Routing phone calls and greeting visitors doesn't have much to do with game development, but you'll find out a lot about what goes on in the business, and you'll eventually meet everyone: they have to come in through the door, after all. For some reason people seem to confide in receptionists, too; they become the company grapevine for all the news and gossip that's going. If you cultivate a friendly and outgoing nature, and pay attention to what's going on around you, you'll soon learn when there are jobs opening up in other parts of the company that might be of interest to you.

Mailroom

No, I'm not joking: you really can work your way up from the mailroom. It may be an entry-level job, but it's not a trivial one: with all the different delivery services and options available, there's quite a lot to know about shipping and receiving documents and packages, especially if some of them are going overseas and there are Customs formalities involved. Even in these days of e-mail, a big company grinds to a halt without an efficient mailroom.

As with reception, the best thing about working in the mailroom is that sooner or later you get to meet everybody. You'll be delivering mail all over the building, so you'll find out who does what. If your job gives you time, stop to chat with people and ask questions. Keep your ears open for news about hiring in other departments.

WRAP-UP

In this chapter, I've tried to describe the key jobs you can have in the game industry, whether they're directly connected with making games, or are in an ancillary, but still important, role. Remember, I haven't been able to cover everything! Many companies will have jobs that I haven't had room to discuss here, or specialized positions that are combinations of the ones I've listed. If you see an ad for an open position that isn't mentioned in this book, don't assume it's not for you. Follow it up and find out what's involved. If it sounds like something you want to do, go for it!

CHAPTER

7

How to Get a Job

THE title of this book is *Break into the Game Industry* because, when you're on the outside, that's what it feels as if you have to do. Like breaking into a bank vault, there are several ways to go about it.

You can try to break in with explosives—make a lot of noise with self-promoting gimmicks, telling everyone how incredibly brilliant you are, and how unbelievably stupid *they* are if they don't give you a job right this instant. It's seldom a good idea: you set off alarm bells and attract a lot of negative attention. Trying to blast your way in, either as a safe-cracker or a game developer, is strictly an amateur approach.

Another way to get in is to get to know someone who already works there and will open the door for you. With bank vaults, this is called an "inside job"; with games, it's called "networking." It is undoubtedly the quickest and most reliable way to do it, and in this chapter I'll talk a lot about networking.

The third way to break into a bank vault is to dig your way in with steady, determined effort. The truth is that looking for a job in the game industry is a lot like looking for a job anywhere else: you read job ads, research companies, send out résumés, and go to interviews. Job-hunting is a job in itself: you have to show up every day and work hard at it in order to see results. However, not all of the advice in traditional job-hunting manuals applies to the game industry; there are a few important differences. I'll discuss them in this chapter.

PACKAGING YOURSELF AS A PROFESSIONAL

You may be an amateur now, but you need to think of yourself as a professional—a professional who's just temporarily out of work. Before you begin job-hunting, you must create a professional appearance: a package of materials that shows off your talents and skills, and represents you to the world. These materials consist of the following items:

> **Your résumé and cover letter** All job-hunters need these things, and I'll discuss them in depth later in this chapter.

> **Your portfolio or demo** You won't need a demo if you're applying for a position in testing or customer service (although it certainly can't hurt), but you will absolutely need one if you're applying for any development position like programmer, audio engineer, or level designer. I'll discuss demos in detail also.

) **A business card**   You may wonder why you need a business card if you don't have a job yet. The reason is simple: you need something to hand to people that will remind them later that you exist, and that tells them how to get in touch with you. If you can design a clever card that will intrigue people or make them laugh, so much the better. The game industry is about entertainment, so people appreciate business cards that show some creativity. Still, avoid anything too gaudy or corny. You want them laughing with you, not at you. If in doubt, go for understated elegance—it's always safe and besides, they're the cheapest to print.

) **A professional web site**   A web site isn't absolutely required, but it definitely helps. It doesn't have to be big or complicated. A professional web site allows you to document your experience and show off your work, cheaply, 24 hours a day, all over the world. You can put your résumé on your web site, your portfolio, and anything else that you think shows you off to advantage. Most Internet service providers offer a little web space along with their accounts, and you can craft a perfectly decent web site with pure HTML if you want—no need to buy a fancy package unless you want fancy features. One word of warning, however: If you do put your résumé on your website, you may not want to include your home address, for privacy reasons. Also, if your résumé, or any part of your web site, includes your e-mail address, you will probably begin to receive "job-seekers' spam"—advertisements for worthless degrees and doubtful business opportunities. You can discourage this by writing your e-mail address as *janedoe "at" janedoecorp.com* and not including a "mailto:" tag.

Introducing Mary Margaret Walker: Recruiter Extraordinaire

I'm a game developer, not a human resources person or a recruiter, so when the time came to talk about specific job-hunting techniques, I turned to an expert: Mary Margaret Walker. She's an old friend and the owner of Mary-Margaret.com, a recruitment and business services firm. She knows everything there is to know about getting work in the game industry, and she's also got a great web site that's full of useful information for newcomers: www.mary-margaret.com. Throughout this chapter, you'll be seeing snippets of her wisdom. Oh, and if you get in touch with her, don't call her Mary!

NETWORKING: IT'S NOT WHAT YOU KNOW...

I used to think that the old saying "It's not what you know, it's *who* you know" was one of the most cynical things I had ever heard. I thought it meant that the old-boy network would always win out; it didn't matter how well-qualified you were for a job, somebody with the right connections would get it instead. Later on I realized I was only half-right. It's true that occasionally someone prefers to hire his incompetent friends instead of better-qualified strangers. But if that's going on, you probably don't want to work at his company anyway. Any business that consistently puts friendship ahead of ability in its hiring decisions is headed for trouble.

There isn't much of an old-boy network in the game industry anyway. This is a young, ambitious, entrepreneurial business. Results are what count—can you do the job or can't you? The industry is competitive enough that people who consistently perform well are among the mostly highly prized. Nobody gets a fat salary just by knowing the fraternity handshake, and nobody gets to retire on the job. Game companies can't afford it.

The truth about "it's not what you know, it's who you know," which I came to realize after I had been working for a few years, is more subtle than simple cynicism. What it really means is that the most important factor in finding a job is not being well-prepared, it's knowing where the jobs *are*, and that means knowing people—lots of people, the more the better. In tribal societies, and in many non-western societies still, people keep track of their extended family relationships very carefully. That's because in those societies even your distant cousins are a resource, people you can call on if you need help. In the western world, we've replaced family with professional contacts. They're your most important business resource—the people you get in touch with if you need something.

This is one of the reasons that professional conferences and trade shows have so many parties. The first time you go to a convention, it may seem as if the whole thing is just a non-stop beer bash. But the companies throwing these parties aren't just spending their money for fun; they're doing it to get their employees together with other people: to renew old relationships and make new ones. This process is called "schmoozing." One of those chance meetings over the wine and cheese platter could turn into a contract worth millions, or a new employee who can bring something really valuable to the company.

INSIDE iNFO Make a friend in the industry. It's just too tough to get in without one ... Get in any way you can, prove yourself, and start going after the job you *really* want once you are on board.
—Lee Rossini, Director of Marketing, Sierra Entertainment

Where to Meet Game Developers

So, how do you start networking? You hang out where game developers hang out. Here's a list of things you can do. Some of them cost money, but others are free.

> ❯ *Read game development web sites, participate in on-line forums.* On the Internet, nobody can tell if you're a raw newcomer or a seasoned pro, so dive in. Don't take any one person's opinion as gospel; find out what the

common wisdom is. Use your real name, and give extra credit to other people who use theirs; it's easy to hide behind an anonymous handle, but someone who uses her own name is putting her professional reputation on the line with everything she says. Avoid flame wars; you won't learn anything from them. Ask for help if you need it—lots of people do, professionals and amateurs alike—and give help if you have it to give. The game industry thrives on shared information.

❱ *Attend local developers' group meetings; if there isn't one, start one!* In cities all over the world, developers get together on an informal basis once a month or so for pizza and beer and to shoot the breeze. Find out where this is happening and go to a meeting: the IGDA has a list of chapters around the world. (Visit www.igda.org/chapters for details.) The meetings normally don't cost anything and in my experience they're always welcoming to newcomers. If you can't find a group, see if you can start one. Look for a pizza place or a pub with a back room that will let you use it for free if you'll bring in a bunch of people who will buy food: weekday nights are best because the room will probably be idle anyway. Unless you live in a really small town, chances are there are at least 10 or 15 other people in your area working on games, none of whom are aware of each other. Pin a note on a bulletin board at the public library or community center, and at the local college's computer science and art departments. Post to the community web site. Put a free announcement in the local paper.

❱ *Join the IGDA.* The IGDA is *the* professional society for the interactive entertainment industry, and it doesn't have any admissions restrictions: if you say you're interested in game development, that makes you a game developer as far as it's concerned. The IGDA has all sorts of programs and activities to advance the state of the profession in various respects, which you'll be welcome to participate in once you're a member. There's a discount rate for students.

❱ *Go to conferences and trade shows.* This is the most expensive option, but it also gives you the most direct exposure to a lot of developers at once. The gold standard is the Game Developers' Conference, held annually in San Jose, California. It has a range of fee levels, and if you're really strapped for cash, you can volunteer to work at it part-time, which gets you into everything for free. Volunteering is a great way to meet people, too. There's also the Electronic Entertainment Expo (E3), which is cheap if you only go to the trade show. Many of the people staffing the booths are in marketing and sales rather than game development, but there are still a lot of developers around and their badges are distinctive. Look in Appendix C for more information about industry events. Travel and lodging, rather than the price of admission, will probably be your biggest expense.

Researching a Company

A key part of job-hunting is knowing what companies you want to work for, and doing research on companies that you've learned are hiring. The place to start is the company's web site for the most direct look at the company's products. Visit the "Jobs" or "Careers" page—most companies have one—to check out the current openings and learn the names of the people they want you to send your résumé to (this isn't the *only* person you should send it to, however). This will also tell you in what format they want it (mail, fax, or e-mail) and whether or not you should include a demo with it.

Go to the "Contact Us" page to find out where the company is located, although a surprising number of small development companies don't list their office addresses; you may have to do a little spadework to dig this up. Large corporations with multiple offices may have a "Locations" page. If they have a "Corporate" or "About Us" page, read it to learn about the management; this will tell you about their experience, philosophy, and company goals. Read the "News" or "Press" page to see their press releases and find out what they've been up to lately.

Also, check out the company's magazine advertisements. This will tell you a little about the company's corporate culture. Even though the ad may have been created by an ad agency, it had to be approved by someone at the company. If they have sexist ads or stupid ads, somebody at the company is sexist or stupid. It may not matter to you unless you're planning to work in marketing, but it's something to consider.

Scan the Internet for news about the company. You can check out the gamer bulletin boards, but take what you read there with a grain of salt: gamers love to complain. Obviously, you want to know if the company's products are any good, but it's better to rely on the published game reviews or even corporate news for that. Use the search features on business web sites like Yahoo! Finance or CBS Marketwatch to find out how they have been performing as a corporation.

Build yourself a database, or even just a spreadsheet, of companies. Include their official contact information, plus the names, e-mail addresses, and telephone numbers of everyone you have ever heard of there. Include the names of their key products, and add any other notes that you think might be useful. Once you have this information, you'll be much better armed to make a pitch to them: companies really appreciate it when a potential employee already knows a lot about them.

About Recruiters

A recruiter—also known colloquially as a headhunter—is a person or firm hired, almost always on a commission basis, by a game company to help them find talented people to fill open positions. If you get a job through a recruiter, it won't cost you anything: the employer will pay them a fee for having found you.

Recruiters spend a lot of time talking in a friendly way to game developers, which can lead to the misapprehension that their role is to find jobs for them. Rather, their role is to find developers for jobs. As such, they seldom are looking for entry-level people; they have been hired to find rarer, more difficult-to-locate senior people.

Recruiters are a great resource for information about the industry, particularly current information like salary ranges and job markets in different parts of the country. Because their whole job is schmoozing, they are usually chatty, well-informed people, who are happy to give you a little of their time and advice for nothing. Don't abuse this privilege, however: they have to earn a living, too. When you're talking to a recruiter about job opportunities, tell her frankly that you're a newcomer so that you and she both know where you stand. Don't send a résumé to a recruiter and then call her up once a week asking if she's got anything for you—if she does, she'll certainly let you know, because that's how she gets paid. Remember, recruiters are working for the companies that hire them; they're not your agent or career coach.

A few unscrupulous recruiters grab all the résumés they can get and spam them to as many employers as they can, hoping to make their money through sheer numbers. This is bad for you, as it means your résumé gets sent out—along with a ton of others—for jobs for which you aren't qualified. Rather than present your application in the best light, your résumé comes to the employer as part of a slush pile—it might not even be read. The only way to prevent this is to carefully choose your recruiter. A good recruiter will want to talk to you and get a feel for your qualifications and career goals, so as to match you up with appropriate job opportunities. She will also assure you that your résumé will not be sent anywhere without your permission.

How to Schmooze

To schmooze you have to attend the industry events where developers congregate, particularly the Game Developers' Conference and E3. But before you schmooze, you need to do some preparation. First, figure out which companies you're interested in. Once you have your business cards, a list of companies you want to talk to, and you're at the event, you're ready to go. If your memory is poor, like mine, make yourself a cheat sheet with a couple of quick facts about each of the companies you're interested in. Keep it in a pocket and glance at it surreptitiously before you go talk to somebody from one of those companies.

If a company is throwing a party at a conference or trade show, that's the place to start, because that's where the largest concentration of its employees will be—generally. In a few cases the company will intend the party specifically for the press or for VIPs and they will have told their less-presentable employees—the developers—to stay away from it. However, if that's the case, you probably won't be able to get into the party anyway.

What you're looking for at a party is a company employee who doesn't seem to have anyone to talk to at the moment: someone getting food or a drink, for example. Your next best bet is to approach two employees talking together. You might find an employee who's talking to someone from another company, but in many cases these are old friends who are seeing each other for the first time since the previous year's convention, and they won't feel like chatting with a stranger. You'll have to eavesdrop a little to see if it sounds as if they know each other; if it doesn't, hang around and wait for your opportunity. The worst situation is to try to break into a group of people all from the same company—like as not they're talking shop about something confidential, or gossiping about their management, and really won't appreciate the intrusion.

When you've spotted your target, just go up and introduce yourself. Tell them flat out that you're really interested in their company, because it sounds like the kind of place you might want to work. There's no benefit in trying to hide the fact that you're a job-seeker; if the person doesn't know about any open positions they'll tell you so right away, and that will save you a lot of time. On the other hand, if they're looking to hire someone, they'll want to find out more about you. Don't start off by handing them your business card—that looks pushy—but wait and see if the conversation seems promising. If it does, ask at the end, "May I give you my business card?" and "Can I get one of yours?" Trade cards, and tell them you'll get in touch after the event is over. Then be sure and do it.

Don't bother giving out copies of your résumé at a party or trade show booth: the people there won't have any place to put it, and the chances are about 80 percent that it'll get lost as they're packing up to leave anyway. Get their business card, and send your résumé to them in the mail or via e-mail afterward. Wait at least a couple of days after the event is over, however: most people work phenomenally hard getting ready for a show and need a couple of days to decompress afterward, as well as catch up on all the e-mail they missed while they were gone.

Your follow-up is incredibly important; odds are these people will not remember you, since they'll have been incredibly busy, stressed, and meeting a lot of other people for the first time at this event. For the best chance of a response, send them a polite, brief e-mail message. (Phone calls are often an intrusion for busy game industry people.)

Talking about Yourself

Don't rehearse a line of patter; it's not natural conversation and will make you sound like a used-car salesman. However, you do need to be able to describe yourself and your experience smoothly and articulately when someone asks you about it. Before you go talk to someone, imagine that you're them, and ask yourself the kinds of questions they're likely to ask: Where did you go to school? What did you study there? What have you been working on? Which tools do you use? What made you choose them? How did that work out? Know the answers ahead of time so that you'll be ready.

Be Real!

There's an old joke that sincerity is the key to success: if you can fake that, you've got it made. I'm sure you've met people who seemed perpetually on the make: eager to further their own ends, indifferent to anything else, and who lost interest in you the moment they discovered you couldn't do anything for them—oily, insincere, so-cial-climbers. Whether fairly labeled or not, Hollywood has a reputation for being full of such people.

The game industry is not, thank goodness. We don't have "who's hot and who's not" lists; we don't have "best-dressed" lists; we don't care who has been seen with whom at what nightclub. Because of its large technical component, game develop-ment is about performance, not personalities. For the most part, game developers, es-pecially those in the trenches building the content, are honest, direct, sincere people who tell the truth and expect the same of others.

I bring this up because I don't want you to think that schmoozing is just a means of greasing your way into the industry. The contacts you make won't necessarily become your friends (though undoubtedly some will), but they are real human beings, not just a way to get a job. You're a professional now, and they are your colleagues. Give them the same degree of respect and attention that you want them to give you. Be real.

YOUR RÉSUMÉ AND COVER LETTER

There are dozens of web sites and job manuals out there telling you how to write a résumé, so I'm going to concentrate on résumé-writing for the game industry. Most of the rules are the same as for any other business, but a few things are different.

Mary Margaret's Résumé Tips

Great résumés are not lists of facts; rather they are a collection of powerful assertions that convince the employer that you have what it takes to be successful. Prepare your résumé as professionally as you can. Be truthful.

This is the résumé structure that we have found works best:

1. Summary

2. Employment History

> ‣ Position, company, location, dates (the first line in each job listing)

> ‣ Treat multiple positions within the same company as separate jobs

> ‣ Lead paragraph, only if you feel it is necessary

> ‣ Bullet items of responsibility

3. Skill Set

> › Areas of expertise
>
> › Specific technical skills (tools you know, and so on, how long you've used them, and whether you've used them professionally or in a classroom)
>
> › Platforms
>
> › Programming Languages

4. Education

5. For experienced developers: Project History or Chart. There is a link at www.mary-margaret.com where you can fill in some fields and generate a project chart.

More tips:

› In the experience section, list your previous employers, your job title at those employers, and your dates of employment. Most recent experience should come first.

› Avoid using paragraphs. Instead, create bullets of your tasks and accomplishments. Incorporate the titles on which you've worked and your role on them.

› In the education section, note the school and degree awarded. If you are still in school, include the degree on which you are working and the anticipated date of completion.

› Strive to present your qualifications in a verbally powerful, visually enticing, accurate, symmetrical, and easy-to-read manner.

› Do not list your age or date of birth on a résumé meant for U.S. employers.

› If you are female and concerned about discrimination, do not list your gender. If you would like to remove the focus from your gender, consider using your initials rather than your first name: B.E. Davis rather than Bette Davis.

› Do not list your salary history on your résumé. You may be asked to provide that at a later time.

› It is not necessary to say that references will be provided upon request. Either include your references or wait to be asked for them.

› It is not necessary to list jobs older than 10–15 years, particularly if they are not relevant to your job search. You may indicate that you have a longer work history by adding "Previous job experience details on request," or something similar.

Don't Get Cute

You may read advice in other job-hunting books that suggests strange ways to make your résumé stand out—printing it on colored paper, doing it in a funny font, and so on. They're hoping that amid a large stack of résumés, such tricks will make yours look different, and the hiring manager is more likely to pick it up.

That kind of thing might work if you're applying for a job at Wal-Mart, but I wouldn't try it in the game industry. All too often this sort of gimmick is just an attempt to distract the reader from the fact that the applicant doesn't have much to say. The minute I see a résumé printed with multiple colors of ink, or folded into origami, it makes me suspicious and inclined to read it with a distrustful attitude—can't this person's record speak for itself?—exactly the opposite reaction from what the applicant was hoping for.

The bottom line is that there is no substitute for real content, saying clearly and cleanly what you can bring to the job. Spend your time polishing your portfolio or demo, not thinking up ways to make your résumé look cool.

Never Lie, but Always Spin

Never, *ever,* tell a lie on a résumé. Don't make up jobs you never had; don't make up degrees you don't hold. The industry is still small enough that most hiring managers can verify any fact on your résumé with a phone call or two. Apart from being immoral, lying on your résumé is dangerous. Your résumé forms part of your job application, and lying on a job application is a firing offense. Even worse, if you get caught, the word will get around. Your company will refuse to give you a reference, and people will talk about you in hushed tones and giggle. You may find it hard to get another job. It's not worth the price.

I've always said that your goal in writing a résumé is *to put the best possible face on the truth.* You don't lie, but you spin: choose to emphasize the things that show you in the best light, and eliminate anything that doesn't. For example, several years ago I got a letter from someone saying that his college grade point average wasn't that good, and wondering how to handle this fact on his résumé. I told him the answer was simple: leave it off! There's no rule that says you have to put your GPA on your résumé, and I certainly never have—mine's not that great either. If the company wants to know what it is, they can ask you.

Job-Hunting Tip: Show Them You're Adaptable

When I'm interviewing job applicants, I'm looking for … smart people who can cope with day-to-day variation. In a small company like CogniToy, you can't get too comfortable doing only one task. I wouldn't normally ask a programmer to design the color palette for a new title, but a willingness to step up and do whatever task needs doing is pretty important to an entrepreneurial organization.

—*Kent Quirk, President, CogniToy*

More Suggestions about Résumé Content

Here are a few other things to know about writing a résumé:

> **Include the tools you know as a separate item.** Mary Margaret said this in her list of tips, but it bears repeating. Experience with particular tools—audio, art, programming, database, whatever—is distinctly valuable in the game industry, and if you bury this information inside your employment history, it might get missed. Back when I was a software engineer, I used to list the languages I knew and the operating systems I had worked with as a separate item above my employment history. But whether above or below, be sure to include it!

> **Revise it as appropriate to match the job you're applying for.** Obviously, you shouldn't make up work you didn't do, but if some aspect of your experience closely matches what the company says it's looking for in the job ad, revise your résumé to highlight that fact. Use the same keywords they do, where appropriate.

> **Highlight key points with boldface or underlining, but don't go nuts.** You want the reader's eye to jump to the most important facts about you, but you don't want your résumé to look like a blotchy mess. The titles of games you've worked on, such as *Total Age of Doomcraft & Conquer: Romero Alert,* should be set in italics just as book titles are; that makes them stand out automatically.

> **Don't worry about keeping it to one page.** A lot of job-hunting manuals tell you that your résumé shouldn't be more than one page. This is nonsense. If one page is all you need, that's fine—don't pad it—but if you have relevant experience, include it. It would be silly to leave off a detail that could be exactly what an employer is looking for, just in order to meet an artificial rule about length.

> **Don't include irrelevant material.** The flip side of the previous advice is, don't include stuff in your résumé that nobody will care about. As soon as I got my first job as a software engineer, I dropped the items from my résumé that said I had worked packing textbooks and digging up soil samples.

Crafting the Cover Letter

Since the introduction of e-mail, letter-writing has experienced a renaissance, but a formal business letter isn't the same as an e-mail message to a friend. You don't want to shoot yourself in the foot by creating a great résumé and then ruining the effect with a sloppy, inarticulate cover letter.

The purpose of the cover letter is to politely introduce yourself and present your résumé. You should explain how you heard about the job, why you believe you are a good fit for it, and end with a request for an interview or at least some further communication. Your résumé is usually written in a telegraphic style to save time and space, but in a cover letter, you should use full sentences and proper paragraphs.

HR departments get a lot of totally inappropriate résumés from people who just spam all the job advertisements willy-nilly. It's HR's job to weed out these goofballs, and you want to avoid getting weeded out along with them. Part of the function of a cover letter is to reinforce the message of the résumé, which is: *I'm a serious candidate for this job.* The HR person probably won't even send the cover letter along to the hiring manager; they'll just read it and throw it away. As long as it discourages them from throwing your résumé away too, then it has done its job.

Here are some more rules to observe about cover letters:

❱ *Rewrite it for each company you send it to.* Do *not,* under any circumstances, use an obviously generic cover letter. This is the surest proof that you are a résumé-spammer, and will get your materials tossed in the trash in the blink of an eye. Include content that shows you know something about the company.

❱ *Don't be arrogant.* Another common mistake is to try to create an impression of enthusiasm by claiming that you *know* you're the right person for the job. Don't send a cover letter that says, "Your search is over—I'm the one you want to hire." My reaction as a manager is, "I'll be the judge of that, thank you," and to view your résumé with a jaundiced eye. There's an important difference between confidence and arrogance, and a wise job applicant stays on the right side of that line. Never forget: your objective is to get yourself an interview, to make the reader want to meet you in person. Don't do *anything* that is likely to put them off.

❱ *The reader is a stranger, and formal politeness is called for.* She is not your friend or buddy. If the letter is going to Susan Wilson, don't begin it, "Sue," or "Hey Sue," or even "Dear Susan." The correct form of address, until you are told otherwise, is "Dear Ms. Wilson." If you don't know who will be reading it, begin "Dear Sir or Madam," but this is a last resort: you should address it to a specific person if at all possible. *This advice goes double in European countries,* where business styles are more formal than in the United States.

❱ *Use real English words.* No shortcuts like "u" instead of "you." No cell-phone or online d00d-speak. You can use standard game-industry terms like "mod" and "RPG," but avoid slang. You're a professional now, not a fanboy or girl. You want the reader to get the impression that you are serious and that this is important to you.

❯ *Keep it short.* Half to three-quarters of a page is about the maximum; or in e-mail, a corresponding amount of text. Remember, the HR department may be reading dozens or hundreds of these.

❯ *Spell- and grammar-check everything.* And do it twice, once with the spell checker and once by eye, because the spell checker isn't going to catch it if you accidentally write "you're" for "your."

 **INSIDE info** Mary Margaret's proofreading trick: read *backward*. This prevents your eye from seeing what it expects to see.

BUILDING YOUR PORTFOLIO OR DEMO

You've learned how the industry works, you've gotten the training you need, but how do you prove that you can do what you say? In other industries, they rely on long, long interviews. In the CIA, they give lie detector tests. In the game industry, they look at your demo or portfolio. I can't emphasize this enough: *you must create a demo or portfolio to break into the industry in a skill-based position.* People who have already held a job in the industry can rely on their experience and, of course, their game credits, but newcomers need material.

Mary Margaret's Tips on Demos

Demo—Reel—Portfolio: These are terms that are often used interchangeably, but they can also be considered three different things. The term "portfolio" is most often used to describe the actual folder, or portfolio, of traditional works that all professional artists should have. "Reel" most often means the VHS tape of an animator's work, though its definition has expanded to include files of animations carried on a CD-ROM. "Demo" is the most all-encompassing term, and can be used in any circumstance. It is generally your entire presentation, a "reel" of animations or stills and a "portfolio" of other work.

❯ Have your demo in as many different formats as possible—have a web site, have a CD reel and have a file that can be transferred to videotape easily. Use a video transfer service—you can find them in the Yellow Pages.

❯ Pay attention to how your target company wants to receive your demo or reel—the easier you make their job, the easier it will be to get your demo seen. Do not assume you know better.

❯ Demo files on CD: test your disc across different computers to make sure your content works!

> Only include your very best work. Never include anything on your demo or reel that you have to make excuses for.

> Always give credit where credit is due. Include a credits list and a shot list. If everything on your demo or reel was created by you, make that clear as well.

> Having a reel on VHS takes away many of the technical headaches at the viewing end of the process. Once you make your first videotape, keep it and do not give it away. Instead, use it as a master so you will not have to make a copy of a copy—this way you ensure the quality of your video.

> Substance over style! Make sure the demo material you include shows the wide range of your talents, and your well-rounded skills.

> Display many different genres and art styles in your demo or reel—do not let one particular genre hijack your demo. If you have only worked on one kind of game, you need to spend time outside of work expanding your reel.

More about Demos

I have just a few more points to add to Mary Margaret's advice. You can mail in a demo with your résumé, or save it for the interview. *Be sure to check the Jobs page of the company's web site to find out which they want, and in what format.* If they ask for one and you don't send it, or send it in the wrong format, they may ignore your application entirely. If it goes in with your résumé and your résumé is only going to HR, however, there's a good chance nobody will see it and you almost certainly won't get it back. You have a much better chance of getting it looked at if you're sending your résumé directly to the hiring manager. If you *are* mailing it in, it needs to be self-running, and as foolproof as possible. As Mary Margaret points out, this is one of the benefits of VCR tapes or video DVDs: they work in any machine. It's also a good reason for putting your material on the Web. The instant access of the Web is incredibly useful to a busy hiring manager. However, when you're creating your web site, avoid unusual plug-ins that require the hiring manager to download new software. It's annoying and potentially time-consuming, and some companies also prohibit downloading of any software not authorized by their IT department.

Whether you send your demo with your résumé or not, you should always bring it to your interview, and be prepared to talk about it. I'll discuss the actual presentation at greater length in the section called "Handling the Interview," but here are some tips on building a demo for presentation purposes:

> *A self-running demo should show your best work in the first three to five minutes, and have the best material first.* Longer than that and you're likely to lose your viewer's attention.

❯ *A demo or portfolio that you present in person shouldn't be longer than ten minutes or so.* You can afford for this to be a bit longer than a self-running demo because a) you have a captive audience; and b) by the time you've gotten to the interview stage you already know they're interested in you. However, don't overdo it. Build in natural cut-off points—transitions between projects or styles—at which you can stop if your interviewer is looking impatient.

❯ *Be sure it illustrates and supports your message.* Don't throw in everything you've ever edited, drawn, or programmed. Think of your demo as a kind of visual résumé: you want it to show you in the best possible light.

❯ *Like your résumé, tune your demo for your audience.* If the job is making artwork for a gory first-person shooter, leave out the cute bunnies you did during that project in college—unless they clearly demonstrate a talent that transfers over to gory first-person shooters.

What about Nudes or Erotic Material?

If you're an artist, a knowledge of anatomy and the ability to draw from life are valuable attributes. Art directors prize these qualities, and if you possess them, your portfolio should reflect it—especially if you're applying for jobs where you will be drawing or animating people.

However, use some discretion! Nudity is one thing; blatant sexuality is another. As in everything else about job-hunting, you want to avoid offending your interviewer, and your presentation should be tailored to your audience. Few games call for erotic material, so there's no need to include erotic material in your portfolio unless you *know* that that is what your interviewer wants to see.

I know of one case in which an artist proudly showed off his collection of photographs of celebrities, which he had retouched to make them look naked. The interviewer was completely repulsed by this display of adolescent lubriciousness, cut short the interview, and showed him the door. While it did demonstrate a certain facility with *Adobe Photoshop,* there are plenty of other ways to illustrate the same skill without giving offense.

In short: life drawings and classical poses are okay, and even recommended, as part of a portfolio; porn is not, unless you're interviewing at a company that makes porn itself.

Job-Hunting Tip: Don't Mail in a Mountain of Stuff!

When I'm interviewing job applicants, I'm looking for … somebody whose single-minded mission is clearly to make my life easier and my product better. Nothing else is important to me. Long demo tapes and lots of info to sort through show me that the applicant is thinking of his own well-being, not mine. So when I establish

> that I am dealing with somebody who doesn't realize how busy I am, and who wants some of my time for nothing, I get all panicky and I freak out and throw his promo pack into the furnace.
>
> —*George Alistair Sanger, Legendary Audio Guy, The Fat Man*

ON THE HUNT: FINDING AND APPLYING FOR JOBS

Once you have your résumé written and your demo prepared, you're ready to start job-hunting seriously. This is the long, hard, and sometimes discouraging part of the process: tunneling into the bank vault. Ultimately, only persistence is guaranteed to pay off. But there are more and less intelligent ways to go about it, too.

How Do You Find the Jobs?

Here's how you look for job openings in the game industry, in order from most to least effective.

> *Network, network, network!* I can't make this point often enough: the majority of jobs in the game industry are obtained through personal contacts, not through mailing résumés in blindly. Get to know as many people as you can by the means that I suggested in the "Networking" section earlier in this chapter. Talk to people you know at different companies. Ask them if they're hiring or if they have any projects that will be staffing up soon. If they don't know about anything, ask them if they know anyone else who does. Don't make a nuisance of yourself, pestering one person repeatedly; gather more leads, and move on to them, and so on.

> *Read the industry news.* Is a game company opening a new studio somewhere? They'll probably be hiring at that location. Has a publisher just signed a major license? They'll need people to build that product. Did a famous designer leave his employer to set up a company of his own? He'll probably have brought several senior people with him, but he may need junior ones. Did a publisher just hire a major name from Hollywood to run some part of their business? That person may be building his own empire.

> *Check company web sites. Frequently.* Most companies have a "jobs" or "careers" page on their web site. If there's a company that you're interested in working for, check its web site often. You'll want to be able to respond promptly when an opportunity comes up.

> *Read job ads in developer magazines and web sites.* A job announcement in a magazine like *Develop* or a web site like Gamasutra is tightly targeted to the developer community; you can be pretty confident they're serious.

❱ ***Read job ads at job web sites.*** General job web sites aren't nearly as useful as developer web sites, but don't ignore them entirely. They will also have jobs in fields that are only tangential to the game industry, but that you still might find interesting: educational software, multimedia, web site design, and so on.

❱ ***Read job ads in newspapers and the general media.*** Something of a last resort, but game companies do occasionally advertise in the newspaper. You can't call your job search truly thorough unless you're checking the paper along with everyplace else.

INSIDE iNFO   A job ad that doesn't give the employer's name has been posted by a recruiter. This isn't necessarily a bad thing, but it does mean that you can't do any research on the company, and in order to find out more about it, you'll have to contact the recruiter. Don't just send in your résumé; contact the recruiter first. Try to find out more about the position, and if you really are a suitable candidate. Only once they've demonstrated to you that it's really worth pursuing should you send in your résumé.

Mailing out Your Résumé

If at all possible, you should try to get your résumé into the hands of the hiring manager directly, rather than into the gaping maw of the HR department. The function of the HR department—among many other things—is to filter out applicants whom they believe to be unsuitable, and you want to avoid being filtered. When you know about a job opening that looks interesting to you, try, by all legal and ethical means, to find out who the hiring manager is and send your résumé directly to him or her. You should *also* send one to the HR department as a matter of courtesy. HR people can get really annoyed if you completely ignore them, and, as ever in job-hunting, the last thing you want is to annoy a potential employer. But your primary goal is to get it into the hands of the person who really has the power to hire you, by the most direct means possible.

Do Not Spam Your Résumé

As I said earlier, an awful lot of people send out their résumé to any and every job ad they see, regardless of whether they're really interested in the company or a good fit for it. Don't do this. The first time an HR department sees your résumé, they may take it seriously until they realize that you aren't appropriate for the position, but every time they see it after that, they'll know you're just a spammer and toss it in the trash. Only apply for jobs you can make a solid case that you are appropriate for.

How to Send It

You can send in your résumé by a variety of means, and each has advantages and disadvantages. Many companies have a preferred method, which they'll specify in their advertisements or on the Jobs page of their web sites—be sure to check first.

❭ **Fax**   Quick but expensive on account of the phone call if it's long distance. Faxes also have the downside that the fax machine at the other end is sometimes jammed and often shared among several people; all too often, the pages get picked up by the wrong person. Faxes don't look that nice, either: if you use images, they will be degraded; if you use colors, they will be lost.

❭ **Mail**   The classic, although it's slow and costs money. This can be a good choice if you know it's going straight to the hiring manager. People at game companies don't get that many real letters in the mail any more, so yours will probably stand out. Crisp white paper looks and feels good and can be part of your professional image if you want it to be. Another benefit of mail is that, if your résumé doesn't go straight into the trash, the recipient actually has to *do* something with it: it's likely to float around her office reminding her of your existence, unlike an e-mail message. One disadvantage is that if she wants to show your résumé to other people, she can't conveniently forward it, but has to make photocopies. Don't expect to continue the conversation by mail, however; if they get back to you it will be by phone or e-mail.

❭ **E-mail**   Fast, cheap, and convenient: you can send documents, images, even executable files or PowerPoint presentations containing your demo (though some e-mail systems reject attached executables as a security measure). The one disadvantage of e-mail is that the recipient probably gets one or two hundred messages a day—many more if it's the HR department—and your mail may get lost amid the spam. That's why it's important to follow up every message.

❭ **Couriers or overnight delivery**   Save your money. Don't try this as a tactic to impress people—they won't be impressed, they'll just think you're rich. Unless the company says they're only accepting applications up to a certain date, and you have to get a compact disc or tape to them before that deadline, it's not worth it.

HANDLING THE INTERVIEW

So you've gotten over the first hurdle and scored yourself an interview! Instead of being one of a hundred applicants, you're one of about five. Now you have to convince them in person that you're the right candidate for the job.

The traditional job-hunting manuals are full of advice about interviews, so I'll just reiterate the key points quickly, and then turn to the areas in which the game industry is different from other businesses. The standard rules about interviews are

❭ *Show up on time.* This doesn't only mean arrive five minutes before you're due; it also means to allow yourself plenty of time to get there and find the place. If there's any question at all about where it is, ask for directions when you set up the interview. If you're driving, find out in advance where you should park. If you're relying on public transportation, take normal service delays into account. The last thing you want is to arrive flustered, rumpled, and out of breath from having to run the last block.

❭ *Bring three or four copies of your résumé.* At least one of the people you'll be talking to won't have one, or will have left it in her office.

❭ *Smile. Be positive. Sit up straight. Shake hands and look 'em straight in the eye.* You want to seem cheerful but not flippant, sober but not dull, well-informed but not a know-it-all, confident but not arrogant. At entry-level you don't have a whole lot of experience to offer the company, and they know it. What they're looking for is a bright, attentive, friendly person who will work hard and fit in well. Your personality has to stand in for the experience you lack, so make sure it shines!

About Phone Interviews

Your first interview may be over the phone. Even if you live near the company, the HR department is likely call you to perform a sort of reality check before they invite you in for an on-site interview, especially if there are many candidates for the position. In some cases, the caller will be reading from a script provided by the hiring manager and writing down your answers without actually knowing what they mean, which can be a little disconcerting.

When you send in your résumé, be aware that you might get a phone call from the HR department at any time. This is yet another stage at which you can be filtered out of the pool of applicants, so be prepared. If you don't want to be phone-interviewed without warning, have a conventional excuse prepared in advance. ("Sorry, I was just on my way to the hospital to visit my grandmother—when would be convenient for me to call back?")

Mary Margaret's Interviewing Tips

Background, preparation, and presence combine to help you win the job you desire in the game of interviewing.

❭ Be prepared! Gather as much information about a company as you can prior to an interview. Play the game or games that the company has made.

❭ What to wear: Business casual is the norm for interviews in our industry. Avoid jeans with holes or rips, but be comfortable.

❭ The following web sites offer basic information and sample questions for interviews:

> › www.careerbuilder.com/gh_int_htg_questions.html
>
> › www.job-interview-questions.com/list.htm
>
> › http://content.monster.com/jobinfo/interview/questions/

❭ Artists should bring their best work along to the interview. Ask ahead of time what format the hiring manager would prefer: VHS, CD, traditional portfolio, or something else.

❭ Engineers should be prepared to discuss both code and contributions to recent projects. Expect to answer a few code questions on the white board during the interview.

❭ Always ask a lead for more leads. If you meet someone helpful and useful, ask them if they can refer you to anyone else who may be able to assist you in your job search.

❭ Send a thank-you note after the interview. It can be a handwritten card or an e-mail message. This is also a good place to fill in or correct what you didn't say but should have said.

The game industry is a heavily environment-driven one, so it is important to get a feel for the people, the culture and the corporate structure. To get to the heart of these issues, ask such questions as:

❭ Is there anything you wish you had known before you came to work here?

❭ Describe the corporate culture to me.

❭ Tell me about a recent internal event that made an impact on the company.

❭ Describe some of your star performers to me.

❭ When top performers leave, why do they leave and where do they go?

❭ What are the biggest problems facing this department over the next two years?

❭ What does the company plan to do over the next year to make things better?

❭ If you were my best friend, what would you tell me about this job that you haven't already said?

Dress Properly: Neither Too Poorly nor Too Well

There's an old saying that when you're hitchhiking you should dress like the people that you want to pick you up. People are more comfortable around their own kind, and one of the ways they determine who their "kind" are is through clothing. The same is true in an interview. I've never worn a suit to a job interview in my life, because I knew none of the people who would be interviewing me would be wearing suits either.

The game industry is famously informal, but a job interview is still a slightly official occasion: two strangers meeting for a business purpose. Therefore, you need to walk a middle ground between the T-shirts you'll see on the people in the office and the business suit that all the job-hunting manuals will tell you to wear. If you're a man, a polo shirt is about the minimum, unless you already know the company and what kind of reception you'll get.

A lot depends on the local culture, too. The east coast of America tends to be more starchy than the west coast, and small companies tend to be more relaxed than big ones, so adjust accordingly. Obviously, if you're applying for a job outside the United States, do some research to find out what's expected of you—but in all cases, the game industry will be less formal than other software industries in the same country.

Who Will Interview You?

When you go to an on-site interview, chances are you'll be interviewed by several different people, not just one. It's not an efficient use of your time or theirs to keep having you come in to meet different people; instead they'll have you meet them all on the same day. When you set up the appointment over the phone, ask how long to plan for, because it could be two or three hours. Also be sure to ask who to ask for when you arrive; it will probably be someone in HR.

The people you'll talk to are likely to be the following:

> **Your prospective boss** Naturally, the hiring manager is the most important interview. If you don't already know who this is, be sure to find out! Game developers can be socially clueless at times, and it's not unusual for someone to walk into the room and say, "Hi, I'm Joe," without ever mentioning that he's actually the boss. Under ordinary circumstances you will meet this person one-on-one, particularly once you start talking about salaries.

> **Someone from Human Resources** This person's role won't be to assess your qualifications for the job but to tell you about the company's benefits and policies. He'll know them better than the hiring manager will, and you can ask lots of questions.

> **Your prospective boss' boss** This is less likely for a low-level position like tester or customer service, but in positions with more responsibility, there's a good chance your boss' *own* boss will want to meet anyone being considered for the team. She's unlikely to make the final decision, but she may exercise veto power over anyone she doesn't like. This interview will probably be short, and more about assessing your personality than your skills or experience.

❭ **One or more prospective coworkers**   Since game development is a such a collaborative activity, it's essential that you get along well with your coworkers. Their opinions count, but during the interview they'll see you as more of a colleague than an employee. With them you can let your hair down just a fraction, and ask questions like, "Do you feel the company has given you the equipment you need to do your job?"

Be prepared for the possibility that you may be interviewed by committee: three or four people in a room at once to save time. Psychologically, this is disadvantageous because you'll be outnumbered, but there are ways to handle it. Imagine that you're a professor and they're the students. If people start firing questions at you, take your time responding, and say calmly, "Just a moment, please, I want to finish answering his question first."

Showing Your Demo or Portfolio

The interview is your opportunity to show off your talents and skills through the preparation you've done. It's your big chance, and you don't want to blow it.

Here are some things to keep in mind to make sure your presentation goes well:

❭ *Rehearse and practice.* A demo or portfolio isn't just a random collection of material; it's a presentation, and it should be structured to make a point. Know your material thoroughly, and be able to move through it smoothly. Rehearse, both by yourself and in front of someone else—preferably a colleague who will understand what you're talking about. Don't over-rehearse to the point that you sound bored or glib, though. Your goal is to seem comfortable, confident, and justifiably proud—but *not* conceited—about your work.

❭ *Anticipate questions.* Get someone obnoxious and unpleasant—we all know someone!—to ask you hard questions as you practice your demo on them. Prepare your answers in advance. If the demo does something the viewer doesn't expect and might see as a flaw, be ready to explain it.

❭ *Bring your own computer if at all possible.* You don't want to delay things, and run into problems, trying to make your software work on someone else's machine. Bring your own laptop and everything you need. The only thing the company should have to provide is an electrical outlet. If your demo runs on a console machine, then you can use one of the company's own machines, but let them know in advance that you'll need one. The same goes for a videotape, audio CD, or DVD.

❭ *Be sure of your gear.* You never want to begin a demo, or any other presentation for that matter, with the words, "I hope this works." Be absolutely certain that your equipment works right the first time. And put a shortcut to your demo on the desktop so you don't spend 20 seconds opening folders while your interviewer twiddles her thumbs.

>) *Bring copies you can leave behind.* There's no better way to keep your name in someone's memory than by having a copy of your work floating around their office. If your demo is really unusual or spectacular, they'll probably want to show it off to other people after you've gone.

What about Tests?

Personally, I don't believe in giving people tests in interviews, but some companies do it to determine how well an applicant does what he says he can do. It's one thing to say you've been programming C++ for 5 years, but have you been doing it well, or have you been depending on other team members for a crutch? Also, many companies send a test *before* any interview. If you are sent a test, take it, and then talk intelligently about the questions and answers in the phone call.

The areas in which a job applicant is most likely to be tested are programming (to see if you know the language and concepts required) and art (to see if you know how to use the tools). If taking tests bothers you, then use the phone call when you're setting the date of the interview as an opportunity to ask if they're planning to give you one. That way at least you'll know it's coming. Unfortunately, there's no good way to get out of a test, and the company is perfectly within its rights to ask that you take one.

INSIDE iNFO Number-one tip for white-board interviews: If you don't know the answer, don't make your interviewers wait while you try to figure it out. Just tell them you don't know off the top of your head, or tell them where you would expect to look up the answer, and move on to the next question. Most reasonable interviewers will give you points for not wasting their time.

Some people just have a hard time with written tests; their scores don't reflect their actual ability. (The smartest girl in my high school didn't do nearly as well on her SATs as you would have expected from her excellent grades.) If you're one of these people, don't make excuses for yourself; that just looks weak. Instead, say as little as possible about it. Act confident, as if it were no more than a formality like filling out the application form. Emphasize your qualifications, your demo or portfolio, and your enthusiasm for the position and the company. If you feel you've done badly on the test, and they do want to talk about it during your interview, you can point out that working on hypothetical problems by yourself for an hour doesn't have much to do with working in collaboration with a team for a year or so.

Job-Hunting Tip: Show Them You're a Team Player

Being able to fit in with the other people on the team, both in their own department (art, design, whatever) and in other departments, is at least as important as being good at the work itself, in my opinion. Someone who is brilliant at what they do but is unapproachable or precious about their work, or who has very rigid opinions, is a potential team-breaker and that can cost the company far more time and grief than many people imagine.

—Kim Blake, Producer, Particle Systems

THE COMPENSATION PACKAGE

Your compensation as an employee of any company actually consists of a lot more than just your salary; it's a whole package of benefits. Some of them may be new to you if this is your first full-time job. When you're computing the value of a job offer, it's important to take *all* the compensation into account, not just the salary. If a company doesn't offer any health insurance, for example, then you'll have to spend a lot of money out of your own pocket to buy some. What's more, health insurance premiums aren't tax-deductible unless (along with other medical expenses) they add up to more than 7.5 percent of your annual income, which isn't very likely. On the other hand, if the company buys health insurance for you, it's tax-free.

In this section, I'll describe the various kinds of compensation you may be offered. One caveat, though: I'll only be talking about American companies. Employment regulations vary considerably from country to country, and many nations have government-mandated vacation policies, for example.

Financial Compensation

"So how much am I going to get paid?" you're probably wondering. The answer, of course, is "It depends." It depends on what kind of job you're looking for, how much education and experience you have, how big your employer is, and what part of the country you're looking in—among other things. These are not questions you should ask in your initial interview, but if it looks like the company may be serious about you, get answers to these questions!

INSIDE INFO   To get a general idea of what you'll be paid in your chosen field, read *Game Developer* magazine's annual salary survey. You can download the most recent edition at www.igda.org/biz/salary_survey.php.

Money is the thing most people think of first when they consider compensation, but it can come to you in several different forms. Not all companies offer all of the following:

❱ **Salary**   Obviously the primary ingredient, your salary is simply the base amount you get paid to do your job. A larger company will have a salary scale that ties job titles to particular salary ranges. Your salary also normally goes up with promotion and good annual performance reviews—though not necessarily, if the company is having a bad year. If you're a full-time employee, you'll be classed as "exempt," which means exempt from government regulations about wages for hourly workers. You won't have to punch a clock, but you won't get overtime, either.

❱ **Bonuses**   A bonus is just a flat cash payment in addition to your salary, often made on an annual basis. It's the company's mechanism for rewarding good performers. Some companies will have detailed bonus plans that compute the size of your bonus based on your salary, seniority, or some measure of your performance; at others, it's awarded entirely at your boss' discretion. Still others do not offer bonuses at all. Bonuses are subject to all the same tax rules that salaries are.

❱ **Royalties**   If you get royalties, this means your employer pays you a percentage of the money that the game you worked on earns in sales. (This isn't the same as royalty deals between a development company and a publisher.) Royalty plans made multimillionaires of the early Atari programmers, but they're not so common any more. Royalties have the disadvantage that if an employee is taken off one project that they know will be a big seller, and assigned to another one that seems likely to make less money, they resent it bitterly: the reassignment is actually costing them money.

❱ **Profit-sharing**   A better arrangement than royalties, profit-sharing doles out a certain proportion of the company's total profits to the employees, regardless of what individual products the employees were working on. If the company has a bad year, of course, there may be no profits to share.

❱ **Stock options**   A stock option is an opportunity to buy a certain number of shares in the company at a certain price. The hope is that the value of the company will go up, the shares will be worth more over time, and you will be able to buy them cheaply and sell them again for much more. *If a company does really well, a stock option can be worth many times your actual salary.* If it does badly, on the other hand, it can be worthless. Normally, you don't get a whole stock option as soon as you join a company; you earn it over time, a process called *vesting*. This period is typically four or five years. For example, suppose I join a company and receive an option to buy 1000 shares at $1 a share, vesting in yearly increments over four years. At the beginning,

I can do nothing; the option has not vested at all. After I have been there a year, the first 250 shares have vested. I can *exercise* the option and buy 250 shares from the company for $250. If, in the meantime, the value of the stock on the stock market has gone up to $2 a share, I can immediately turn around and sell them again for $500: a $250 profit for me (less taxes). But I don't have to exercise if I don't want to; I can just wait and exercise another time if I like. The following year, another 250 shares will be vested, and so on. If a company's stock isn't traded publicly on the stock market, however, you may be limited in who you are allowed to sell the shares to. If you leave the company, you have to either buy your vested shares or lose them. There's a lot more to know about stock options, so ask the company's HR department for full details.

❱ **Employee stock purchase plan**   An employee stock purchase plan (ESPP) is a government-regulated scheme in which you can choose to have a certain amount of your salary (usually between 1 and 10 percent) withheld by the company for a fixed period (usually six months to a year). At the end of that time, the company will use the money to buy shares in the company for you at a discount, typically 85 percent of its publicly-traded price. If the value of the stock goes up during that period, you pay 85 percent of the original, lower price that it had at the beginning of the period; if the value has gone down, you pay 85 percent of the current price at the end of the period. In other words, it's a no-lose situation for you as long as you can do without the money in the meantime. You can also pull out of the program in the middle and get your money back. If you leave the company, you must pull out.

Time-Off Benefits

It's considered bad form to go to a job interview and immediately start talking about taking a vacation, but companies must have some policy or other, and you'll need to find out what it is. Ask the HR person, if there is one, rather than the person who will be your boss. In European countries, time-off benefits are usually regulated by the government and will be the same everywhere.

❱ **Vacation**   This is simply paid time off. You normally get a certain number of weeks per year, and that number goes up the longer you work for the company. Typically, you don't get it in a lump at the beginning of every year, but earn it over time as you work. Different companies will have different rules about how it accrues, and the amount of vacation you have available will usually appear on your pay stub as a certain number of hours. The company will also have a maximum amount that you can save up, and beyond that point you won't earn any more until you've used some. You can't take vacation any time you want; the company has to approve it in advance.

❱ **Holidays**   This is paid time off for the whole company. In America, this is typically about ten days per year. A common scheme is to get Memorial Day, Independence Day, Labor Day, two days at Thanksgiving, and five days between Christmas and New Year's Day. People who want to observe other religious holidays can usually work out some kind of deal by working weekends, but talk to HR about it.

❱ **Sick leave**   Some companies have sick leave policies in which you only get a certain number of paid days per year, usually five or ten. However, I've found that it's more common for companies just to use a "reasonable good sense" approach: they don't keep track unless it starts to seriously affect your job. Sick employees who come to work anyway tend to infect other employees, which only makes things worse. If you're sick, stay home!

❱ **Sabbatical**   A rare but wonderful benefit, borrowed from the academic world. After you've been at a company for a certain number of years, they may give you several weeks off with pay as a reward, or some similar form of compensation. When I had been at Electronic Arts for seven years, they gave me seven weeks off. I used that time to start writing this book!

❱ **Comp (compensatory) time**   When people have been working really hard, wise bosses give them a few days off after the project is done, usually "under the table." Don't bother asking HR about this; as far as the company is concerned, it doesn't officially exist. This is one of the things you can ask a prospective coworker about. Be subtle about it, however. Don't say, "So, do we get comp time for working so hard, or what?" Instead say, "So what happens when a project is over? Is it straight on to the next one?"

Health-Related Benefits

It's a sad fact that in America, the spiraling cost of health care has a powerful effect on people's employment plans, especially if they have dependents. Many people don't dare leave their jobs without having another job lined up first, because they'll lose their health insurance. However, there is a law called COBRA (which stands for Consolidated Omnibus Budget Reconciliation Act—how's that for gobbledygook?) that enables you to continue on your company's health plan—at your own expense—for up to 18 months after you leave, as long as the company employs 20 or more people.

There are actually quite a few health-related benefits that companies can offer:

❱ **Health insurance**   This is the big one, and almost every American company will offer it. Some companies have just one plan; others let you choose between a traditional insurance scheme, in which you pay a small part of all your medical bills and they pay the rest, and a health-maintenance organization (HMO), in which most treatment is free but you are restricted to certain doctors and hospitals. Normally, you get to choose between one plan or the other when you are hired, and can switch at one other fixed time during the year, a period called "open enrollment." If you already have an illness of some kind (a "pre-existing condition"), many plans won't cover treatment for it until you've been with them for as much as two years. Check with the plan documents for details.

❭ **Disability/Long-term illness**   This is another important benefit that young people tend to overlook. If you are unable to work for a long period, either through an accident or illness, disability insurance kicks in after several weeks (usually around six) off the job. It pays you a percentage of your salary, typically between 66 and 75 percent, for as long as you are unable to work, up to the rest of your life in some cases.

❭ **Life insurance**   This is typically a flat-cash death benefit to your heirs if you die while you're employed by the company. It's usually not as much insurance as you really need, however, especially if you're the sole earner for a family.

❭ **Dental care**   Dental plans often pay for 100 percent of the cost of routine preventive care, and a large percentage of other treatment. Specialist treatment, such as orthodontia and treatment for temporomandibular joint syndrome (TMJ), is frequently excluded, however.

❭ **Vision care**   This typically consists of free eye exams once a year, cheaper glasses, and more sophisticated care, if needed. Not many companies offer this.

❭ **Employee Assistance Program (counseling)**   A few companies offer limited psychological counseling services should you suffer extremely stressful events—a natural disaster or the death of a relative, for example. These services are only sufficient to help you through a crisis; they're not intended to be a substitute for therapy.

Find out Who Is Covered!

To judge the value of a company's health benefits, it's essential to find out whom they actually cover. In a few cases, they only cover you, the employee, full stop. This is rare, however. More commonly, the plan will cover you, and you can add your spouse and children at an extra cost, which will be deducted from your paycheck. (It will almost certainly be cheaper to do this than to try to purchase health insurance for them on the open market.) Larger, more successful companies will offer complete protection for you and your whole family.

Be sure to take this into account when you're calculating the *actual* value of your salary: if you have numerous dependents, it could add up to several hundred extra dollars per month.

Retirement Plans

Okay, you're just getting started, so the last thing on your mind is retiring and getting a gold watch. Think again. The population of America is aging. The number of people taking money out of Social Security is going up faster than the number of people putting money in. You're going to have to take responsibility for your own retirement; you can't be sure Social Security will be around when you need it.

Very small companies won't have any kind of retirement plan at all; you're on your own to manage your own savings. The best way to do this is with a traditional or Roth IRA, and a tax advisor can explain the benefits of each.

Larger companies will offer a retirement plan, but it's unlikely to be the traditional pension scheme in which the company holds the money and pays you a certain percentage of your salary after you retire for as long as you live. Those have been discredited in the scandals of the past few years, as some companies were caught mismanaging the pension fund or even misappropriating the money.

In the game industry, the retirement plan is much more likely to be what's called a *401(k) plan*. In a 401(k) plan, you contribute a percentage of your salary (that you get to choose) into a personal fund that is managed for you by a financial services company. The money you put in isn't subject to income tax. Once you retire, you can start taking money out of the fund, and only then is it taxed. You can also transfer the fund to another company's 401(k) plan if you change jobs. You can go on using the same fund even if you quit, too. Best of all, you, not the company, get to choose how your money is invested, usually from a suite of available opportunities ranging from safe but slow-earning instruments such as certificates of deposit, to high-risk things like aggressive-growth stock funds. You can even borrow money out of your own fund for certain approved items like medical expenses or buying a house.

Company Retirement Contributions

Many game companies are too small to be able to afford to contribute to your retirement fund: you'll have to do it all on your own through salary deductions. Bigger companies, though, will match a certain percentage of your own contribution They may tie it to the company's own financial performance, though—so, if the company is doing badly, they won't contribute. HR will tell you what their policy is.

Miscellaneous Benefits

Most companies have a variety of other fringe benefits. These can include things like education reimbursement, child care facilities, a subsidized cafeteria, membership in a gym, discounts on the company's products, trips or events for the employees and their families, and so on. These benefits are only really worth taking into account if you know you will use them and they actively save you money. Subsidized child care, for example, won't be of any use to you if you don't have children, but could save you a fortune if you do. Such benefits do give you an idea of how successful the company is and how much it values its employees, however. If the company's holiday party consists of a free bottle of beer for everyone who's still working on Christmas Eve, that's one thing; if they rent out a nightclub and have dinner and a band, that's another.

Work Policies

Game development is hard work; schedules are tight and hours are long. Very few people put in 40 hours a week and go home. Most people's work week is 44–48 hours during normal periods, and 48 to even 60 or more during crunch time.

To compensate for this a little, and to make it easier to manage, most game companies have *flextime:* flexible working hours. Some are completely flexible; as long as you get your job done, they don't care when you come in or leave. The collaborative nature of game development means that you will spend a surprising amount of time in meetings and just talking things over with your teammates. In order to make sure people are there when they're needed, a lot of companies have a "core hours" policy: they require you to be present between 10 A.M. and 4 P.M. every day, for example. As with compensation issues, the HR manager should explain all this at your interview. If your personal life dictates a strict schedule—picking up children from day care at a certain time, for example—be sure to ask about it.

NEGOTIATION

As an entry-level employee, you won't have a lot of flexibility here. A big game company will have a standard set of salary ranges they offer, and their attitude is likely to be, "There are plenty more where you came from; take it or leave it." Obviously, you want to earn what you're worth, but at this point you simply don't have the leverage to bargain hard. That doesn't mean you shouldn't bargain at all, however! Don't take a bad offer just because you're grateful for any job you can get. A year down the road, when you're working 16-hour days and a little of the shine has worn off the job, you may regret your haste. Remember, they wouldn't offer you the job if they didn't think you could do the work.

The two key principles in salary negotiation are

1. Defer salary discussions for as long as you can.

2. Know your value in the job market.

The reason for the first principle is simple: the longer your discussions with the company are, the more seriously they'll take you as a candidate, and the more reluctant they'll be to write you off for purely financial reasons. On the other hand, if you state your salary requirements directly on your résumé, the company is likely to eliminate you immediately if your target is outside their range. You want to pique their interest and make them want to talk to you. A flat salary demand is likely to cut that short.

As for the second principle, it's essential you understand your value for two reasons: one, because it will help you to set a realistic goal; two, because it will give you ammunition when the subject of salary finally comes up. Do the research. Read the *Game Developer* salary survey. Discuss it with recruiters—they have up-to-the-minute information. Talk to other developers who have held a similar job in a similar part of the country.

As a newcomer, you do have one advantage: they can't ask you what your current salary is, because either you don't have a job at all, or the job you have isn't relevant to the game industry. Here are some traditional ploys for avoiding naming a salary early in the process:

❱ *"I don't really know enough about the position to know what to ask for. Obviously, I want to be paid in line with the market for this sort of job. Could you describe it in more detail, and tell me what range you consider appropriate?"*

❱ *"I'm quite flexible about salaries; it depends a lot on other things such as the benefits plan, opportunities for promotion, and other forms of remuneration like bonuses or stock options. Perhaps we could talk about them first, and then I can form a better idea."*

❱ *"As long as its consistent with the going industry rate I don't think we'll have a problem, but let's make sure we're right for each other first."*

❱ *"Well, as an employer I imagine you have a better idea of industry standards than I do. What do you think would be appropriate for someone with my education and qualifications?"*

Here are some more tips for salary negotiation:

❱ *The basis of your salary is the way in which you will contribute to the company's bottom line—how you are going to make them richer.* Forget the L'Oreal ads that say, "Because I'm worth it." Intrinsically, you're not worth anything to the company. What's worth something is your personality, energy, skill, and experience. Your approach must demonstrate that: make it clear you will make a valuable contribution to the company's enterprise.

❱ *Find out other details as well.* Ask how often you'll be reviewed, how, and by whom. Get them to tell you what promotional opportunities are available—how they perceive the career ladder at their company (remember, my examples in Chapter 6 were all hypothetical). Ask what sort of salary progression they would expect for someone in this position over the next three years or so. Take all this data into account when you're weighing up the value of their offer.

❯ *If you get two job offers, don't try to start a bidding war between the companies.* You might conceivably be able to pull this off if you're a senior executive, but at entry level, forget it—they'll just cross you off and pull another résumé out of the stack. One of the reasons a company wants to hire you is because you've demonstrated that you really want to work for *them.* If you make it obvious that you'll work for whoever pays you the most, it doesn't demonstrate much commitment or interest.

Reasons to Accept a Lower Salary

You obviously want to get the best salary you can, but it shouldn't be your only consideration. Suppose you get two job offers and one of them includes a higher salary. Should you take it automatically? Absolutely not. Nor should you reject an offer for salary reasons alone until you're sure you understand their entire offer and you haven't missed anything. There are many reasons to accept a lower salary in exchange for some other, often longer-term, benefit.

❯ *The other company benefits are excellent.* Never forget that company benefits often have an actual cash value, especially if you expect to make use of them. As I said earlier, if company A offers you a good salary but no health insurance, and company B offers a slightly lower salary but does include health insurance, company B's offer is probably better. With company B, you won't have to pay for your own insurance, you won't be taxed on it, and the insurance company can't turn you down—they have to take *all* the company's employees. Weigh the cash value of the company's other benefits, and factor them into your salary calculations.

❯ *The product you'll be working on is highly respected.* Working on a well-respected product is good for your long-term career growth. There's nothing like being credited on a hit game. In the long run, it's usually worth a few dollars off your salary to work on *Command & Conquer* than on a real-time strategy game no one has ever heard of. Future employers will brighten up and pay more attention.

❯ *The company itself is highly respected.* As with a respected product, there's prestige in working for a respected company. If you get a job for Sony, Activision, or LucasArts, you won't have to explain who they are to future employers: they'll know.

❯ *The company's future looks bright.* A big salary at a company that's circling the drain isn't worth much: you could be out of a job in a few months anyway.

If the company really looks solid, however—it's well-funded, sensibly managed, and has a steady track record of successes—then it can be worth sacrificing a few dollars for the sake of that stability. The company's growth will mean higher salaries and more benefits in the future. This is particularly true if you're offered a stock option at a public company: if you have a great deal of faith in the company and their performance has been good for several years, then a stock option can be well worth trading away some immediate cash for.

❭ *You won't have to move.* This is mostly a consideration for people with families. Moving is expensive, and at entry level, companies seldom offer a relocation allowance. It also causes a lot of emotional wear and tear, particularly if your spouse also has a job that he or she will have to give up, and you have children who will lose their friends and have to change schools. In both financial and personal terms, there can be good reasons for taking a job in an area where you already live.

❭ *The job comes with considerable creative freedom.* As I've said repeatedly, few people get to work on their own ideas in the game industry; they're usually working on someone else's ideas. Having the freedom to develop your own ideas is a rare privilege, and one that can be well worth giving up some cash for, if you can afford it.

❭ *The job sounds like exactly what you want to do.* Don't underestimate the importance of quality of life. If you're typical, you'll spend nearly 40 percent of your waking life every year at work, and on occasion it will be much more than that. Which is more important to you: spending that time doing something you love, that makes you feel happy, positive, and energized, or getting more money to do something you simply tolerate?

Reasons NOT to Accept a Lower Salary

Small companies in particular look to shave costs wherever they can, and may try to persuade you to accept a lower salary in exchange for other things. Some of those things aren't worth having, as follows:

❭ *A cool-sounding title.* Titles in the game industry aren't exactly meaningless, but they're not standardized, and a fancy title won't impress anybody unless you're working for a really big company. Being "Senior Creative Director" at a ten-person shop doesn't say much. It's certainly not worth trading away money for. Ignore the title and concentrate on the actual job responsibilities.

❭ *Vague promises of a big bonus or a raise later on.* Never count on any bonus unless the company has a bonus plan explicitly spelled out in writing. The plan should state how much you'll get (typically as a percentage of your salary), when you'll get it, and if there are any circumstances in which you *won't* get it, such as a poor performance review or low profits for the company. In that case, the bonus is something you can factor in, and may be worth accepting a lower salary for. But remarks like "We'll see how things look in three months," are meaningless: leave them out of your calculations.

❱ *A big stock option at a privately held company.* It's difficult to judge the value of a stock option if the company isn't publicly traded. You'll have to ask to whom you are allowed to sell the stock—and if so, whether anyone will want to buy it. You'll also have to find out what the owners' long-term plans are, and judge whether or not the company has much chance of succeeding at them. If the owners want to eventually go public or sell the company, then there's a chance you could make a fortune—*if* they succeed. If they want to keep it private indefinitely, then while the stock may appreciate in value, there may not be any way to recoup that value. (This advice doesn't apply to startups in which you get in on the ground floor as one of the principals. As a newcomer, however, you're unlikely to be offered that opportunity unless you make it for yourself by founding your own company.)

Get It in Writing

Don't accept a job offer on a handshake alone. When you get an offer that you like, and you agree to take it, end the conversation with something like, "So, I'll watch the mail for your offer letter." If they look surprised or uncomfortable, be suspicious: any company with an ounce of professionalism mails out formal offer letters—for full-time work they may even be required by state law. An offer letter is the company's stated commitment to hire you at the salary and other terms you've agreed upon. It should also include your start date.

DISCRIMINATION AND WORKPLACE ISSUES

In this section I'm going to address some of the concerns that women, members of minority groups, gays and lesbians, and non-westerners (people from Asia, not people from New York!) might have about trying to find work in game development. For the most part, the news is good. Although the game industry is primarily an entertainment business, it was founded by engineers and to some extent their pragmatic ethos still pervades the workplace. As with other high-tech industries, interactive entertainment is largely a meritocracy. If you can write tight, bug-free software that does amazing things, you can be a three-headed alien from planet Zweeble for all that other programmers will care. They'll be much more interested in your code than in you. This attitude tends to spill over into art, music, writing, and the other development crafts as well: people respect performance.

Here are a few tips to help you spot whether a game development company might discriminate against you, or be an uncomfortable place to work:

❱ *Company culture flows down from the top.* Obviously, your job interview will tell you a lot about your immediate coworkers, but if you want to get a sense of the company's values as a whole, find out what you can about the man or woman at the helm. Bosses set the tone and pace of an organization, and they tend to surround themselves with people who think and work the way they do. If the CEO cracks dirty jokes himself, you can be pretty sure there'll be a lot of dirty jokes around the office.

❱ *Big companies tend to be more professional than small ones.* This isn't always the case, but on the whole, the bigger a company is, the more likely it is to enforce the workplace rules and regulations. That's partly because a large company has deep pockets; it has to toe the legal line or risk being sued by a disgruntled employee. Aside from that, big game companies have experienced HR staff who are trained to prevent these kinds of problems and to resolve them when they arise. I don't mean to suggest that small companies are bad, only that three-guys-in-a-garage are not going to think about these issues much, and may not be prepared to deal with them when they come up.

❱ *Keep your eyes open when visiting a prospective employer's offices.* Don't snoop, but pay attention to everything you see. How many women and minority employees do you see, and what positions are they occupying? Are there racist or sexist posters or other decorations around? Where are they—in public places like the hallways, inside individual offices, or nowhere to be seen? This tells you something about the company's degree of tolerance for such things. Bear in mind that a lot of games use pictures of women in tight clothing as part of their own advertising, so they may be legitimate posters for the company's own products—in which case you'll have to decide if you want to work for a company that makes such games. Don't jump to unwarranted conclusions, but take mental notes for comparison with other companies you visit.

Women

The game industry is, to put it bluntly, male-dominated, and as a result, our games don't appeal to women as well as they might. In order to reach more female gamers, we need more female developers. It's not that every woman telepathically knows what all women want from a game, but taken collectively, a game company with female developers is more likely to get it right than one without any. *The Sims,* the best-selling PC game of all time, appeals equally to men and women, and its development staff at Maxis is just about equally balanced as well. This is not a coincidence.

However, Maxis is something of an exception. Although the sex ratio in the industry is beginning to change, a woman who wants to be a game developer needs to be aware that she will probably work with a lot of men and comparatively few women, especially at smaller companies. There's nothing inherently wrong with that, but it can leave female developers feeling rather isolated. Make no mistake, however: women can, and do, make it to positions of real power in the game industry. The Director of the Xbox Advanced Technology Group at Microsoft is a woman, as is the Director of Development at Sony Computer Entertainment of America. The Executive Vice Presidents of Publishing at THQ, Activision, and Electronic Arts are all women. Numerous women run their own companies as well. If you have the drive and dedication for it, there's no limit to how far you can go.

INSIDE INFO
While there isn't much of an old boys' network, there is very much a quiet network of veteran industry women. Many of us faced serious challenges breaking into the industry, especially those who entered the business over ten years ago (when very few women were working in games), so we're willing to help newcomers, especially younger women. If you are at a trade show or conference, look for the women who are especially dynamic, and approach them politely. At the Game Developers' Conference, Microsoft organizes the "Women Celebrating Women in Gaming" event, where they specifically introduce some key industry women and invite newcomers to ask them questions.
—Ellen Guon Beeman, Producer, Monolith Productions

Overt hiring discrimination based on gender is comparatively rare, especially in America. It's slightly more likely to occur in hardcore graphics programming than in any other field, because there is still something of a macho culture about it, and there are fewer women there than in general gameplay programming or art, for example. At the résumé stage, you can defend against this by using only your initials rather than your name on your résumé. Once you get an interview, let your demo speak for itself. As I said before, people respect performance.

You're more likely to experience sexist attitudes from fellow students in school, or from amateur coders, than from companies. These guys are usually kids who treat game development as a form of showing off rather than a profession. Do *not* waste your time and energy arguing with adolescent trolls on message boards. Instead, channel that energy into building a great demo that will get you a job. They'll still be shooting off their mouths while you're getting paid to make games.

The IGDA has a committee dedicated to supporting female game developers, and an active e-mail discussion forum. Membership is not limited to IGDA members. For details, visit www.igda.org/women.

Inside the Job: Advice for Women in the Game Industry

1. *Business was only a man's world because it used to be profitable to keep it that way. That's no longer true.* The western world could not keep the standard of living that it has grown accustomed to if women didn't work. The United States government has put many laws in place to stop discrimination and encourage women to enter the workforce based on that belief. It also gives both women who work in a traditionally male field, and their managers, a way of reframing this thorny issue in concrete terms. Legal and moral issues aside, a company will most clearly understand that discrimination is not in its best interests when they realize that it is unprofitable. At the individual level, every company needs each worker to be their most enthusiastic and productive from the moment they step through the door to the moment they leave. Photos of nude women as screensavers lead to low morale, which leads directly to poor work. Glass ceilings mean that a company loses the benefit of having a qualified and productive employee in the place where she does the most good. For both the employee and the company, it's not a personal matter but a cost/benefit issue, with tangible rules that help make decisions.

2. *Don't doubt that you can do the job.* Women won't apply for a job they don't think they can do; men just assume they can do the job they get. It's trite but true. Aim for the higher, better job and figure it out when you get there. It really is what everybody else does.

3. *Toot your own horn.* When you do a good job, crow about it (or at least mention it to your manager). Don't assume people will notice. It's up to you to publicize (and put on record) your own successes.

4. *Never be the office mother, martyr, hussy, or feminist activist in the office.* Having a style is useful and comfortable, but it doesn't pay to be stuck in a stereotype. Many coworkers, managers, and underlings really want to put people in boxes. It's easier for them to relate to, because they have an internal template for dealing with those types of relationships. The main roles women can fall into are mother, martyr, hussy, or feminist activist.

   › Don't become the office counselor or confessor. Even if someone seems really pathetic, send them to their manager or human resources, or the employee assistance program. It's not your job.

   › Don't clean the kitchen, or volunteer to organize social events any more than your fair share. And when the toilet backs up, and he comes to you saying he doesn't know what to do, smile and tell him what a plunger is for.* When someone does you a disservice, professionally and courteously correct him on the spot and if that doesn't work, talk to your manager immediately. Suffering in silence is unprofitable and unnecessary.

) As hard as it is to say, a woman in the office can be discounted through her sexuality. Realize that people draw conclusions from the clothes you choose. Just as a sloppy dresser is viewed as lazy and disorganized in the office, a woman who wears something low-cut will have a hard time getting her male coworkers not to stare at her breasts.*

) Resist the urge to speak for all women—even if you know that the e-mail sent around (the one about the remote control for girlfriends*) is beyond the pale of decency. Women shouldn't feel they have to carry the burden of political correctness in the office. That's management's job; they get paid for it.

5. *Decide what makes you happy, what makes you content, what you can live with and what you can't.* Women have a larger burden in trying to balance home and work life. Often they want to meet every request and can't meet them all and end up disappointed and guilty. One way to sort out all the competing needs is to make them concrete. Think about them, write them down, and then create plans for execution. Issues move from being emotional, unconquerable messes to concise, small tasks.

* All examples taken from real life!
—*Clarinda Merripen, Human Resources Manager, Cyberlore*

Minorities

When the game industry was founded in the late 1970s, it consisted almost exclusively of young white men as game developers, and middle-aged white men as producers and publishers. Of course, there were a few exceptions, but they were so rare as to be almost oddities. Today, a quick look around the Game Developers' Conference makes it clear that this is changing: there are definitely more African-American developers than there used to be, although they remain under-represented, while Hispanic developers are even more under-represented.

Darrell Porcher is a developer with a longstanding interest in improving the diversity of the game industry, and he runs the Harlem Game Wizards group in New York. Darryl Duncan worked his way into games from the music industry, and is now the owner of GameBeat, a highly regarded audio and music firm. Since they know more about the subject than I do, I asked them to contribute their thoughts.

iNTERVIEW WITH DARRELL PORCHER AND DARRYL DUNCAN

Do you believe there are barriers that face minorities in game development?

Darrell Porcher, Harlem Game Wizards   I have two good friends who aspired to be game developers. One was fronted money and allowed to stay rent-free and job-free as he pursued his dream. The other was laughed at and scolded, and had no choice but to continue to work, and create in spare moments. It's a question of support and opportunity. The barriers that face minorities in game development are not always "black and white."

Do you think members of minorities experience barriers in education for game development?

Darryl Duncan, GameBeat   I feel the opportunities to learn game development are equally available to minorities as well as to non-minorities. But from an economic point of view, perhaps fewer minorities are able to take advantage of these opportunities than their non-minority counterparts.

Darrell Porcher, Harlem Game Wizards   Educational barriers exist in communities where there is no access to computers and software. Growing up in Harlem, New York City and the south Bronx, there were minimal computer resources other than arcade video games. These were some of the very few sources of any appreciation for what computers could do. While most educational systems had some minimal computer classes, they seldom went into any depth about any career paths, other than data entry or spreadsheet manipulations. In my case, game development as a career was a joke, much more so than wanting to play sports or get a "good job." In the urban community, we are sometimes taught to focus on flash over substance.

Do you feel there are barriers in hiring and job opportunities for minorities, especially at entry level?

Darryl Duncan, GameBeat   I think that you could ask five different African-Americans in the industry and get five different answers. My opinion is that, yes, discrimination does in fact exist in the game industry and it's hard to think that it wouldn't when you talk about a business where only a very small percentage are non-white. The only true tool a minority can use to overcome such obstacles is to make sure that his or her talent is at such a level that no one can deny what their contributions can and will be. It's the skill and quality of one's work, be it audio, graphics, or programming, that is often the measurement that places them at a particular social level (and salary level) within the company. So, I personally feel that a minority can use his or her talents and skills to rise above any discrimination that might exist and achieve the level of respect that he or she deserves. Any discrimination comes from not knowing or wanting to know about another race or culture, and often a shared art form or common respect for one's work can bridge these gaps. To be honest, while others do not and would never "see" it, an African-American employee knows in his or her own heart and mind when this sort of bias or discrimination exists, even if it appears nonexistent to non-minorities.

Darrell Porcher, Harlem Game Wizards The game development community is largely blind to ethnicity if you can truly get the job done, or show something cool to get in the door. But the exposure to the game development world has only recently changed and thus, minorities, particularly in urban communities, do not see gaming as a career—other than becoming a sports figure to appear in a game, or quite recently, a hip-hop star.

There is a common belief that Japanese people possess stereotypes about black people. Given the dominance of Japanese console companies, do you think this is true and if so does it represent an obstacle to the careers of black developers?

Darrell Porcher, Harlem Game Wizards Having worked for some major Japanese companies, I have found there is more of a stereotype associated with Western culture as a whole. Americans are lazy, undisciplined, and so on. It's a case where we need to prove ourselves up front more than our counterparts in Japan do. But fortunately, I have found that if I can make the screen sing with art, music, and amazing programming feats, everyone is appreciative and respects what I have done. In fact, they try to take it to the next level or, better yet, challenge me to produce the next cool thing.

Darryl Duncan, GameBeat I don't feel there are any working conditions that are biased for minorities. I mean a cubicle is a cubicle and social cliques will form within any company. I remember when I first started working at EA Florida, I was one of only two African-Americans there. During my lunch breaks I would often observe seven or eight guys in a circle all sort of looking down at the floor, giggling and seemingly enjoying themselves. One day I decided to head over to see what the heck this seemingly ritualistic gathering was all about. As I approached the outside of the circle I noticed they were kicking around some type of little bean bag object to each other using their feet. I asked a couple of passers-by what they were doing, and they looked at me like I was from another planet. Of course they were playing hacky sack, and I had never seen this played in my life. For some reason, just about every white guy in the building participated in this lunchtime event at one time or another and I was the weird one. Yeah, I felt like an alien from outer space, but this was simply something that was never done or heard of where I grew up. I tried it a couple of times and always kicked the darn thing across the room as if I was a field goal kicker. Needless to say I gave up and decided to just watch.

What do you think about racial stereotyping in games, and the general "whiteness" of games as a whole? Is this a problem? Would the industry benefit from a game designer equivalent of Spike Lee?

Darrell Porcher, Harlem Game Wizards   There is a definite problem in how heroes and game characters have been portrayed in games. I have seen numerous studies showing that when major fashion magazines use non-white models on the cover, sales drop at least 20 percent for that issue. Games are big business these days. The problem is, when a hero is of color these days, it's typically an exaggerated version of an iconic character. In game design, people have said, half the player wants to escape and be someone they could never be, and the other half wants someone they can identify with. Shuane Anderson, from the Culture Rock Network Yahoo forum (which is dedicated to minorities in gaming) refers to characters speaking in Ebonics to cater to the existing mindsets. The fact that these images are allowed is very much due to the fact that the amount of diversity, specifically non-Asian or non-Caucasian developers, is relatively small. The good news is that it is increasing with more information. Organizations like the IGDA make an effort at outreach. Grassroots organizations like Culture Rock and my own organization, the Harlem Game Wizards, provide game development as career outreach programs.

Darryl Duncan, GameBeat   Well this is a heated topic of debate among African-Americans, but my take on it is this … I think all games make fun of one cultural stereotype or another. I do not feel blacks are the only group who have games that use stereotypical characters. I can think of many games that pick fun at white stereotypes, too, so I think we as a race get a little too sensitive when a game that depicts black stereotypes is released. This is an issue that is very connected to the motion picture industry, too. The problem is when there are *zero* games with black characters or black heroes in them. I would like to see some games where the *main* character or the central figure of a game is a black (or other minority) character.

But I personally do not expect an all-white development team to make a main game character that is black unless they, in their personal lives, had heroes or role models that were black. Since most white kids are not raised with these types of role models or figures in their lives, I can't say I expect them to make them central characters or heroes in the games they develop. I feel we cannot change any imbalances in the game industry or the motion picture industry until we change the imbalances in the real world, and that is an entirely different issue indeed.

Gays and Lesbians

In my experience, the majority of game developers are not particularly well-informed about gay and lesbian issues; they're mostly just interested in games. So while developers may be ignorant about the subject, I doubt that gays and lesbians will experience any direct hiring discrimination in the game industry. It is extremely unlikely that you'll be asked in a job interview what your sexual orientation is. On the whole, game developers tend to be either liberal or libertarian (although there are exceptions). Whatever their political bent, they have a wide streak of individualism and a distinct distrust of authority. Passing judgment on how other people live isn't part of game developer culture.

As far as I have been able to discover, relatively few game companies have implemented equal benefits policies for same-sex partners. Many smaller companies don't have enough clout to demand changes from their insurance providers, and some are so small they cannot offer benefits to employees' dependants in any case.

Non-Western Game Developers

Here, at least, the news is quite good. For the last twenty years the game market has been dominated by the presence of Japanese consoles—it was Nintendo that revived the video game industry's flagging fortunes after the Atari crash of 1983. This close relationship with Japan has necessarily led to a great many connections between America and the Far East. East-Asian game developers are welcomed and highly respected, for both their creative and technical skill. The recent explosive growth of online games in South Korea has led to increased numbers of contacts between that country and America as well.

We're also starting to see growing numbers of developers from India and elsewhere in South Asia. This has long been the case in other areas of high technology; when I worked for a Silicon Valley CAD company in the 1980s we had a sizable number of Indian employees even though the company was situated in America and Belgium. It makes perfect sense that South Asians should be moving into game development as well, particularly since South Asia will become a huge market for games in the next decade or two. Also, because English is widely spoken in South Asia and many

Commonwealth countries, developers from those regions seldom experience the language problems that complicate relations between American and Far Eastern companies. I have never heard of any difficulties for South Asian game developers in either the Western job market or Western workplaces.

Another rapidly growing area of game development is in the former Warsaw Pact nations, many of which are now joining the European Union. In fact, there is so much programming talent there, and it is so much less expensive than development in California or Boston, that there is starting to be concern about American publishing companies looking for developers overseas. Most of these people are working in their own countries, however, rather than coming to the United States. I am not aware of any of them encountering difficulties working in the U.S., however, apart from the need to learn English, of course.

WRAP-UP

Job-hunting can be a long, discouraging, and emotionally demanding task. In order to prevent it from wearing you down, you have to go into it with the right attitude: it's professional, not personal. If someone doesn't return your phone calls, it's almost certainly because they're too busy, not because they have anything against you. Try again in a day or so. If you get nowhere with a company, don't rule them out for life, just make a note by their name that says "not this time." Move on to the next company. Keep at it—both the networking and the digging.

Almost everybody I've spoken to in the game industry believes that their own "breaking in" story was a special case. They think that they didn't get their job in the "normal way"; they just got lucky. They met somebody at a party; they just happened to hear about a job from a friend; they saw an ad in a magazine left on a bus, or whatever. After hearing enough of these stories, I came to realize that there *is* no "normal way." These people didn't just get lucky; they made their own luck by keeping their eyes and ears open, and actively pursuing their dream. There's always a little bit of luck required in job-hunting, but the effort you put into it can change the odds in your favor. Don't give up: with patience, persistence, and a positive attitude, you *will* get a job in the game industry one way or another—and then you, too, will have a "breaking in" story to tell.

CHAPTER

8

Legal Issues for Creative People

I get a lot of letters from people who've had great game ideas, or written a game design, asking how to protect their work from being stolen. Chances are you've already got some material too: a portfolio of artwork or music that you've created, or some code under construction. You'll need to be able to show this material to other people, especially during interviews, while at the same time protecting your ownership of it. And even if you don't have anything like that, there are still some legal issues surrounding your status as an employee that you should know before you start a job. In this chapter, I'm going to give you a few pointers on legal issues for creative people. These will touch on two subjects: protecting your own property, and your rights and obligations as an employee.

FIRST, THREE DISCLAIMERS

Before I get into the subject, I need to warn you about the limitations of what I know.

> *This isn't formal legal advice.* I'm not a lawyer, and what I'm about to say here doesn't constitute legal advice. The law changes all the time, such as when the Digital Millennium Copyright Act was recently passed. For qualified professional advice and the latest information, talk to an attorney—preferably one specializing in intellectual property matters.

> *This material only applies to the United States.* I'm not familiar with the patent, trademark, and copyright rules of other countries, so I can't meaningfully comment on them. If you live outside the U.S., you should consult the appropriate legal advisors in your area.

> *Every state is different.* Although the laws about copyrights and patents are nationwide, trademark and employment issues are regulated at both the federal and state level. If you have questions or concerns, look at your state government's web site to see what information they have online, and if you need formal advice, consult a lawyer licensed to practice in your state.

YOU CAN'T PROTECT AN IDEA ALONE

To begin with, you have to understand that, in the United States at least, you can't legally prevent other people from having and acting on the same ideas that you have. Ideas are as free as the air. The artistic, intellectual, and industrial life of our nation depends on people being able to think up ideas for things, both aesthetic and practical, without constantly worrying about whether someone else has "laid claim" to them. There is one exception—the patent (a special case, which I'll discuss next). But patents are of little use to video game developers.

Years ago, my wife and I were standing in line waiting for a movie and talking about computer games, and she had a great idea: make an adventure game in which the player was a detective trying to solve a crime. No such game had ever appeared before. We talked it over and thought it would be fun, but neither of us had time to do anything about it; we were both in college. Not long after that, Infocom published a game called *Deadline,* the first commercial game in which the player was a detective. They didn't steal her idea; they just had it independently. There was no way to prevent them from doing it, nor should there have been. If someone could lay permanent claim on the idea of detective computer games, or anything else for that matter, the whole medium of gaming would have died long ago.

On the other hand, you *can* protect an expression of an idea: words, pictures, music, and other forms of creative representation. That's what I'll talk about next.

THE THREE TYPES OF INTELLECTUAL PROPERTY PROTECTION

There are three formal mechanisms provided by U.S. and state law to protect intellectual property: copyrights, trademarks, and patents. Each is designed to protect a different kind of property in different ways. In this section, I'll discuss each in turn.

To begin with, you need to understand that these "protections" don't actually stop anyone from doing something unless you go to court to enforce them! If someone violates your copyright, you can't ask the police to make them stop, because it's a civil matter, not a criminal one. You have to show the violator your copyright and ask them politely to stop, and if they don't, you have to sue them. In short, enforcement is up to you. However, the copyright, trademark, and patent systems do allow you to register something as yours: they are evidence in the form of government records. And in the case of patents and trademarks, the U.S. Patent and Trademark Office is supposed to make sure that once you have a patent or trademark, no one else can register one if it conflicts with yours.

Finally, you can lose a copyright or trademark if you *don't* take steps to protect it. If you know that someone is violating your intellectual property rights and you let them get away with it, it creates a presumption that you don't care. In a famous case, the family of deceased science fiction writer E.E. "Doc" Smith was made aware that an unauthorized TV show based on Smith's "Lensman" series of books was being made in Japan, but did nothing about it. When they finally did sue, they lost in court, because they hadn't aggressively protected their property.

Copyright

Copyright is the best option for protecting your work from being copied or closely imitated. You own the copyright on anything you write, draw, or compose from the moment you create it. You don't have to do anything to make it yours; it's already yours. However, it's a good idea to *claim* it as yours, so other people who see it know it belongs to you. All you have to do is put "© [*the current year*] by [*your name*]" on the title page, or, if you're concerned that a printed document might be disassembled, at the bottom of every page. If you're really anxious to make sure that there's an unmistakable record of your ownership, you can register the copyright quite inexpensively with the U.S. Copyright Office at the Library of Congress. (Visit www.copyright.gov for details and further information.)

You have to realize, though, that copyright doesn't protect the ideas in the document, only the words, images, or sounds in the document—that is to say, the *expression* of the ideas. The copyright means that you are the only one entitled to publish, display, or perform the work (with certain exceptions under "Fair Use" rules). Someone can still read your document, get a brilliant idea from it, and create something using that idea. They're not violating your copyright unless they duplicate part of your original material.

Any work you create for hire, either as a contractor or as an employee, belongs to the person or company that paid you for it—meaning the copyright resides with them. When you get a job in the game industry, your employer will own the copyright on everything you do for them.

Trademark

A trademark is a means by which a company associates particular names, logos, and slogans with itself. A trademark is used at either a local or a national level, depending on whether it has been registered with the U.S. Patent and Trademark Office or not. For non-registered trademarks, a certain amount of common sense applies in determining how far the trademark extends. If "Joe's Garage" fixes cars in the tri-county area (whatever that may be), then it's reasonable that there should only be one "Joe's Garage" in that region, even though someone else can have their own "Joe's Garage" a hundred miles away. On the other hand, "Activision" distributes video games all over the United States and, indeed, the world. Therefore, there can only be one video game company named "Activision" in the United States.

The protection of a trademark is also limited to the line of business that the company is in, although this is more of a gray area. If two companies have the same name, the governing factor is whether the public is likely to be confused and assume that the companies are related. For example, if you look up "Ultima" in the trademark database, you'll find that its use isn't restricted to the *Ultima* video game series. There are Ultima cosmetics, Ultima telescopes, even Ultima toilet paper! On the other hand, if you founded the Coca-Cola Mineral Water Company, the real Coca-Cola company would send you a letter telling you to cease and desist so fast your head would swim.

Trademarks (or service marks for services) aren't intended to protect large amounts of material; rather, their purpose is to identify the company that produced the goods or services in question, and the ™ and ® symbols are used to inform the public that the trademark is being reserved. The ® symbol indicates that the trademark has been registered with the U.S. Patent and Trademark Office for exclusive use nationwide. You may *only* use the ® symbol once the trademark has actually been registered. (Visit the U.S. Patent and Trademark Office's web site at www.uspto.gov for more details.)

If you have created a character, name, or logo that you want to trademark, all you have to do is use the ™ symbol when you publish or reproduce the item. This doesn't guarantee you anything, however, it only asserts that you consider it a trademark. If you are infringing on someone else's trademark, you'll hear from their lawyer; if they're infringing on yours, you'll have to hire a lawyer yourself and be prepared to prove that you really had it first and that their use creates confusion. If you register your trademark with the U.S. Patent and Trademark Office, it creates much better protection for you, but it costs several hundred dollars to do so. Also, you actually have to be "in commerce," using the trademark to identify your goods or services; you can't trademark a whole lot of names and logos simply to prevent others from using them.

As with copyright, a trademark doesn't protect an idea, only a logo, name, or slogan that identifies a business or a product of that business. You're perfectly free to make a video game about an Italian plumber as long as a) his name isn't Mario, and b) he doesn't look like Mario.

Patents

A patent is a legal mechanism for preventing other people from importing or manufacturing something you have invented. There are two types of patents that concern us, design patents (ornamentation of manufactured objects) and utility patents (inventions that accomplish something useful).

A design patent is unlikely to be of any use to you as a video game developer. You can't patent an ornamental design for use on anything at all; it has to be for use on a specific manufactured object. Unless you're designing some cool-looking game hardware, you won't get a design patent. A video game isn't a manufactured object; it doesn't have any physical existence. If you have a picture that you would like to protect, you're better off copyrighting it.

Unlike copyrights and trademarks, a utility patent *does* protect an idea, but it has to be an idea for accomplishing something practical. You can't patent an image, general game concept, story, or character. Filing for a patent takes a long time, and several hundred dollars' worth of filing fees plus (usually) the services of a patent attorney. You have to submit a great deal of documentation, and be able to prove that nobody else has ever invented whatever it is you're proposing to patent. If your invention, or one substantially similar to it, already exists or has even been described in print anywhere else in the world, the U.S. Patent and Trademark Office will deny the patent. Again, visit the U.S. Patent and Trademark Office web site at www.uspto.gov for more information.

Game-related patents do exist. The game designer Jon Freeman has patented a new deck of cards that enables people to play games not possible with the standard 52-card deck (Patent No. 5,887,873) and Chris Crawford has patented a mechanism for algorithmically generating storylines from story fragments called "substories" (Patent No. 5,604,855). But unless you have invented something so radically new that it has never been seen before in any video game, it's almost certainly not worth the time and expense to patent it. The application will take several years to work its way through the system, and even if it's approved, it's still up to you to exploit it commercially. Having a patent doesn't actually get you any closer to making money out of it.

TRADE SECRETS AND NON-DISCLOSURE AGREEMENTS

The best way to protect your ideas and prevent someone else from stealing them is to treat them as a trade secret. A trade secret is some fact or information of value to your business that it would help your competitors to know. If you have some ideas you consider to be a trade secret, then you have to treat them like one. Keep any written material under lock and key (locked in your house is enough). Don't discuss it on the Internet, send e-mail to friends about it, or write about it for publication. If someone can show that you've been talking openly about your ideas, then they aren't a trade secret and you have no cause for complaint if she uses them for her own purposes.

Having a trade secret doesn't prevent anyone else from having the identical idea on their own and exploiting it themselves, of course. It's just a way of protecting your own ideas from getting out and being used by others.

When you do need to talk to someone about a trade secret (a potential investor or partner, for example), you can ask them to sign a non-disclosure agreement, or NDA.

An NDA is a short, simple contract in which the person promises not to reveal the secret in exchange for getting the opportunity to hear about it. There's no money involved; being in on the secret is their compensation for promising to keep it secret. You can find sample NDAs on the World Wide Web, or you can have a lawyer write one for you.

NDAs and Job Interviews

If you've got a portfolio or a demo that you want to show in an interview, don't treat it as a trade secret, or ask your interviewer to sign an NDA. Unless you're being interviewed by the president or a senior executive, she probably won't have the authority to sign on behalf of the whole company anyway. Most companies won't sign NDAs because they don't want to risk a legal entanglement just to hear some piece of information they may or may not care about anyway. Besides, your interviewer isn't going to be impressed if you apply for a job at their company and you make it clear you don't even trust them!

On the other hand, you yourself may be asked to sign an NDA during a job interview, if the company wants to show you something secret that they're working on. You should do this (you probably won't get the job if you don't!), and then honor it by not talking about whatever they show you. It may sound unfair that they won't sign one for your property while expecting you to sign one for theirs, but realistically, theirs is probably worth a lot more than yours. They are investing hundreds of thousands, or even millions, of dollars into it, so they've got more to protect.

DON'T WORRY TOO MUCH ABOUT PROTECTING YOUR IDEAS

The bottom line is that your ideas aren't in much danger of being stolen. Remember, as Ellen Guon Beeman says, "Ideas are easy, production is hard." The real value in a video game isn't the idea but all the effort that went into making the game.

There's a limit to how much you can protect your ideas, and all the work you create is automatically protected by copyright anyway. In my opinion, you're actually better off talking about your ideas. Explaining them to others will help you to refine them. Write them down and show them to anyone who'll listen. Ask for other people's opinions and advice. Even if you don't end up making a fortune from an idea, it's useful to discuss it in an interview: it shows that you're a creative, imaginative person. Somebody who walks in with a brain bubbling over with good ideas, and is eager to share them, is going to seem like a much more desirable employee than someone who has none, or acts suspicious and secretive about them.

Any one idea is unlikely to be worth a fortune. The right attitude to have about ideas is this one: more is better.

UNDERSTANDING YOUR EMPLOYMENT CONTRACT

The first real job I ever held was packing college textbooks into boxes in a warehouse. Employment there was pretty straightforward: when they hired me, they said, "You're hired," and when I quit, I said, "I quit." That was about it so far as the paperwork went. Everything was done on a handshake.

However, once I got a programming job in Silicon Valley, I was quite surprised on my first day of work when the personnel manager shoved a contract under my nose and told me I had to sign it. When you get a job in the game industry, the same thing will almost certainly happen to you. You'll be going through the company's new-employee process, setting up your health insurance and so on, and among all the other things you'll be asked to sign will be this contract. It may not be called a contract; it may be called an "employment agreement," a "proprietary information and inventions agreement," or something similar. In any case, it's a legally binding document and although it looks like a bunch of boring gobbledygook, it's very important. So what's it about?

It's Not about the Money

It's unlikely to be about money. The contract won't promise to pay you a specific amount, or to employ you for a specific length of time. Your position and starting salary are set out in your offer letter, but they can change over time as your company's labor requirements change. (Don't worry, though, they can't lower your salary to a penny a day and not tell you about it; your rights are protected by state and federal labor laws.) Only in the upper echelons of management do companies have negotiated employment contracts with people stating explicitly what their salaries and other compensation are. At your level, you'll simply get a wage and other benefits according to whatever the company's normal policy is. Most likely, your employment will be called "at will," which is the legal phrase for a job situation where you can quit at any time, and likewise, the employer can end your employment at any time, without a reason.

Beware: Your Inventions Are Not Your Own!

My company that bought and re-sold college textbooks didn't "invent" anything, so it didn't have any intellectual property to protect, except maybe their trademark. But a game company creates new property out of nothing: characters, worlds, vehicles, game names, and on and on. It also creates program code—reams and reams of it. The copyright on all this material automatically belongs to the company, since they pay you to create it. But most companies go farther than that. In order to avoid disputes later on, they want all new employees to sign a contract giving up their rights to any inventions that they create while they are employed—even if they make them at home on their own time.

When I first saw this I was really shocked, wondering if I should refuse—and lose the job. I had been working on a game at home, and I didn't want my new employer to claim ownership. A closer reading, however, showed that it wasn't strictly true that I had to give up *all* inventions. First, anything that you invent *before* you take employment somewhere is obviously your own property. Second, there were exceptions. The California Labor Code (which applied in my case) does not allow a company to demand ownership of everything an employee does. If I created something on my own time, without using my employer's facilities, trade secrets, or any work I had done for them, *and it was unrelated to my employer's business*, then it was all mine. If I worked for a software company and I invented a brilliant new kind of can opener, they couldn't claim ownership of it. My first programming job was not for a game company, so I could safely create games on the side. But you *are* going to a game company, so you may not be able to. See the upcoming section titled "The Hazards of Moonlighting" for a discussion of this.

Remember also that my experience only applies to California and was many years ago. Check with a lawyer or your state's own labor or employment department to find out what the law pertaining to employee inventions says in your area.

INSIDE iNFO Legally speaking, there is no such thing as a "standard contract" for anything. Every contract is unique and every word is meaningful. Be extremely suspicious of anyone—in any circumstance, whether you're getting a job or buying a mattress—who hands you something with a blasé attitude and says, "Oh, and I'll just need you to sign our standard contract."

Protecting Your Existing Inventions

If you've already got some work in progress when you go to work in the game industry, the best way to avoid trouble is to clearly declare it when you start, so there's no question about who owns what. If the employment contract is written properly, it will say something like, "I have identified on Exhibit A (attached) a list of all the inventions I have made prior to joining the company, which I wish to have excluded from the terms of this agreement." Then there'll be a blank page at the back for you to list your existing work. When I got mine, I wrote in:

> All documents, ideas, computer programs, and methods in my possession applying to:
>
> 1. A computer game simulating the fighting of forest fires.
>
> 2. A computer game simulating fighting medieval castle sieges.
>
> 3. A computer game for playing the guessing game "Botticelli."

These were all games that I had either written or created designs for. Obviously, if you've already done some work for another company, their property is excluded, too—but it's up to them to worry about that. Our concern is with protecting *your* property.

What If They Don't Ask?

If the contract requires you to assign your inventions to the company and it doesn't have any provision for documenting your existing work, write it in! Put it neatly in the margin and initial it—there's nothing that says contracts have to be neatly printed. You're taking a slight risk that some uptight HR person will object to you altering the contract and you'll have to decide how big of a fuss you're prepared to make—but, in truth, all you're really asking is that the company acknowledge that you have some prior inventions that are not their property. By the time you've arrived for the first day of work they've probably told all the other candidates that the position is filled and pulled the newspaper advertisements, so it would be a big nuisance if you walked out and they had to start over. Besides, it's not as if you're flatly refusing to sign it, just making a minor amendment. On the other hand, you don't want to come off looking legalistic and troublesome on your very first day, either. If they question it, be polite, keep calm, and explain that you're just trying to be as honest as possible about your existing projects so there's no misunderstanding later.

Of course, declaring this information doesn't prevent your company from making a game along the same lines, but it does ensure that the material you've created remains your property, no matter what they do later on.

The California Labor Code on Inventions

This is what the California Labor Code actually says about employee inventions made outside of work:

> 2870. a) Any provision in an employment agreement which provides that an employee shall assign, or offer to assign, any of his or her rights in an invention to his or her employer shall not apply to an invention that the employee developed entirely on his or her own time without using the employer's equipment, supplies, facilities, or trade secret information except for those inventions that either:
>
> (1) Relate at the time of conception or reduction to practice of the invention to the employer's business, or actual or demonstrably anticipated research or development of the employer; or
>
> (2) Result from any work performed by the employee for the employer.

(b) To the extent a provision in an employment agreement purports to require an employee to assign an invention otherwise excluded from being required to be assigned under subdivision (a), the provision is against the public policy of this state and is unenforceable.

The Hazards of Moonlighting

Another thing the contract will probably require is that you not work for anyone else, or do any work on your own in the same line of business as long as you're employed with the company. Most companies don't want you moonlighting, for three reasons:

> *You're competing against your own employer.* As an employee, you're supposed to be assisting your company, not working against it. If you make a game at home, they might not mind if you bring it in and offer to let them publish it, but they will object very strongly (and probably fire you) if you try to get some other, competing publisher to do it. They *may* be willing to turn a blind eye if you self-publish it … and then again they may not. If they suspect that you've used any of their trade secrets or facilities, they could claim ownership, sue you, or even try to prosecute you for theft or industrial espionage.

> *They don't like gray areas over ownership of ideas.* Remember, the exemption about inventions I described earlier only applies to inventions that were outside my employer's line of business—and only in California. But what *is* their line of business? If they sell console games and you're building a PC game at home, that's a gray area—they could decide to go into the PC business at any moment, and without any obligation to tell you. In practical terms, they are unlikely to come after you about it—*unless* you suddenly start to make a lot of money, or they suspect you've been using their facilities or trade secrets. But an employer would much rather that you keep the boundaries very clear: they make software, you design can openers.

> *They want you devoting your energy and attention to their projects, not your own.* They're not entitled to tell you what to do on your own time, but they are going to expect a certain amount of loyalty to them and their business. If you're spending a lot of effort on a project of your own, even if you're doing a fine job for them, it may cause them to question your dedication to the cause. Game companies don't have a strong division between labor and management, with both sides at each other's throats all the time; they want to feel as if everyone's pulling in the same direction.

The game industry is a business full of creative people, and it's unrealistic to expect that nobody will ever work on a private little project of their own. People do it all the time for fun and self-education, and most sensible managers would even consider that a good thing—a sign of your enthusiasm for the work. The problems start when you treat it as a separate business or a second job. In short, be discreet and sensible about your extracurricular activities, and you shouldn't have any problems.

Moral Rights

You might have recently noticed a peculiar phrase in the front matter of some novels (on the page where the publisher is identified, and so on): "So-and-so [*the author*] asserts the moral right to be identified as the author of this work." You may also notice in your employment contract that you are being asked to relinquish any moral rights in the work you create. So what in the heck is a moral right?

Moral rights are an idea that originated in Europe in the last hundred years. Some artists began to be distressed about the fact that when they sell a work, they lose all control over it. A painting could be used in pornography, or to advertise shaving cream—purposes which the artist did not intend them for and does not like. The idea behind moral rights is that by creating a work, the artist retains certain rights over the work even if he sells the copyright: the right to prevent it from being distorted (or destroyed, if it is a unique item), and the right to be identified as its creator. The moral rights always remain with the artist, and, in theory, the artist cannot sell or give away moral rights even if he wants to. The notion of moral rights is highly respected in countries where there is a strong cultural belief in the value of art and artists, France in particular.

Unfortunately, the United States is not one of these countries. Until very recently, the U.S. has always taken the position that selling intellectual property rights confers more-or-less absolute control over the property: if you own the rights to an image, even if someone else created it, you can do whatever you like with it. By selling the copyright, the creator gives up all rights, moral and otherwise. However, just to make sure of the point, companies that hire creative people—like video game developers, for example!—have started to include clauses to the effect that as an employee, you give up any moral rights to your work.

This is an area in which the law is changing. California and New York have both passed laws concerning the moral rights of visual artists and authors, and if you are concerned about such things, you'll need, as ever, to seek an attorney. But I wouldn't fight this one. It's not as if you're creating paintings one by one and selling them; the company is paying you a salary to work for them, and they have a reasonable expectation that they own the work and everything about it. If your video game creation turns up in an ad for a soft drink (as Lara Croft has in Britain, for a sports drink called Lucozade), you're just going to have to get used to it.

Your Duty to Protect Your Company's Property

In addition to asking you to work for only one company at a time, the employment contract will also ask you to promise to protect the company's intellectual property—to keep its trade secrets and not let its confidential documents or data get away. As an employee, you will have access to a lot of valuable property and information about what the company is planning to do. In order to beat the competition, the company needs all its employees to be discreet, and that obligation will form a part of the contract.

It may sound obvious, but it's important that you take this seriously. Unfortunately, there have been instances of employees at game companies illegally transmitting gold master copies of games off to pirates—even before the game is officially ready for manufacturing. When such people are caught, they get fired, *and* sued, *and* leave the building in handcuffs under arrest for industrial espionage. Big publishers with millions of dollars at stake have private security staff and they work closely with the police to make sure this kind of thing doesn't happen. So don't even think about it.

How Come You're Being Kept in the Dark?

If you go to work for a big publisher, you'll notice that the management tends to be rather closed-mouthed about some of the company's financial details and plans for the future. If you've ever had a job working for a small outfit, this kind of secrecy may seem unfriendly and bureaucratic—a "big-company" attitude—or even as if they don't trust you.

Don't take it personally. It is bureaucratic, but it's actually intended to protect you. Companies whose stocks are publicly traded on Wall Street have to be extremely careful with the data they release about their plans and financial performance. Rumors about such things can affect the stock price, and somebody who knows "inside information" could use it to get an unfair advantage over other shareholders. Since the insider-trading scandals of the 1980s, the Securities and Exchange Commission has cracked down hard on release of inside information.

The reason that keeping you in the dark benefits you is that it enables you to buy and sell the company's stock freely if you want to. Anybody who is an "insider"— the management—isn't allowed to buy and sell stock without filing special paperwork with the Securities and Exchange Commission months in advance, as a notice to the public that they're about to do so. Insiders also have to watch every word they say about the company in public. Obviously, you shouldn't go around loudly speculating about the company's plans, but since you're not an insider, you don't have to be quite so careful.

WRAP-UP

Legal issues are not the most exciting thing about being a game developer, but they're part of what separates amateur development from professional development. Whenever there's money or property involved, there are rights, duties, obligations, and laws—and, of course, lawyers. You won't spend much time thinking about these things unless you go into the business and legal side of it ... but you'd be surprised how useful it can be to know the basics.

CHAPTER

9

The Future of
Game Development

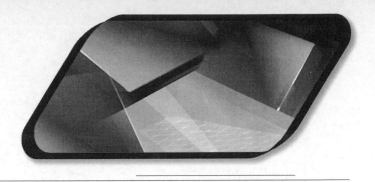

AS I said back in Chapter 1, innovations in gaming hardware have driven the expansion of the game industry, transforming the home console from a toy for children into an amusement center for the family, and the PC from a hobbyist's pastime into a communication and entertainment powerhouse. The growing power of the machines affects every part of the game business, and will continue to do so for the foreseeable future. It determines the way the games look and feel, and it also influences the developer's working environment. In this chapter, I'll take a brief look at how I expect gaming to change in the next few years, and what that means for you as a new developer.

BIGGER GAMES, BIGGER TEAMS

On the PC, our standard distribution medium has gone from floppy disks to compact discs, and will soon move to the DVD. On console machines, it has gone from cartridges to compact discs to DVDs already, except on handheld devices. Bigger storage media mean we can make bigger games, and bigger games require more people to build them. As long as players keep buying the games, this is great news for us: it means there will be more jobs for developers.

Bigger Teams Mean More Bureaucracy

The benefits of bigger games are not unmixed, however. As development teams swell, the game industry enters uncharted territory. Unlike other software industries, we don't have any experience with really big projects. If a software company builds, say, a new air-traffic control system for the FAA, or a new tax-return database for the IRS, the project may require hundreds of programmers and take ten years to complete. Industrial software companies have devised engineering management techniques for working on that sort of scale. Game development companies aren't used to such things, and they can't possibly afford to take that much time. For the moment, the economics of the industry don't allow for hundred-million-dollar budgets or really long-term projects.

Development teams working on a single commercial game tend to range in size from about five people at the very smallest up to about forty people (not counting testers and subcontractors). At the upper end of this scale, not all those people will be actively developing code or content. Big projects require more oversight: team leaders and project managers who maintain the task lists and make sure the schedule is being met.

This phenomenon may not continue indefinitely. There may come a day when we've settled on a standard size for games, just as the movies have settled on two hours as their preferred running time. But for the time being, as storage space continues to grow, game growth looks set to continue along with it: the content expands to fill the space available. Developers who were used to floppies thought the compact disc would give them all the room they would ever need, but now many games require more than one CD. For the next several years, we can expect to see bigger and bigger team sizes on the largest projects, and more management overhead to keep them all organized.

What this means to you, as a developer, is that, on a large game at least, your work will be carefully planned out for you and closely monitored. Companies with multi-million-dollar projects can't afford to give their employees the kind of flexibility that students and small developers have.

The Rise of the Content Creators

One of the major trends in the last 20 years, and one that will continue, has been the flip-flop in the relative numbers of programmers versus content creators (writers, artists, musicians, and so on) on game projects. It used to be that 90 percent of the development budget went into programming and only 10 percent went into art—and usually it was the programmer who created the art anyway. That situation is now reversed. Ninety percent of the development budget goes into content and only 10 percent into programming; the disparity will continue to grow with time.

INTERVIEW WITH ...

A Producer

At the beginning of a project, the focus is to specify all the tasks necessary to complete the game. There are many tasks which remain relatively constant from one project to the next, but equally, depending on the platform, the genre, the experience of the team members, and so on, there are many variables.

Because of this, it is often impossible to specify tasks in detail at the beginning of a project. Therefore, it's important to leave time for researching and clarifying matters later on, and to factor in the estimated time for those tasks as well. Scheduling and project planning are areas in which it is crucial to work closely with the project leads (although, truth to tell, it's important throughout any project!).

Once the initial planning and scheduling is done and the project is under way, the producer's focus shifts to tracking the progress of the tasks and adjusting the schedule so that, hopefully, the end date doesn't shift.

—Kim Blake, Producer, Particle Systems

This doesn't mean that programming isn't important; it's central to the entire process. Without programmers there would be no game. But the number of jobs available will grow faster in the content positions than in the programming positions, simply because more content is needed. The game industry used to be dominated by programmers; now it is dominated by content creators.

Programmer Specialization

With larger and more powerful hardware has come more powerful software: smarter AI, better physics, fancier graphics engines. This means not only more programmers but more kinds of programmers. The industry will always need generalists, people capable of programming a variety of things, but job growth will be faster in specialist areas, and hiring managers will be looking for people with particular kinds of training and experience. This trend is undoubtedly going to continue. If you're a programmer, it would be wise to cultivate your skills in one (or more, if possible) of the specialist areas I mentioned in Chapter 6.

Subcontracted Services

As I've said before, game development teams can't farm out work to subcontractors as much as movies can, because every video game is a unique piece of software engineering. Many development tasks require that people work closely together throughout the process. However, there are certain areas where subcontracting makes sense. Music production is one; there are companies (like Team Fat in Austin, Texas) that

INTERVIEW WITH ...

An Advanced Graphics Programmer

❯ Ambient light does not exist. (0.3f,0.3f,0.3f) gray ambient especially.

❯ Refraction is the only light transport process there is. (Specular Reflection is just Total Internal Reflection between air and an object.)

❯ Lambertian diffuse reflection is the only equation we use with any physical justification.

❯ Nothing in reality has a texture map. All objects are just high detail and flat shaded.

❯ Once you can do diffuse area lighting with self transport, you will never look at buildings, cars and bridges on an overcast day again without thinking "Hey, I can do that!"

—Robin Green, R&D Programmer, Sony Computer Entertainment of America

[If you already know what Robin is talking about here, then you have a great career ahead of you as a graphics programmer!]

The Future of Game Development

specialize in composing and recording music for games. Video production and compression is another. So is motion capture, which is done by companies such as House of Moves. Motion capture gear is expensive and requires a lot of space, but any given game seldom needs it for more than two or three weeks at a time. It makes sense for it to be a subcontracted service. Testing, writing, game design, and some art and animation can also be subcontracted if the circumstances allow it.

If you go to work for a subcontractor, you won't have the sense of being involved in a single project from beginning to end. Instead, you'll work on many different companies' games throughout the year. This actually gives you a larger portfolio, but it doesn't have quite the same sense of personal connection to the project or the team.

As the game industry grows, subcontracting will grow with it. If you're particularly attracted to one of these specialties, and are less concerned about seeing a single game through to completion, be sure to check out the companies that offer the service you're interested in.

SPIRALING DEVELOPMENT COSTS AND CONSEQUENCES

Suppose you start up a small independent grocery store, and during the first year, the rent on the building costs you $100,000. The second year, the landlord raises it to $200,000. The third year, it goes up to $300,000, and so on, rising by $100,000 every year. You could raise prices, but beyond a certain point, the customers wouldn't pay. To cover the rising rent, you'd have to work harder, stay open longer, and sell a lot more groceries.

Something similar has happened to game development in the last 20 years. It now costs 20 times as much, or more, to develop a videogame than it did two decades ago. Publishers can't cover that by raising the price of games 20 times; the players won't pay it. Instead, the publishers have to work harder and sell more games. Rising development costs may mean more jobs for developers, but it's hard on the publishers who pay those costs. This, in turn, affects how they work and what kinds of games they choose to produce.

Publisher Conservatism

It's no secret that publishers have become more and more conservative over the years. You just can't take the kinds of risks with $2 million that you could with $100,000. They're unwilling to fund unusual, quirky games that might not make any money. Not every game needs to be a smash hit, but every game needs to be a steady, reliable seller.

INSIDE iNFO   Back in the old days, games were generally developed by one person—from the code and graphics to the audio. A game was, therefore, very much the vision of an individual. Games were also much, much cheaper to produce, so the commercial risks were generally lower than they are today. This meant that people could come up with wild and wacky ideas, write the game for very little, and publishers would publish them with minimal risk. These days, the cost of development and the commercial risks require a creative pragmatism. This is not necessarily a bad thing—but it means that the games we write are very different in spirit to those of yesteryear.
—*Charles Cecil, Managing Director, Revolution Software Ltd.*

This won't change any time soon, unfortunately. The higher costs go, the more closely publishers have to watch the bottom line. If you've got a truly outrageous idea for a game, you aren't very likely to get funding for it from a big mainstream publisher—especially if it requires a large development budget. Unfortunately, this risk aversion also means that some publishers develop a "copycat" mentality: they see some other publisher's hit game and try to duplicate it, usually by borrowing its formula and changing a few things. It seldom works. Often what made the other game a hit in the first place isn't one particular quality, but the synergy of the whole. This doesn't stop a few of the less scrupulous, or more desperate, publishers from trying it, however.

There isn't really anything you can do about publisher conservatism except to be aware of it. If you're considering working for a publisher, look closely at their products. If they all seem to be clones of the same idea, you know they won't give you a lot of freedom to exercise your own creativity.

Inbreeding

Another way publishers try to reduce their risk is by funding games that borrow and mix ideas from other games—a sort of genetic recombination. In biology, this mechanism (called sex) works well to create diversity in a species—but most species have millions of members. Unfortunately, when the population is too small, the result is inbreeding. The same characteristics appear over and over. In the game industry, old ideas and mechanisms get perpetuated because of a lack of better ones and an aversion to trying new things.

There are a couple of different solutions to this problem, and this is where you come in. One is to expand the gene pool: bring in new ideas from the outside and mix them with the existing ones. Not just ideas for whole games, but ideas for parts of games as well: new user interface elements, new gameplay mechanics, new art styles or musical themes. The game industry needs a steady supply of these if it is not to become inbred, and new developers like yourself are an excellent source of them. That's why I encourage you to get a full, four-year college degree if you can afford to; you will bring the ideas you are exposed to in college into the game industry.

The other solution is *mutation,* an external influence that unexpectedly changes an existing gene and causes a new kind of animal to appear. You're that external influence. When you get into the game industry, don't accept the status quo too easily. Question things that seem questionable to you. Don't be arrogant about it, or insist that you know better than veteran developers, but don't blindly accept the prevailing wisdom just because "this is the way we've always done it." If you see an idea that's stale, or a technique that's inefficient, ask if there isn't another way to do things. A few people will dismiss you as naïve, but that's better than obediently falling into line behind a system you feel could be improved. You may be the genius who revolutionizes some aspect of game development and saves, or makes, millions for your company.

Sequels and Sequels to Sequels

Yet another aspect of publisher conservatism is an emphasis on sequels. As I said earlier in this chapter, publishers sometimes try to duplicate other publishers' hits; in making sequels, they try to duplicate their own hits. A lot of developers find this boring. Having finished a particular game, they want to move on to something new.

You can hardly blame a publisher for wanting to clone something that makes money, but few games can be turned into long-running franchises. Except for the smash-hits, many games never have a sequel at all, or have only one sequel and then stop. For example, Activision had *Interstate '76,* a highly enjoyable game but not a world-beater, followed it up with *Interstate '82,* and then called it a day on that particular franchise. Players want variety, and it's rare that they're content with simply getting more of the same. Part of the appeal of video gaming is experiencing new ways to play and new universes to play in.

The exceptions are games with strong storylines—such as the *King's Quest* adventure games from Sierra Entertainment, or the *Ultima* series from Origin—and sports products. In the case of story-driven games, it's the new story that matters, and if the stories are really good, the series can go on for a long time, especially if the technical quality of the games keeps pace as well. With sports products, the names and abilities of the athletes change every year, so there's always something new to sell to the player. But they, too, have to keep pace. Most sports games add new features a little at a time: a dynasty mode that lets you play through multiple seasons, the ability to trade athletes among teams, and so on.

In short, publishers will go on exploiting an intellectual property for as long as they can. But the game industry thrives on novelty. In spite of all the sequels, you probably won't get stuck developing the exact same thing forever, simply because the players won't buy the exact same thing forever.

NEW OPTIONS FOR NEW IDEAS

The commercial game industry may have become more conservative as it has grown, but it's not the only option available for people interested in game development. There are other ways of working on games that may give you more freedom and flexibility.

Homebrew: Mods, Bots, and Engines

It used to be that all computer games were homemade. Now, amid the hype and glitter of commercial gaming, it's easy to forget that it's still possible. Homebrew games rarely earn enough money to live off of; many provide no income at all. But it's an excellent way to get development practice, and it affords a freedom that you'll find nowhere else.

Until *Doom* was released, few games offered players an opportunity to modify games and release their own data files for them. The publishers, anxious to control their intellectual property, discouraged any monkeying around with their software. Since *Doom*, that has all changed. The publishers have come to realize that there's a great deal of free advertising to be had from gamers who work to extend their games, and indeed it lengthens the shelf-life of the game itself.

You can get a great deal of experience in most aspects of game development simply by doing it yourself—that is, using "moddable" games as a springboard. When you're ready to go beyond making new environments, you can start building bots—AI-driven opponents for games. The step beyond that is creating whole new games, but you don't have to do it from scratch. There are also a number of open-source game engines available, such as Genesis3D and NeoEngine. The open- source community is famous for being encouraging and helpful. If you want to explore strange new ideas in game design, ideas that a publisher would be unwilling to fund, there are many resources to help you go solo. Once you have something you feel has real commercial potential, take it to a publisher, or publish it yourself via the Web.

INSIDE info If you're doing independent game development, be sure to check out the Independent Game Festival (www.indiegames.com). The IGF is an annual contest to highlight the best independently developed games in the world. The top scorers get their works put on display in front of hundreds of professionals at the Game Developers' Conference, and there's a cash prize as well for the best overall game. It costs little to enter and it's an excellent way to get yourself noticed—at the very least, your contest submission will be read by a jury of professional game developers who may be willing to give you advice and commentary.

Academic Research

Until recently, the idea of an academic program on game development would have been considered laughable, and to many academics it still is. But universities are starting to realize that there's money in them thar games; students are demanding to learn about them, and a few professors are interested in teaching and researching them. Unfortunately, academic research is notoriously under-funded unless it has a direct medical or commercial application. On the other hand, it doesn't have to go out and compete for shelf space at Wal-Mart, either. Colleges and universities offer opportunities to do high-risk yet potentially ground-breaking work without a publisher needing to know the ship date or the marketing department breathing down your neck.

It took a while for the movies to become a subject of serious academic study, but they certainly are now, and games will follow. If you're interested in the more theoretical aspects of game development, especially things like animation programming, simulation, and artificial intelligence, and if making commercial products for sale is less important to you, you might consider a career in academe. There aren't the same opportunities to make a lot of money, but as game schools expand—and they will—there will be opportunities to do some interesting and important research.

INSIDE info The academic scene is growing rapidly. If this area is of special interest to you, be sure to check out the IGDA's Education Committee (visit www.igda.org and then select the Academia button on the menu) and the Academic Summit at the Game Developers' Conference. The SIGGRAPH and American Association for Artificial Intelligence organizations, both of which include a large academic contingent, are also starting to pay attention to game development.

Video Games as an Art Form

Video games are (slowly) beginning to be recognized as an art form. The game industry now gives annual awards that, while they can't touch the Oscars for star power, get coverage from the mainstream press and clearly highlight the best that the industry has to offer. The public is beginning to understand that there's real talent in the game industry and some games showcase it. Furthermore, games are starting to appear in art festivals such as Ars Electronica in Austria, and are gaining acceptance as a legitimate form of aesthetic expression. This is partly because there are things you can say in a game, ideas that you can examine, that can't be explored in any other medium.

This won't help you make unusual games any more easily, but it may change the response you get when you try.

WILL THERE BE ANOTHER CRASH? HOW SAFE IS THIS BUSINESS?

Sometimes people ask me if there could ever be another crash like the one that the industry went through in 1983. They wonder if it's a safe career to get into when things like that can happen.

The short answer is no, I don't think there will be another crash. The crash of '83 was caused by a particular set of circumstances, and the industry has taken steps to make sure they don't recur. For example, back then anybody could make Atari cartridges, and many fly-by-night publishers produced a lot of cheesy games that harmed the reputation of Atari and, in fact, the whole medium. Nowadays, console manufacturers enforce quality and content standards in order to make sure that doesn't happen again. If there ever is another crash, it'll be caused by something else—but as the industry matures I think it becomes less and less likely.

A crash like that, whether in the stock market or in the demand for a business's products, is usually a *correction,* not a permanent disaster. Don't forget, two years after the Atari crash, the Nintendo Entertainment System came on the market and the console game industry was reborn. When a crash occurs, it's a sign that the demand for something was inflated beyond its real value, usually by wishful thinking. Atari's financial projections before the crash assumed that the demand for video games would continue to grow at a ridiculous rate; when they didn't, Wall Street freaked out. Since then, most companies have been a lot more careful. Electronic Arts, for example, almost always issues conservative financial predictions, then surpasses them handily. That way the investors are pleased, rather than disappointed, by the news.

Today, most console game developers and publishers see the game industry in terms of generational cycles. These cycles correspond to the lifespan of the console hardware. At first, there'll be an initial sales burst as the new console launches, then a slow ramp-up in sales, followed by a slow decline as the console ages and new hardware is expected on the market. This is why many game publishers publish a mix of console and PC games, because while the PC games sell less than the console games, it's a much steadier market.

The game industry is an entertainment industry, and entertainment companies tend to have a lot of ups and downs. Developers that were the darlings of the media one year are sometimes the dogs a few years later. That's the risk of working for a business that sells luxuries like video games rather than necessities like toothpaste: fashions change. It's difficult to predict what the public is going to like from year to year; all you can be certain of is that it'll be different from whatever it is now. If you're looking for one steady job for life, you're in the wrong business—and, in fact, even traditional blue-chip businesses like General Motors and IBM can't make that sort of promise any longer. But on the whole, the video game industry shows no signs of disappearing. Interactive entertainment is not a fad or a gimmick. It's a medium, like books or radio or television. Radio and television didn't put an end to books; television didn't put an end to radio, it just changed the things that radio was used for. Interactive entertainment will change, individual companies may come and go, but the medium is here to stay.

FEW FINAL WORDS

At the beginning of this book, I talked about the moment when, sitting at a noisy old Teletype, I realized that I had to learn how to make computer games. Playing them was fantastic, incredible fun... but I knew that I wanted to make them, too. It wasn't only the feeling of *being* in the game world that attracted me; I could sense the expressive power of *building* that world, there beneath my fingertips. The computer gave me the means to create an imaginary place, populate it with wonderful things, fill it with challenges, and then set a player loose in there to enjoy it all just as I had.

You'll hear a lot of talk about "passion" in the game industry. I actually think the term is overused. I wouldn't call the way I feel about designing computer games "passion," in the sense of frenzied desire. Frenzied desire is OK, but it tends to burn out after a while. Rather, what I feel is closer to what the great designer Brian Moriarty calls *harmony* "an ineffable sense of proportion and rightness." It's the feeling you get when the last piece of the jigsaw clicks into place, when you understand the riddle, when you find what you have been seeking. Writers on learning, invention, and creativity sometimes call it an "Aha!" moment.

In this book, I've told some hard truths about the video game industry, and given a few warnings about its pitfalls and downsides. There's a gap between knowing, intuitively, that you want to build video games, and actually getting a job and making your living doing it. Don't let that put you off. This book is intended to help you bridge that gap, and, in fact, you may find the gap isn't as wide as it seems. Forewarned is forearmed: it's better to go into game development with an understanding of what it's like, both the good and the bad, than to go in blindly and learn the hard way. But don't let your foreknowledge of the game industry's quirks and foibles destroy your interest in games themselves. Remember your "Aha!" moment and cherish it. You will have more of them as you work, celebrating large and small achievements with the other people on your development team. Holding on to that deeply felt sense of fascination and power is an essential part of getting, and enjoying, a job making video games.

APPENDIX

A

Educational Institutions

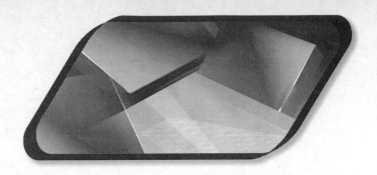

FOLLOWING

are lists of educational institutions that provide training for game developers in one or more fields. Rather than try to divide them up by topics (which is subject to change), I have organized them geographically so that you can find an institution in your area. Visit their web sites for more details of the programs they offer.

This list is derived from the database of educational institutions at the Gamasutra developers' webzine (www.gamasutra.com). Check there for the most up-to-date information.

TABLE A-1

Institute	City	State	Web Site
The Art Institute of Phoenix	Phoenix	AZ	www.aipx.edu
Collins College—A School of Design & Technology	Tempe	AZ	www.houseofedu.com/cc/index.jsp
University of Advancing Technology	Tempe	AZ	www.uat.edu/multimedia/gamedesign
The Art Center Design College	Tucson	AZ	www.theartcenter.edu
Mesmer Animation Labs, Berkeley	Berkeley	CA	www.mesmer.com
Expression Center for New Media	Emeryville	CA	www.expression.edu
California State University, Fullerton	Fullerton	CA	www.fullerton.edu
Academy of Game Entertainment Technology	Hollywood	CA	www.academyofget.com
Gnomon School of Visual Effects	Hollywood	CA	www.gnomon3d.com
Brooks College	Long Beach	CA	www.brookscollege.edu
California State University, Long Beach—University College and Extension Services	Long Beach	CA	www.uces.csulb.edu
Eni Oken's 3D Online Workshops	Los Angeles	CA	www.oken3d.com/workshop
Otis College of Art and Design	Los Angeles	CA	www.otis.edu
University of California, Los Angeles	Los Angeles	CA	www.ucla.edu
University of California, Los Angeles (Extension)	Los Angeles	CA	www.unex.ucla.edu

United States

TABLE A-1

Institute	City	State	Web Site
University of Southern California	Los Angeles	CA	www.usc.edu/dept/cs
Art Center College of Design	Pasadena	CA	www.artcenter.edu
Academy of Digital Animation	Ridgecrest	CA	www.coyote3d.com
Cerro Coso College	Ridgecrest	CA	www.cerrocoso.edu
Platt College	San Diego	CA	http://platt.edu
The Art Institute of California–San Diego	San Diego	CA	www.aicasd.artinstitutes.edu
Academy of Art College	San Francisco	CA	www.academyart.edu
San Francisco State University	San Francisco	CA	http://msp.sfsu.edu
The Art Institute of California–San Francisco	San Francisco	CA	www.aicasf.aii.edu
Core Microsystems	San Jose	CA	www.coremicro.com/training
California Polytechnic State University	San Luis Obispo	CA	www.calpoly.edu
Palomar College	San Marcos	CA	www.edmagnin.com/palomar.html
The Art Institute of California–Orange County	Santa Ana	CA	www.aicaoc.aii.edu
DH Institute of Media Arts	Santa Monica	CA	www.dhima.com
The Art Institute of California–Los Angeles	Santa Monica	CA	www.aila.artinstitutes.edu
Cogswell Polytechnical College	Sunnyvale	CA	www.cogswell.edu
California Institute of the Arts	Valencia	CA	www.calarts.edu
University of Colorado, Boulder	Boulder	CO	www.cs.colorado.edu
The Art Institute of Colorado	Denver	CO	www.aic.artinstitutes.edu
University of Colorado, Denver	Denver	CO	http://carbon.cudenver.edu/mume/multimediastudies.html
The Art Institute of Fort Lauderdale	Ft. Lauderdale	FL	www.aifl.edu
Florida Center for Electronic Communication	Ft. Lauderdale	FL	www.animasters.com
University of Central Florida	Orlando	FL	www.ucf.edu
Ringling School of Art and Design	Sarasota	FL	www.rsad.edu
Full Sail Real World Education	Winter Park	FL	www.fullsail.com
Georgia State University	Atlanta	GA	www.cs.gsu.edu
Georgia Tech	Atlanta	GA	www.cc.gatech.edu
The Art Institute of Atlanta	Atlanta	GA	www.aia.artinstitutes.edu

United States *(continued)*

TABLE A-1

Institute	City	State	Web Site
Savannah College of Art and Design	Savannah	GA	www.scad.edu
Art Institute of Chicago	Chicago	IL	www.artic.edu
DePaul University's School of CTI	Chicago	IL	www.cti.depaul.edu
The Illinois Institute of Art–Chicago	Chicago	IL	www.ilic.artinstitutes.edu
Northwestern University (Department of Computer Science)	Evanston	IL	www.cs.nwu.edu
The Illinois Institute of Art–Schaumburg	Schaumburg	IL	www.ilis.artinstitutes.edu
Indiana University	Bloomington	IN	www.mime.indiana.edu
Purdue University	West Lafayette	IN	www.purdue.edu
The New England Institute of Art & Communications	Brookline	MA	www.aine.artinstitutes.edu
Massachusetts Institute of Technology	Cambridge	MA	http://web.mit.edu/cms
CCBC Essex/University of Baltimore	Baltimore	MD	http://student.ccbcmd.edu/immt
University of Maryland, Baltimore County	Baltimore	MD	www.umbc.edu
University of Michigan (EECS Department)	Ann Arbor	MI	www.eecs.umich.edu/cse
University of Michigan–Dearborn	Dearborn	MI	www.engin.umd.umich.edu/CIS
Michigan State University (Department of Telecommunication)	East Lansing	MI	http://dmat.msu.edu
Minneapolis College of Art and Design	Minneapolis	MN	www.mcad.edu
The Art Institutes International Minnesota	Minneapolis	MN	www.aim.artinstitutes.edu
University of Missouri–Columbia (College of Engineering)	Columbia	MO	www.cecs.missouri.edu
The Art Institute of Charlotte	Charlotte	NC	www.aich.artinstitutes.edu
School of Communication Arts	Raleigh	NC	www.higherdigital.com
The Art Institute of Las Vegas	Henderson	NV	www.ailv.artinstitutes.edu
Pratt Institute	Brooklyn	NY	www.pratt.edu/ad/cgim
Game Institute, Inc.	New York	NY	www.gameinstitute.com
New York Institute of Technology	New York	NY	www.nyit.edu
New York University	New York	NY	www.scps.nyu.edu/dyncon/dime
Parsons School of Design	New York	NY	www.parsons.edu

United States (continued)

TABLE A-1

Institute	City	State	Web Site
School of Visual Arts	New York	NY	www.sva.edu
Rochester Institute of Technology	Rochester	NY	www.rit.edu
Rensselaer Polytechnic Institute	Troy	NY	www.rpi.edu
Mercy College	White Plains	NY	www.mercy.edu/cda
MMDC–Northern Oklahoma College	Tonkawa	OK	www.mmdclab.com
The Art Institute of Portland	Portland	OR	www.aipd.artinstitutes.edu
College of Media Arts & Design at Drexel University	Philadelphia	PA	www.drexel.edu
Philadelphia University	Philadelphia	PA	www.philau.edu
The Art Institute of Philadelphia	Philadelphia	PA	www.aiph.artinstitutes.edu
The Art Institute of Pittsburgh	Pittsburgh	PA	www.aip.artinstitutes.edu
Carnegie Mellon University–Computer Science	Pittsburgh	PA	www.cs.cmu.edu
Carnegie Mellon University–Entertainment Technology Center	Pittsburgh	PA	www.etc.cmu.edu
The Art Institute Online	Pittsburgh	PA	www.aionline.edu
Rhode Island School of Design	Providence	RI	www.risd.edu
3D University	Dickson	TN	www.3duniversity.com
University of Texas at Austin	Austin	TX	www.utexas.edu
The Gemini School of Visual Arts & Communication	Cedar Park	TX	www.geminischool.com
The Art Institute of Dallas	Dallas	TX	www.aid.artinstitutes.edu
University of North Texas	Denton	TX	www.unt.edu
The Art Institute of Houston	Houston	TX	www.aih.artinstitutes.edu
San Jacinto College Central	Pasadena	TX	www.sjcd.cc.tx.us
The Guildhall at SMU	Plano	TX	www.guildhall.smu.edu
University of Texas at Dallas	Richardson	TX	http://iiae.utdallas.edu
The Art Institute of Washington	Arlington	VA	www.aiw.artinstitutes.edu
Virginia Commonwealth University	Richmond	VA	www.vcu.edu
Puget Sound Discreet Training Center (DTC)	Bothell	WA	http://pugetsoundcenter.org
Edmonds Community College	Lynnwood	WA	http://gamedev.edcc.edu

United States (continued)

TABLE A-1

Institute	City	State	Web Site
DigiPen Institute of Technology	Redmond	WA	www.digipen.edu
Mesmer Animation Labs, Seattle	Seattle	WA	www.mesmer.com
Seattle Central Community College	Seattle	WA	www.sccconline.com
The Art Institute of Seattle	Seattle	WA	www.ais.artinstitutes.edu
University of Washington	Seattle	WA	www.extension.washington.edu/extinfo/certprog/gam/gam_main.asp
Madison Area Technical College	Madison	WI	http://matcmadison.edu/matc

United States (continued)

TABLE A-2

Institute	City	Province	Web Site
Banff New Media Institute (BNMI)	Banff	Alberta	www.banffcentre.ca/bnmi
Alberta College of Art & Design	Calgary	Alberta	www.acad.ab.ca
University of Calgary–Department of Computer Science	Calgary	Alberta	www.cpsc.ucalgary.ca
Grande Prairie Regional College	Grande Prairie	Alberta	www.gprc.ab.ca
Ai Center for Digital Imaging and Sound	Burnaby	British Columbia	www.artschool.com
Replica 3D Animation School	Courtenay	British Columbia	www.replica3d.ca
Vancouver Film School	Vancouver	British Columbia	www.multimedia.edu
Vancouver Institute Of Media Arts	Vancouver	British Columbia	www.vanarts.com
Center for Arts and Technology Atlantic Canada	Fredericton	New Brunswick	www.digitalartschool.com
New Brunswick Community College, Miramichi	Miramichi	New Brunswick	www.miramichi.nbcc.nb.ca
Eastern Business Computer Institute	Moncton	New Brunswick	www.ebci.ca
Success College of Applied Art & Technology	Moncton	New Brunswick	www.scaat.ca
Sheridan Centre for Animation and Emerging Technologies	Oakville	Ontario	www.sheridanc.on.ca/scaet

Canada

TABLE A-2

Institute	City	Province	Web Site
Algonquin College	Ottawa	Ontario	www.algonquincollege.com/me-dia/fast_track/animation
Algoma University College	Sault Ste. Marie	Ontario	www.auc.ca
Seneca College of Applied Art and Technology	Toronto	Ontario	http://dmc.senecac.on.ca
The Centre for Creative Communications	Toronto	Ontario	www.bccc.com
University of Waterloo	Waterloo	Ontario	www.softeng.uwaterloo.ca
National Animation and Design Centre (NAD Centre)	Montreal	Quebec	www.nad.qc.ca
New Media Campus–Regina	Regina	Saskatchewan	www.newmediacampus.com
New Media Campus–Saskatoon	Saskatoon	Saskatchewan	www.newmediacampus.com

Canada (continued)

TABLE A-3

Institute	City	State	Web Site
Instituto Tecnológico y de Estudios Superiores de Monterrey–Campus Estado de México	Atizapán de Zaragoza	Estado de México	www.cem.itesm.mx

Mexico

TABLE A-4

Institute	City	Region	Country	Web Site
Polytechnical University of Hagenberg	Hagenberg	Upper Austria	Austria	www.fhs-hagenberg.ac.at
Aarhus University	Aarhus C		Denmark	www.daimi.au.dk
IT University of Copenhagen	Copenhagen	Copenhagen NW	Denmark	www.itu.dk
L.I.S.A.A.–L'Institut Supérieur des Arts Appliqués	Paris		France	www.lisaa.com
Otto-von-Guericke University	Magdeburg	Sachsen-Anhalt	Germany	www.computervisualistik.de

Europe

TABLE A-4

Institute	City	Region	Country	Web Site
Academy of Converging Media	Berlin		Germany	www.academy-of-converging-media.com
Games Academy	Berlin		Germany	www.games-academy .com
Homer College	Athens	Attiki	Greece	www.omiros.gr
Utrecht School of the Arts/ Faculty of Art, Media & Technology	Hilversum	CL	Netherlands	http://emma.hku.nl
Noroff Instiuttet	Kristiansand and Oslo	Vest-Agder	Norway	www.webstudent.no
Enginyeria i Arquitectura La Salle (Universitat Ramon Llull)	Barcelona		Spain	www.salleurl.edu/citem/ area_grafics_rv
Universitat Pompeu Fabra	Barcelona		Spain	www.upf.es
E.T.S.I.Telecomunicación. Universidad de Málaga	Málaga		Spain	www.uma.es
Playground Squad	Falun		Sweden	www.playgroundsquad .com
Halmstad University	Halmstad		Sweden	www.hh.se
PowerHouse	Kramfors		Sweden	www.powerhouse.net
Luleå University of Technology	Skellefteå		Sweden	http://gscept.tt.luth.se
Stockholm University, Multimedia Programme	Tumba		Sweden	www.mmedu.net
University of Teesside	Middlesbrough	Cleveland	UK	http://wheelie.tees.ac.uk
University of Derby	Derby	Derbyshire	UK	http://computing-technology .derby.ac.uk
Bournemouth University– National Centre for Computer Animation	Poole	Dorset	UK	http://ncca.bournemouth.ac.uk
University of Hull	Hull	East Yorkshire	UK	www2.dcs.hull.ac.uk
University of Lincoln	Hull	East Yorkshire	UK	http://dcc.humber.ac.uk
University of Essex	Colchester	Essex	UK	www.essex.ac.uk

Europe (continued)

TABLE A-4

Institute	City	Region	Country	Web Site
Bolton Institute	Bolton	Greater Manchester	UK	www.technology.bolton .ac.uk
University of Salford	Salford	Greater Manchester	UK	www.salford.ac.uk
University of Portsmouth	Portsmouth	Hampshire	UK	www.tech.port.ac.uk/ct
Kent Institute of Art & Design (School of Design)	Rochester	Kent	UK	www.kiad.ac.uk
University of Central Lancashire	Preston	Lancashire	UK	www.uclan.ac.uk
Escape Studios	London	London	UK	www.escapestudios.co.uk
School of Computing at Middlesex University	London	London	UK	www.cs.mdx.ac.uk
The London College of Music and Media	London	London	UK	http://mercury.tvu.ac.uk/courses .html
University of Westminster	London	London	UK	www.wmin.ac.uk
Liverpool John Moores University–International Centre for Digital Content	Liverpool	Merseyside	UK	www.icdc.org.uk/ magames/
Liverpool John Moores University–School of Computing & Math. Sciences	Liverpool	Merseyside	UK	www.cms.livjm.ac.uk
St. Helens College	St. Helens	Merseyside	UK	www.sthelens.ac.uk
Motherwell College	Motherwell	North Lanarkshire	UK	www.motherwell.ac.uk
University of Paisley	Paisley	Renfrewshire	UK	www.paisley.ac.uk
University of Sheffield	Sheffield	South Yorkshire	UK	www.dcs.shef.ac.uk
Glasgow Caledonian University	Glasgow	Strathclyde	UK	www.gcal.ac.uk
University of Abertay Dundee	Dundee City	Tayside	UK	www.abertay.ac.uk
University of Birmingham	Birmingham	West Midlands	UK	www.cs.bham.ac.uk
University of Bradford	Bradford	West Yorkshire	UK	www.bradford.ac.uk/ external
Leeds Metropolitan University	Leeds	West Yorkshire	UK	www.lmu.ac.uk

Europe (continued)

TABLE A-5

Institute	City	Region	Country	Web Site
Hong Kong Polytechnic University–Multimedia Innovation\Centre (MIC)	Hong Kong	Kowloon	Hong Kong	www.mic.polyu.edu.hk
Digital Hollywood	Kanda-surugadai	Chiyoda-ku	Japan	www.dhw.co.jp
Kyoto University	Sakyo-ku	Kyoto	Japan	www.kyoto-u.ac.jp/index-e.html
Multimedia University	Cyberjaya	Selangor	Malaysia	www.mmu.edu.my
Stamford College Malaysia	Petaling Jaya	Selangor	Malaysia	www.stamford.edu.my
Nanyang Polytechnic	Ang Mo Kio		Singapore	www.nyp.edu.sg/sdn/sdn_main.htm
Ngee Ann Polytechnic	Singapore	Singapore	Singapore	www.np.edu.sg
Ajou University	Suwon	Kyungido	South Korea	www.ajou.ac.kr
SungKyunKwan University	Seoul	Seoul	South Korea	http://eng.skku.edu
Korea Advanced Institute of Science and Technology	Taejon		South Korea	www.kaist.edu

Far East

TABLE A-6

Institute	City	Region	Country	Web Site
Academy of Interactive Entertainment	Watson	ACT	Australia	www.aie.act.edu.au
Charles Sturt University Bathurst	Bathurst	NSW	Australia	www.csu.edu.au
QANTM	Brisbane	QLD	Australia	www.qantm.com.au
Queensland University of Technology	Kelvin Grove	QLD	Australia	www.creativeindustries.qut.edu.au
Media Design School	Auckland		New Zealand	www.mediadesign.school.nz
University of Otago	Dunedin	Otago	New Zealand	www.otago.ac.nz

Australia and New Zealand

TABLE A-7

Institute	City	Country	Web Site
GameEDU	New Delhi	India	www.gameedu.org

South Asia

TABLE A-8

Institute	City	Country	Web Site
Hebrew University (CG Lab)	Jerusalem	Israel	www.cs.huji.ac.il/labs/cglab

Middle East

TABLE A-9

Institute	City	Country	Web Site
Technikon Natal	Durban	South Africa	www.ntech.ac.za
5th Dimension College of Visual Arts	Johannesburg	South Africa	www.5dcollege.co.za
University of the Witwatersrand	Johannesburg	South Africa	www.wits.ac.za
University of Natal Pietermaritzburg	Pietermartizburg	South Africa	www.cs.unp.ac.za
Technikon Pretoria	Pretoria	South Africa	www.techpta.ac.za
University of Pretoria	Pretoria	South Africa	www.up.ac.za

Africa

APPENDIX

B

IGDA Curriculum Framework

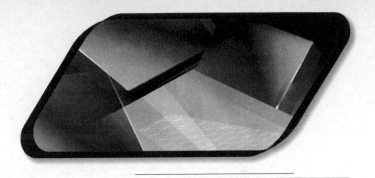

THIS appendix is a slightly edited form of the IGDA Education Committee's Curriculum Framework document (February 2003 version). As I explained in Chapter 5, you can use it in two ways: to decide what you want to study in college or other training programs for game developers, and to compare academic programs with the recommendations listed here. This isn't what the Education Committee intended it for, but I think it should be useful to you all the same.

At press time, this was the latest version of the Curriculum Framework, but it will continue to be revised from time to time. If you want to see if a new edition is available, visit the IGDA web site at http://www.igda.org/academia.

From this point on the text is taken directly from the IGDA Education Committee. In some places I have made editorial comments, and that text looks like this paragraph.—Ernest

WELCOME

The Education Committee of the International Game Developers' Association came into being three years ago, an unprecedented cooperative effort between the game industry and academia. At that time, only a few pioneering educators viewed games as a sophisticated medium of expression—a cultural and economic force that deserved study and attracted increasing numbers of students. Similarly, only a handful of game developers saw the value in forging relationships with academia, jumpstarting valuable research programs, creating a common language, and building a shared knowledge base for discussing games.

These two communities were highly motivated to work together, but how could they establish contact? Some developers and publishers succeeded in reaching out to universities, and select academic programs and schools found ways to work with industry partners. At the same time, individual developers and academics found themselves participating in conferences, teaching, consulting, and working on degree programs. But there were no roadmaps and progress was slow.

In 2000, the Education Committee was created to improve collaboration and communication between industry and academia. Reinforcing the goals of the IGDA charter, the Committee began building bridges between game developers and academics from a variety of fields.

Our initial goal was to create a template for creating lectures, courses and degree programs in game-related fields. Based on feedback from a roundtable at the 2001 Game Developers Conference, our emphasis shifted. The result of this new approach is a "curriculum framework," designed to delineate all of the topics related to games in an educational context—with the details of implementation left to individual readers.

The document you're about to read is the result of the Committee's efforts, anchored by Committee co-chairs and game developers Doug Church and Warren Spector, Northwestern University PhD candidate Robin Hunicke, game designer and academic Eric Zimmerman and the IGDA's tireless Program Director Jason Della Rocca. In addition, this draft was revised (and improved) many times thanks to insightful comments from the Education Committee at large, dozens of friends and colleagues, the 200+ attendees at least year's Academic Summit and a similar standing room only crowd at SIGGRAPH 2002.

This document is also very much a work in progress. There is still plenty of work to do. We've received enough feedback on this draft of the Framework to see that further revisions will emerge. We look forward to your continued guidance and feedback. With your help, we can attract and serve an ever wider audience. We thank you for your participation to date and look forward to crossing bridges with you in the future.

—Doug Church
—Jason Della Rocca
—Robin Hunicke
—Warren Spector
—Eric Zimmerman
...and the members of the IGDA Education Committee

Contact Info

International Game Developers Association
  600 Harrison Street
  San Francisco, California 94107
  USA

  Phone: (415) 947-6235
  Fax: (415) 947-6090
  E-mail: info@igda.org

  www.igda.org
  www.igda.org/academia
  www.igda.org/students

INTRODUCTION

Electronic gaming, a curiosity twenty years ago, is now one of the most popular forms of entertainment and a pervasive component of global culture. The ubiquity and growth of games requires that we understand them not just as commercial products, but that we appreciate them from many points of view. Games are aesthetic objects, learning contexts, technical constructs and cultural phenomena—among many other things.

For gaming and the study of gaming to reach their full potential, industry and academia must cultivate a deeper understanding of the ideas that drive electronic gaming, the experiences games can offer and the implications of those ideas and experiences on the social and cultural significance of this young medium. This kind of progress will only come about when academia and industry work together.

This cooperation has already begun. Developers, spurred by increasing risk and skyrocketing development costs, turn with greater frequency to academics for conceptual and technical inspiration. Similarly, as academics begin to recognize the cultural importance of games, they are enriching their research and studies through dialogue with developers. As universities begin to create programs for game study and research, many institutions are including voices from the industry to help shape their curricula.

The primary goal of the IGDA's Education Committee is to help foster interaction between developers and educators, to speed and help direct the evolution of games. Interaction between industry and the academy has countless benefits—facilitating the transition of new technologies from the lab into real products, enriching education by bringing industry experience into the classroom, engendering more critical approaches among game creators, enhancing understanding of contemporary media culture and overall, fostering a deeper exchange between academics and game developers.

About the Framework

The curriculum framework we present in this document is a conceptual guide for game-related educational programs.

Though the field of game studies is young, the number and variety of game-related educational institutions is already vast. No single curriculum can apply to them all. This document therefore presents a modular curriculum *framework,* not a single detailed curriculum. We have described knowledge areas and practical skills required to make and study games, in a format that can be adapted to the resources and curriculum offerings of a range of institutions.

We have not suggested specific courses, appropriate credit hours or specific degree program requirements. Nor is this framework an attempt to tell developers what areas of knowledge should be important to them. Instead, this framework proposes a set of *Core Topics*—a list of general areas relevant to the construction of a game-related curriculum. We intend for you to mix and match the Core Topics according to your needs, to include and exclude as you see fit. Rather than a menu of *necessary* ingredients, this document lists *possible* ways to grow or focus your program.

As a practical document, the framework is designed to assist educators and students on a variety of levels—from the creation of individual courses to the development of full degree programs, within a single department or across several. It is also a guide for students creating individualized courses of study at institutions without game-related majors.

In such a complex set of fields, there is no "silver bullet" approach. It is our hope that individual teachers, administrators and students can adapt appropriate aspects of this framework to their particular educational needs and institutional contexts.

OVERVIEW OF CORE TOPICS

Games are interdisciplinary on many levels. To create games requires collaboration among diverse existing fields, from audio and visual design to programming and project management. At the same time, digital gaming has given rise to new kinds of hybrid disciplines, such as game design and interactive storytelling. And considered as cultural media, a full critical understanding of games requires that we appreciate them in all of their social, psychological, historical and aesthetic complexity.

For this reason, we strongly advocate a *cross-disciplinary* approach to game-related education. For us this means an educational approach that respects what established fields bring to games but that also pays attention to new realms of study that games make possible.

The set of Core Topics we propose below reflects this approach. Some of the Core Topics are derived directly from existing disciplines like Computer Science. Others combine disciplines or synthesize new ones. We acknowledge that there are other ways to organize these overlapping fields of knowledge. However, we feel that the set of Core Topics listed below intuitively addresses the unique practical and theoretical concerns of gaming. As a whole, the Core Topics provide a birds-eye view of the immense landscape of games-related education. These Core Topics are

> Critical Game Studies

> Games and Society

> Game Design

> Game Programming

> Visual Design

❭ Audio Design

❭ Interactive Storytelling

❭ Game Production

❭ Business of Gaming

Following is a general description of each of these topics.

Critical Game Studies

Criticism, analysis, and history of electronic and nonelectronic games.

This interdisciplinary Core Topic combines approaches from history, literature, media studies and design. A key goal of Critical Game Studies is to develop and refine a critical vocabulary for articulating the aesthetics of games. This includes both the distinctive features unique to games as well as those they share with other forms of media and culture. Game Studies, for example, offers insight into the textual analysis of game play, while established work on other media, such as literature, film, television, theater and interactive arts can provide rich critical frameworks. Also included here are the history of computers and electronic games and toys; the construction and critique of a canon of significant and influential games; and game criticism and journalism.

Games and Society

Understanding how games reflect and construct individuals and groups.

In this Core Topic, Sociology, Anthropology, Cultural Studies and Psychology offer important insights into worldwide gaming culture. Games and Society includes scholarly work on online economies and community building, fan cultures and their creative reworkings of game content, the role of play in human culture and the relationship between online and offline identity. Also found here are issues of representation, ideology and rhetoric as they relate to gaming. Finally, this Core Topic covers the psychological facets of games including studies of media effects and the ongoing debate about the psychological impact of games on individuals and groups.

Game Design

Principles and methodologies behind the rules and play of games.

This Core Topic addresses the fundamental ideas behind the design of electronic and non-electronic games. It touches on relevant formal fields like systems theory, cybernetics and game theory. Game Design also includes basic interactive design, including interface design, information design and human-computer interaction. Perhaps most important for Game Design is a detailed study of how games function to create experiences, including rule design, play mechanics, game balancing, social game interaction and the integration of visual, audio, tactile and textual elements into the total game experience. More practical aspects of Game Design, such as game design documentation and playtesting are also covered. This is the Core Topic most intrinsic to games themselves and is therefore in some ways the heart of the curriculum framework we outline here. On the other hand, because it is the least understood, trained instructors and quality reference materials are sorely lacking, making it among the most challenging Core Topics to teach.

Game Programming

Aspects of traditional Computer Science—modified to address the technical aspects of gaming.

This Core Topic includes mathematics, programming techniques, algorithm design, game-specific programming and the technical aspects of game testing. Much of the material in this area could be taught under the auspices of a traditional Computer Science curriculum. However, games do present a very specific set of programming challenges, such as optimization of real-time 3-D rendering, that are addressed here.

Visual Design

Designing, creating, and analyzing the visual components of games.

This topic includes visual design fundamentals, both on and off the computer, across a broad range of media. Content areas include history, analysis and production in traditional art media such as painting, drawing and sculpture; communication fields like illustration, typography and graphic design; other design disciplines such as architecture and industrial design; and time-based media like animation and filmmaking. Special emphasis is placed on how visual aesthetics play a role in game experience. Use of 2-D and 3-D graphics programs can be an important part of a Visual Design curriculum. However, our emphasis is on fundamental visual design principles rather than on specific software packages.

Audio Design

Designing and creating sound and sound environments.

This Core Topic includes a range of theoretical and practical audio-related areas, such as music theory and history; music composition; aesthetic analysis of music; recording studio skills; and electronic sound generation. Audio relating specifically to digital game technologies, such as 3-D sound processing and generative audio structures are also included. Throughout, special emphasis is placed on the role of audio experience within the larger context of a game. As with Visual Design, the emphasis is on design fundamentals rather than on specific technical knowledge.

Interactive Storytelling

Traditional storytelling and the challenges of interactive narrative.

Writers and designers of interactive works need a solid understanding of traditional narrative theory, character development, plot, dialogue, backstory and world creation, as well as experimental approaches to storytelling in literature, theatre and film with relevance to games. In addition, interactive storytelling requires familiarity with new tools and techniques, including the technical aspects of writing for this new medium, algorithmic storytelling and collaborative story construction. In this Core Topic, these approaches are applied to the unique context of interactive storytelling in games.

Game Production

Practical challenges of managing the development of games.

Games are among the most complex forms of software to create and game development and publishing are complex collaborative efforts. Along with all the technical challenges of software development, issues of design documentation, content creation, team roles, group dynamics, risk assessment, people management and process management are addressed in this Core Topic. While there is growing literature on Game Production, there are also rich traditions in software engineering and project management from which to draw for this Core Topic.

Business of Gaming

Economic, legal, and policy aspects of games.

The economics of the game industry—the ways that games are funded, marketed and sold and the relationships between publishers, developers, distributors, marketers, retailers and other kinds of companies are addressed here. Market and industry trends, licensing management, dynamics of company and product value and business differences between major game platforms are all important aspects of the Business of Gaming. In addition, legal issues that affect games, developers and players, such as intellectual property and contract law, are part of this Core Topic. Lastly, social and governmental forces that impact the legislation and regulation of game content are included here.

CORE TOPICS BREAKDOWN

Note: The following breakdown section is a continual work in progress. Due to the many ongoing revisions, there may be inconsistencies in language or level of specificity. Further, the Committee continues to receive significant feedback, which will be incorporated into future revisions of the Framework.

In this section, we present the complete, expanded list of Core Topics. As we said earlier, we do *not* expect any institution to adopt the entire Curriculum Framework. By selecting appropriate elements from this list, educators can craft lectures, courses and/or programs that meet their needs and the needs of a wide variety of students and game developers. Students can acquire the knowledge and skills necessary to accomplish their goals, whether academic or vocational.

The order in which the material is presented in each Core Topic below reflects a rough sequencing of study, beginning with basic knowledge and proceeding to more advanced topics in a particular study area. These more advanced topics form the heart of the Framework within a Core Topic. Last in the list are topics that delve deeper into the material of a study area but which may not be necessary for all students or for all career paths.

Critical Game Studies

Criticism, analysis, and history of electronic and nonelectronic games.

Game Criticism

Game studies/"Ludology":

> Critical theory and research

> Critical vocabulary for discussing games and play, including the evaluation of game mechanics and game play, flow and game design

> Establishing and critiquing the canon of influential and/or important games

Experience-centered criticism:

> Study of interactivity

> Function and uses of exploration

❭ Encouraging and supporting player "agency"

❭ Creating and sustaining player immersion

❭ Supporting the suspension of disbelief

Consumer-oriented criticism:

❭ Analyzing and understanding the function and current state of the gaming press

❭ The function and current state of game reviews

❭ Tools, techniques and standards of print and media journalism

Genre analysis:

❭ What genres exist?

❭ How are game genres defined?

❭ History of game genres (genres that have come and gone)

❭ Are genres useful? How does the application of genre analysis differ when applied to games as opposed to other media?

Auteur studies:

❭ Given the collaborative nature of game development, who actually creates a game?

❭ Does the concept of authorship apply to individual games?

❭ Does the concept of authorship apply to an individual's body of work as a whole?

Media Studies

History:

❭ Non-electronic games

❭ Computers

❭ Electronic games

❭ Preservation of Digital Technologies

History, theory, and criticism of mainstream/commercial and experimental media:

❱ Literature

❱ Radio

❱ Movies

❱ Television

❱ Art

❱ Theatre

❱ Comic Books

❱ Architecture

Research:

❱ Introduction to mass media/pop culture research

❱ General media effects research

❱ Game-specific research

Games and Society

Understanding how games reflect and construct individuals and groups.

Players and Effects

Gaming demographics:

❱ Gender and diversity

❱ Childhood, education and child development

❱ Understanding the choices and patterns of buyers and players

The "Cultures" of Gaming:

❱ **Pop Culture**   Games as icons and cultural artifacts

❱ **Fan Culture**   Game communities and the people who inhabit them

› Why communities form

› How to encourage the creation of fan communities and how to sustain them

> ⟩ Fan communities from related media

> ⟩ **Mass Culture**   Cultural dialogue about games

>> ⟩ Games in other media (film, television, books, etc)

>> ⟩ Games in the larger perspective of computer acclimation into culture

Experience of Play

Historical aspects of the experience of play:

> ⟩ History of play:
> ⟩ Cross-cultural anthropology of play
> ⟩ Commonalities and differences of games across national boundaries

Social aspects:

> ⟩ How games create "safe spaces" for play
> ⟩ How they are used in social settings
> ⟩ How they support and break traditional social roles

Emotional aspects:

> ⟩ How emotional responses are triggered and manipulated by games

Cognitive aspects:

> ⟩ Theories of intelligence
> ⟩ Applicability of developmental models

Psychological aspects:

> ⟩ How games rely upon and affect our understanding of ourselves and others

Human/machine interaction:

> ⟩ Uses of games in medical, training, therapeutic and other non-entertainment applications

Game Design

Principles and methodologies behind the rules and play of games.

Conceptual Game Design

Play Mechanics:

❯ What are game "rules"?

  ❯ How should they be structured?

  ❯ How do you create the right balance of obstacles/aids, penalties/rewards?

❯ When are games too hard, too easy? Why?

❯ What sorts of play mechanics work best for what sorts of people?

Boardgame and Roleplaying design:

❯ Thinking about design algorithmically

Ideas:

❯ Generating new ideas

❯ Turning ideas into game concepts

❯ Evaluating game concepts

Game theory:

❯ The study of strategic decision-making in competitive and cooperative situations

Abstract design elements:

❯ Positive and Negative feedback systems

  ❯ Game balancing tools

  ❯ Player rewards and punishments

❯ Emergent complexity

> ❯ Interactions among systems that lead to unique player experience

❯ Simulation and Emulation

> ❯ Using systems that allow flexible response versus specific behaviors for preconceived situations

Psychological design considerations:

❯ Operant conditioning

❯ Addiction in gaming

❯ Rewards and penalties

❯ Creating diverse social systems

❯ Bringing players back to the game

Interface design:

❯ Computer UI theory

❯ Balancing player control schemes—simplicity versus expressiveness

❯ The impact of specific hardware constraints—controllers, keyboards, headsets, etc.

Practical Game Design

Spatial design:

❯ Gameplay spaces

> ❯ Representational spaces

> ❯ Abstract spaces

> ❯ Space and pacing

> ❯ Space and narrative

❯ Creating densely interactive, highly responsive worlds

Task design:

❯ Action and interaction

> ❯ World/geometry interaction

> › Character interaction

> › Puzzles

❱ Providing adequate feedback to players

Design integration:

❱ Melding space and task

❱ Integrating art and gameplay

Control schemes:

❱ Movement

❱ Items and item manipulation

❱ Inventories

Training:

❱ Supporting learning with consistent challenges and appropriate feedback

❱ Communicating with the player regarding challenges, actions and abilities within the game world

Game tuning:

❱ Understanding games as dynamic systems

❱ What makes a balanced game

❱ Working with Quality Assurance and understanding play-test feedback

❱ Applying game tuning strategies in light of feedback from actual play

Play testing and player analysis:

❱ Understanding who your audience is

❱ Selecting test subjects

❱ Designing for diverse populations

❱ What criteria to use to measure success with a given audience

❱ Play test procedures

> › Design implications of platform choice

Game Programming

Aspects of traditional Computer Science—modified to address the technical aspects of gaming.

Math and Science techniques:

❱ Basic Newtonian physics

❱ Computational mechanics

❱ Linear algebra

❱ Differential equations

Style and design principles:

❱ Information design

❱ Data structures

❱ Environmental models, spatial data structures

Prototyping:

❱ Tools and skills for fast, iterative development

❱ Building flexible systems, configurable by others

Testing:

❱ Code review and test harnesses

❱ Designing tests and incorporating feedback from Quality Assurance

❱ Bug fixing, bug databases, creating stable code bases

  ❱ Programming teams—structure and working relationships

Design/Technology synthesis:

❱ Supporting player goals and actions

❱ Building intelligent, coherent, reactive game environments

❱ Platform issues

  ❱ System architecture for real time game environments and simulations

Data-driven systems:

> Building flexible systems for non-programmers to use

  ﹥ Game logic

Multimedia programming:

> Graphics

  ﹥ Rendering

  ﹥ Animation

  ﹥ Graphics System Design

> Sound

Artificial intelligence:

> Path planning

> Agent architectures

> Decision-making systems

Networks:

> Networking and Server design

> Performance metrics

> Topologies

> Protocols

> Security

Tools for designers and play analysis:

> 3-D GUI creation

> Play testing to monitor player frustration, progress and enjoyment

Visual Design

Designing, creating, and analyzing the visual components of games.

Basic Visual Design:

> Art history and theory

> Fundamentals of drawing

❭ Painting techniques

❭ Sculpting

❭ Anatomy and life drawing

❭ Physiology and kinesiology

❭ Visual design fundamentals

  ❭ Composition

  ❭ Lighting and color

  ❭ Graphic design

  ❭ Visual design in an interactive context

Motion Graphics:

❭ Animation

❭ Cinematography

❭ Camera angles and framing

❭ Visual narrative

❭ Non-narrative graphics/Abstraction as expressive tool

  ❭ Fundamental principles of architecture

Introduction to visual asset generation:

❭ 2-D graphics

❭ 3-D modeling

Architecture:

❭ History of architecture

❭ Real-world spaces vs. game spaces

Advanced Visual Asset generation:

❭ Textures

❭ Interface design

❭ Character design

  ❭ Conceptual design

> Character modeling

> Character animation

Working with 3-D Hardware:

> Procedural shading

> Lighting

> Effects

> > Game Art (digital based art with game content)

> > Visualizing Information

Audio Design

Designing and creating sound and sound environments.

Audio history and theory
Basic technical skills
Basic studio skills:

> Familiarity with hardware and software (e.g., microphones, mixers, outboard gear)

> Recording, mixing and mastering.

> Studio organization

Audio Design Fundamentals:

> Setting mood, managing tension and resolution

> Processing, mixing and controlling sound for aesthetic effect

> General workflow for game creation

> Audio engine terminology and functionality

Introduction to Interactive Audio:

> Designing sound for interactivity

> Sound effects

> Music

> Voice recording

Sound Effects:

❭ Simulation of sound environments

❭ Ambience versus musicality in soundtracks

Music:

❭ Composition

❭ Interactive scoring

3-D Audio:

❭ Fundamentals of 3-D and multi-channel sound

❭ Modeling for effects, echo, room size simulation

Interactive Storytelling

Story in Non-Interactive Media:

❭ Literary Theory and Narratology

   ❭ Aristotle

   ❭ Traditional narrative "act" structure

   ❭ Thinking abstractly and concretely about "story"

❭ Characterization in fiction, film and theatre

❭ Introduction to film and literary theory

❭ Theories of game and narrative

❭ Context-setting versus traditional storytelling

❭ Back-story and fictional setting design

❭ Creating compelling characters

Approaches to interactive narrative:

❭ Alternating fixed story with interactive game

❭ Branching trees

> ⟩ Branching narrative

> ⟩ Branching conversation

⟩ Emergent narrative approaches

⟩ Object-oriented approaches

⟩ Hypertext

⟩ Interactive fiction

Writing for other media:

⟩ Fiction-writing

⟩ Screenwriting

⟩ Playwriting

Game Production

Practical challenges of managing the development of games.

People management and collaborative development
Team make-up:

⟩ Job descriptions

⟩ Recruiting

⟩ Balancing talent, experience, budget

The phases of game development:

⟩ Pre-production

⟩ Production

⟩ Testing

Work flow:

⟩ Knowing which tools to use and when

⟩ Problem evaluation and investing appropriate resources

Group dynamics:

❯ Team building

❯ Establishing clear roles and clear goals

❯ Realities of development teams

❯ Building effective teams

  › Working as a team to realize a unified gameplay vision

  › Delegation and responsibility

Design documentation:

❯ Why document?

❯ What should you document?

❯ How much documentation is enough/too much?

❯ To storyboard or not to storyboard?

Scheduling:

❯ Creating a schedule

❯ Goals of a schedule

❯ Balancing quality and reality

❯ Working with a schedule, using it to help you ship

Communication skills:

❯ Rhetoric

❯ Communicating with peers, supervisors and subordinates

  › Communicating clearly in print and in speech

  › Collaboration skills—speaking the same language

  › Coordinating the efforts of development, quality assurance, sales, marketing, public relations and finance

  › Localization issues, processes, and skills

Product post-mortems:

❯ Evaluating decisions, after the fact

　❯ Design decisions

　❯ Process decisions

　❯ Business decisions

Business of Gaming

Economic, legal, and policy aspects of games.

Basics of game industry economics:

❯ Marketing and sales: How games currently reach an audience

❯ Retailers, shelf-space: How audiences currently reach the games

❯ Platform choices—the tradeoffs of developing for consoles, PCs and handheld devices

❯ Internationalization/globalization of development

Audience:

❯ Understanding audiences for different game genres

❯ How to reach and keep given audiences

❯ Consumer behavior and psychology (what do consumers of various sorts and various populations want?)

Publisher/Developer Relationships:

❯ The deal

　❯ What it covers

　❯ How it gets done

　❯ What it is likely to say

❯ Day-to-day: Once signed up, what interactions and processes occur

Intellectual property:

❯ Technology

❯ Content

❭ Licenses

> ❭ Acquisition of licenses

> ❭ Use of licenses

> ❭ Working with licensors

❭ Patents and the game industry

Contracts:

❭ Publisher/developer

❭ Employer/employee

❭ Contractors

Content Regulation:

❭ Industry Ratings

> ❭ U.S.

> ❭ Overseas

❭ Government regulation

> ❭ U.S.

> ❭ Overseas

TYING CORE TOPICS TO CAREER OPTIONS

This section was temporarily omitted from the February 2003 version of the document and has been revised from the earlier July 2002 edition. —Ernest

The next section of this document addresses how these Core Topics might be organized as preparation for specific professional roles. There are many more jobs, career paths and roles that can and must be filled in game development, criticism and education—the list below is in no way meant to be definitive or complete. These are simply examples to show how the curriculum framework can be "sliced" in different ways to meet different needs.

Courses we feel are not required but merely recommended for adequate education and training are presented in *italics*. All other listings represent elements of gaming education the specialties can't do without.

Game Studies Scholar and Educator

As universities and colleges add courses and even majors in game studies, this creates a need for trained educators in the field. We will discuss what an educator or scholar with a specialization in game history, theory and criticism might expect to study.

Ideally, though not necessarily, a game studies scholar would have practical experience developing games. Any instructor at the college/university level should take *all* courses in his or her field of expertise but, more importantly, understand the material at a fundamental level.

Critical Game Studies:

❯ All courses

Games and Society:

❯ All courses

Game Design:

❯ Conceptual Game Design

❯ *Optional: Practical Game Design*

Interactive Storytelling:

❯ Story in Non-interactive Media

❯ *Optional: Approaches to interactive narrative*

Game Production:

❯ People management and collaborative development

Optional: Business of Gaming:

❯ All courses

Game Technology Educator

We define this position as an instructor who specializes in training the next generation of game programmers and technologists. It might also include someone who engages in games-oriented research projects. This position requires a deep understanding of the current state of technical innovation and procedures in the field of game development. Also desirable is knowledge of game theory and design and the people/process issues surrounding game development. Ideally, this person would be capable of building and directing a group engaged in research into next generation game and simulation technology.

The technical requirements for this position are higher than for a programmer and require delving deeply into research-oriented projects at the graduate level. Game industry experience is a definite plus.

Game Design:

> ❭ Practical Game Design
> ❭ *Optional*: *Conceptual Game Design*

Game Programming:

> ❭ All courses

Visual Design:

> ❭ Visual design fundamentals

Audio Design:

> ❭ Audio design fundamentals

Game Production:

> ❭ All courses

Game Journalist

The gaming press has traditionally been dominated by self-taught fan/writers. We believe that journalistic standards, generalized tools, critical methodologies and formal training should be available to people who want to write about games. In this example, we focus on the training and skill set needs of someone who aspires to be a game critic.

In addition to the courses listed below, a game journalist should take appropriate journalism and creative writing classes.

Critical Game Studies:

> ❭ All courses

Games and Society:

> ❯ All courses

Game Design:

> ❯ Conceptual Game Design
> ❯ *Optional: Practical Game Design*

Interactive Storytelling:

> ❯ Story in Non-interactive Media
> ❯ *Optional: Approaches to interactive narrative*

Optional: Business of Gaming:

> ❯ All courses

Producer

This title means different things at different studios and publishing houses. For purposes of this example, we define a "producer" as the person responsible for managing the people and processes associated with the development of the game. The producer works with the development team to create and manage schedules, maintain the budget and ensure that the finished product meets the needs of the publisher funding it.

Business of Gaming:

> ❯ All courses

Game Production:

> ❯ All courses

Game Design:

> ❯ Practical Game Design
> ❯ *Optional: Conceptual Game Design*

Game Programming:

❯ Basic programming techniques

Visual Design:

❯ Visual design fundamentals

Audio Design:

❯ Audio design fundamentals

Interactive Storytelling:

❯ Story in Non-Interactive Media

❯ *Optional: Approaches to interactive narrative*

Optional: Critical Game Studies:

❯ All courses

Optional: Games and Society:

❯ All courses

Game Designer

Like "Producer," this title has many different interpretations. For our purposes, we will define a "Game Designer" (sometimes referred to in the game industry as the "Project Director" or "Lead Designer") is the person responsible for conceiving the overall vision of a game and then coordinating the efforts of the team members to ensure that the vision is realized to the highest degree of fidelity and quality. In addition to the courses listed below, a game designer should take at least an introductory programming course and probably more advanced courses focusing specifically on the needs of gaming.

Game Design:

❯ All courses

Interactive Storytelling:

❭ All courses

Game Programming:

❭ Basic programming techniques

Visual Design:

❭ Visual design fundamentals

Audio Design:

❭ Audio design fundamentals

Game Production:

❭ Collaborative development

❭ Process management

Optional: Business of Gaming:

❭ All courses

Optional: Games and Society

❭ All courses

Level Designer

A different kind of game designer, a Level Designer is the person who actually implements a game's minute-to-minute player experience. This job is most typically associated with the creation of 3-D worlds for first-person shooters or third-person action games. We define "Level Designer" as the person who uses content-creation tools crafted by programmers to place and manipulate assets generated by artists. The level designer creates the game world and engineers the player's gameplay experience, working in the service of an overall vision that is typically crafted by the Game Designer.

As was the case with game designers, in addition to the courses listed below, level designers should have some structured training in programming.

Game Design:

❭ All courses

Game Programming:

❭ Basic programming techniques

Visual Design:

❭ Visual design fundamentals
❭ Architecture

Audio Design:

❭ Audio design fundamentals

Game Production:

❭ Collaborative development
❭ Process management

Optional: Interactive Storytelling:

❭ Story in Non-Interactive Media

Optional: Games and Society:

❭ All courses

Programmer

Despite increasing specialization in the industry, most beginning programmers need a broad base of skills in order to get a job in game development. For the purposes of this discussion, we focus on the skills and training required to get a job as an entry-level programmer with a mid-size game development studio.

Game Design:

> Practical Game Design
> *Optional: Conceptual Game Design*

Game Programming:

> All courses

Visual design:

> Visual design fundamentals

Audio design:

> Collaborative development
> Process management

Optional: Interactive Storytelling:

> Story in Non-Interactive Media

Optional: Critical Game Studies:

> All courses

Optional: Games and Society:

> All courses

Game Graphics Artist

As is the case with programmers, the context in which an artist works determines the specific skills he or she requires. For our purposes, it is enough to say that a beginning game artist should have a broad understanding of his or her field. Again, we focus on the skills and knowledge expected of an entry-level graphic artist at a midsize game development studio. Such an artist wouldn't be expected to be master of any one aspect of his or her field but should have a working knowledge of a variety of specializations.

Game Design:

> ❯ All courses

Game Programming:

> ❯ Basic programming techniques

Visual Design:

> ❯ All courses

Audio Design:

> ❯ Audio design fundamentals

Game Production:

> ❯ Collaborative development
> ❯ Process management

Optional: Games and Society:

> ❯ All courses

Optional: Interactive Storytelling:

> ❯ Story in Non-Interactive Media

Game Audio Engineer

This career option was not included in the original document, so I have added it. The recommended courses are my own opinion and not that of the Education Committee. —Ernest

Audio engineers must have a thorough grasp of the basic principles of sound recording, mixing, and editing. They also require an understanding of the physics and psychology of sound perception. Unlike most game artists, some audio engineers also do programming to support the specific sound hardware in their target machines.

Game Design:

> ❯ Practical Game Design

Game Programming:

> ❱ Basic programming techniques
> ❱ *Optional: Multimedia programming for sound*

Visual Design:

> ❱ Visual design fundamentals

Audio Design:

> ❱ All courses

Game Production:

> ❱ Collaborative development
> ❱ Process management

Optional: Games and Society:

> ❱ All courses

Optional: Interactive Storytelling:

> ❱ Story in Non-Interactive Media

Two appendices in the original Curriculum Framework, titled "Usage Case Studies" and "Next Steps" respectively, have been omitted at this point, as their content does not apply to students or prospective developers. —Ernest

THANKS

The Education Committee would like to extend a heartfelt thanks to all the academics, developers and students who have provided input and support throughout the development of this document. Apologies in advance if anyone has been mistakenly forgotten.

Espen Aarseth, University of Bergen	Ernest Adams, Designer's Notebook
Clint Bajaikian, CB Studios	Karthik Bala, Vicarious Visions

Ranjit Bhatnagar, gameLab	John Buchanon, Electronic Arts
Michael Capps, Naval Postgraduate School/ Scion Studios	Rob Catto, Full Sail Real World Education
Mary Clarke-Miller, Art Institute of California	Dustin Clingman, Full Sail Real World Education
Sebastien Doumic, SupInfoGame	Christopher Erhart, DigiPen Institute of Technology
John Feil, LucasArts	Nick Fortugno, gameLab
Austin Grossman, University of California, Berkeley	Ian Horswill, Northwestern University
Henry Jenkins, MIT	Jesper Juul, IT University of Copenhagen
John Laird, University of Michigan	Frank Lantz, gameLab
Marc LeBlanc, Visual Concepts	Andrew Leker, Mind Control Software
Janet Murray, Georgia Tech. University	Ray Muzyka, BioWare Corp.
Rob Nideffer, University of California, Irvine	Kirk Owen, Octagon Entertainment
Celia Pearce, University of California, Irvine	Ken Perlin, NYU
Jon Purdy, University of Hull	Simon Redmon, Liverpool John Moores University
Nicolas Rioux, Ubi Soft Montreal	Dave Rorhl, EA.com
Katie Salen, Mint	Matthew Southern, Liverpool John Moores University
Kurt Squire, MIT	Michael Sweet, Audiobrain
Raphael van Lierop, The Idea Foundry	Mark Voelpel, CUNY
John Welsh, Shockwave.com	

APPENDIX

C

Jobhunting Resources and Development Tools

IN this appendix, I've assembled a collection of tools and resources to help you get that job.

MAJOR EMPLOYERS IN THE GAME INDUSTRY

Table C-1 is a list of more than 100 publishers and development companies in the game industry. It is by no means complete, however! There are many hundreds more around the world, as well as subcontractors that offer particular services—sound design or motion capture, for example. I have concentrated on large publishers and developers in the U.S., Canada, and the UK, as well as a few others. Gamasutra (www.gamasutra.com) has a much larger database, which I encourage you to visit for more information. You can also find a long list of developers and publishers at Yahoo's directory. Visit http://dir.yahoo.com, then navigate to Business and Economy > Shopping and Services > Computers > Software > Games > Developers and Publishers.

Now that interactive entertainment is big business, the game industry is subject to just as much corporate merger-mania as any other enterprise. Publishers often buy up smaller publishers and key developers; the large media companies are getting into the act too. It is getting harder and harder to keep track of who stands in what relationship to whom. For your purposes as a job-seeker, however, it doesn't really matter that Blizzard

TABLE C-1

Company	Location	Web Site
The 3DO Company	Redwood City, CA	www.3do.com
3D Realms / Apogee	Garland, TX	www.apogee1.com
Acclaim Entertainment (HQ)	Glen Cove, NY	www.acclaim.com
Acclaim Audio	Cincinnati, OH	www.acclaim.com
Acclaim Studios Austin	Austin, TX	www.acclaim.com
Acclaim Studios Cheltenham	Cheltenham, UK	www.acclaim.com
Acclaim Studios Manchester	Manchester, UK	www.acclaim.com

Game Development Companies

TABLE C-1

Company	Location	Web Site
Activision	Santa Monica, CA	www.activision.com
Argonaut Games PLC	Edgware, Middlesex, UK	www.argonaut.com
BioWare	Edmonton, AB, Canada	www.bioware.com
Black Cactus	Morden, Surrey, UK	www.blackcactus.co.uk
Black Isle	Irvine, CA	www.blackisle.com
Black Ops Entertainment	Santa Monica, CA	www.blackops.com
Blizzard Entertainment	Irvine, CA	www.blizzard.com
Blizzard North	San Carlos, CA	www.blizzard.com
Bungie Studios	Redmond, WA	www.bungie.com
Capcom Entertainment	Sunnyvale, CA	www.capcom.com
Check Six Studios	Venice, CA	www.checksixstudios.com
Cinemaware	Burlingame, CA	www.cinemaware.com
Climax Brighton	Brighton, UK	www.climax.co.uk
Climax London	London, UK	www.climax.co.uk
Climax Nottingham	Nottingham, UK	www.climax.co.uk
Climax Solent	Fareham, UK	www.climax.co.uk
Codemasters	Leamington Spa, Warwickshire, UK	www.codemasters.com
Computer Artworks	London, UK	www.artworks.co.uk
Criterion Software	Guildford, Surrey, UK	www.csl.com
Crystal Dynamics	Menlo Park, CA	www.eidosinteractive.com
Cyberlore Studios	Northhamton, MA	www.cyberlore.com
Deep Red Games	Milton Keynes, UK	www.deepred.co.uk
Disney Interactive	Burbank, CA	www.disney.com/DisneyInteractive
Dreamcatcher Interactive	Toronto, ON, Canada	www.dreamcatcherinc.com
Dreamcatcher Europe	Paris, France	http://dcegames.com
Eidos Interactive (HQ)	Wimbledon, London, UK	www.eidosinteractive.com
Eidos Interactive (USA)	San Francisco, CA	www.eidosinteractive.com
Electronic Arts (HQ)	Redwood City, CA	www.ea.com
EA Australia	Gold Coast, Australia	www.electronic-arts.com.au

Game Development Companies (continued)

TABLE C-1

Company	Location	Web Site
EA Canada	Vancouver, BC, Canada	www.ea.com
EA Los Angeles	Los Angeles, CA	www.ea.com
EA Pacific	Irvine, CA	http://westwood.ea.com
EA Europe	Chertsey, Surrey, UK	http://europe.ea.com
Empire Interactive	North Finchley, London, UK	www.empireinteractive.com
Firaxis Games	Hunt Valley, MD	www.firaxis.com
Fox Interactive	Beverly Hills, CA	www.foxinteractive.com
Funcom (HQ)	Oslo, Norway	www.funcom.com
Funcom USA	Durham, NC	www.funcom.com
Funcom Switzerland	Zurich, Switzerland	www.funcom.com
Gas Powered Games	Kirkland, WA	www.gaspowered.com
Garage Games	Eugene, OR	www.garagegames.com
Humongous Entertainment	Bothell, WA	www.funkidsgames.com
id Software	Mesquite, TX	www.idsoftware.com
Impressions Games	Cambridge, MA	http://games.sierra.com/games/impressions
Infogrames Inc. (US HQ)	New York, NY	www.infogrames.com
Infogrames Interactive, Inc.	Beverly, MA	www.infogrames.com
Infogrames Hunt Valley	Hunt Valley, MD	www.infogrames.com
Infogrames Inc.	Plymouth, MN	www.infogrames.com
Infogrames Inc.	Santa Monica, CA	www.infogrames.com
Infogrames QA	Sunnyvale, CA	www.infogrames.com
Interplay Entertainment Corp.	Irvine, CA	www.interplay.com
Ion Storm	Austin, TX	www.ionstorm.com
Koei Corporation	Burlingame, CA	www.koeigames.com
Konami (HQ)	Tokyo, Japan	www.konami.com
Konami Gaming (HQ)	Kanagawa, Japan	www.konamigaming.com
Konami of America	Redwood City, CA	www.konami.com/usa
Konami Honolulu Studio	Honolulu, HI	www.konamihwi.com

Game Development Companies *(continued)*

TABLE C-1

Company	Location	Web Site
Legend Entertainment Co.	Chantilly, VA	www.legendent.com
Lionhead Studios	Guildford, Surrey, UK	www.lionhead.co.uk
LucasArts Entertainment	San Rafael, CA	www.lucasarts.com
Maxis	Walnut Creek, CA	www.maxis.com
Microsoft Game Studios	Redmond, WA	www.microsoft.com/games/home
Midway Games	Chicago, IL	www.midway.com
Midway Games West	Milpitas, CA	www.midway.com
Midway Home Entertainment	San Diego, CA	www.midway.com
Monolith Productions	Kirkland, WA	www.lith.com
Namco Cybertainment	Bensenville, IL	www.namcoarcade.com
Nihilistic	Novato, CA	www.nihilistic.com
Nintendo of America	Redmond, WA	www.noa.com
NovaLogic	Calabasas, CA	www.novalogic.com
Oddworld	San Luis Obispo, CA	www.oddworld.com
Origin Systems	Austin, TX	http://origin.ea.com
Papyrus Racing Games	Concord, MA	www.papy.com
Paradigm Entertainment	Carrollton, TX	www.pe-i.com
Particle Systems	Sheffield, South Yorkshire, UK	www.particle-systems.com
Radical Entertainment Ltd.	Vancouver, BC, Canada	www.radical.ca
Relic Entertainment	Vancouver, BC, Canada	www.relic.com
Remedy Entertainment Ltd.	Espoo, Finland	www.remedy.fi
Revolution Software	York, UK	www.revolution.co.uk
Rockstar Games	New York, NY	www.rockstargames.com
Rockstar Games North	Leigh, Edinburgh, UK	www.rockstarnorth.com
Rockstar Vancouver	Vancouver, BC, Canada	www.rockstarvancouver.com
Rockstar Vienna	Vienna, Austria	www.rockstarvienna.com
Sammy Studios	Carlsbad, CA	www.sammystudios.com
Sammy Studios	Sherman Oaks, CA	www.sammystudios.com
Sega of America, Inc.	San Francisco, CA	www.sega.com

Game Development Companies *(continued)*

TABLE C-1

Company	Location	Web Site
Shiny Entertainment	Aliso Viejo or Newport Beach, CA	www.shiny.com
Sierra Entertainment	Bellevue, WA	www.sierra.com
Sony Computer Entertainment America	Foster City, CA	www.us.playstation.com
Sony Computer Entertainment Europe	London, UK	www.scee.com
SquareSoft	Tokyo, Japan	www.squaresoft.com
Stormfront Studios	San Rafael, CA	www.stormfront.com
Strangelite	Runcorn, Cheshire, UK	www.strangelite.com
Sunflowers GMBH	Obertshausen, Germany	www.sunflowers.de
Take2 Interactive	New York, NY	www.take2games.com
Tecmo	Torrance, CA	www.tecmoinc.com
Tiburon Entertainment	Maitland, FL	www.tiburon.com
Turbine Entertainment	Westwood, MA	www.turbinegames.com
Ubi Soft	Worldwide jobs page	http://corp.ubisoft.com/jo_offer.htm
Valve Software	Bellevue, WA	www.valvesoftware.com
Virgin Interactive	London, UK	www.virgininteractive.com

Game Development Companies *(continued)*

Entertainment is owned by Vivendi Universal, as long as they're hiring! Rather than try to clarify it all—which would be out of date in two months anyway—I've simply listed the larger publishers and developers in alphabetical order, along with their locations and web sites, so that you can see if there's anyone developing games in your area. In some cases these companies will be owned by other companies on the same list, or will simply be different offices where development is taking place. Finally, many of these companies have subsidiary offices that I didn't have room to include. UbiSoft, for example, has facilities all over the world. When in doubt, check it out!

THE IGDA BREAKING IN PAGE

No matter what else you do, be sure to visit the IGDA's Breaking In web page at www.igda.org/breakingin. There you'll find an extensive list of schools, career paths (with salary information!), developer profiles, and other resources. This is the single most useful site on the entire Internet for prospective game developers.

FREE OR INEXPENSIVE DEVELOPMENT TOOLS

I've put a lot of emphasis on the importance of a demo or portfolio, but I know students and wannabes can't always afford the big professional packages. Fortunately, you don't have to. There are a lot of free or inexpensive development tools available, and in this section I've assembled a collection of them. They won't have all the features that the high-end tools have, nor will they have much in the way of manuals, training, or customer support. But you can still get a heck of a lot done with them and make yourself a pretty spectacular demo if you have the talent.

Programming Tools

There are literally hundreds of free software development tools available. The best-known of these are the GNU C and C++ compilers, but there are also editors and debuggers, as well as development tools for every language from the most ancient (FORTRAN) to more recent ones like Python and Lua. To obtain programming tools, you need look no further than SourceForge (www.sourceforge.net). This web site is a gigantic database for the Open Source movement, and it contains pointers to many more resources.

Following is a short list of game-specific programming tools that you may find useful as well. Not all of them are free:

Graphics Engines	Web Site
Genesis 3D	www.genesis3d.com
CrystalSpace	http://crystal.sourceforge.net/drupal/
Ogre	http://ogre.sourceforge.net
Nebula Device	www.radonlabs.de/nebula.html
XEngine	http://xengine.sourceforge.net
Torque	www.garagegames.com
Destiny3D (coming soon)	www.destiny3d.com

Gameplay Engines	Web Site
3D Rad	www.3drad.com/
RPG Toolkit	www.rpgtoolkit.com
FreeCraft real-time strategy gaming engine	www.freecraft.org
Verge role-playing engine	www.verge-rpg.com

Art Tools

Thanks to the mod community, there are loads of good 3-D modeling tools to choose from. Milkshape 3D is one of the most popular and supports a wide variety of file formats.

3-D Modeling Tools and Utilities	Web Site
Blender	www.blender3d.com
Milkshape 3D	www.swissquake.ch/chumbalum-soft
Anim8tor	www.anim8tor.com
Art of Illusion	www.artofillusion.org
3DMatrix	www.digitalscores.com/jcsoftware/
UVMapper texture mapping tool	www.uvmapper.com

2-D (Image Editing/Pixel Painting) Tools	Web Site
GNU Image Manipulation Program (GIMP)	www.gimp.org
Pixia	www.ab.wakwak.com/~knight/
PhotoPlus and DrawPlus (Serif Software)	www.freeserifsoftware.com

Resources for Finding Tools	Web Site
3D Café	www.3dcafe.com
3dcgi	www.3dcgi.com/learn/free/free-3d.htm
Ultimate 3D Links	www.3dlinks.com

Audio Tools

Following is a list of free or inexpensive audio tools, for both waveform editing and music creation:

Waveform Editors and Tools	Web Site
Encounter 2000	www.waschbusch.com/software.asp
Sound Engine (Cycle of 5th)	www.cycleof5th.com/download
Audacity	http://audacity.sourceforge.net
Goldwave	www.goldwave.com

MIDI and Music Tools	Web Site
Jazz++ MIDI sequencer	www.jazzware.com
Cubasis InWired	www.steinberg.net/en/ct/support/downloads/freeware

Resources for Finding Tools	Web Site
Steinberg's freeware page	www.steinberg.net/en/ct/support/downloads/freeware
Database Audio	www.databaseaudio.co.uk
AnalogX freeware page	www.analogx.com/contents/download/audio.htm

Office Tools

Can't afford Microsoft Office? You don't have to. Try OpenOffice.org for a completely free, full-featured word processing program that is compatible with Microsoft Word. It doesn't have *all* the bells and whistles (no thesaurus), but what do you expect for nothing? As with programming tools, visit SourceForge.net for dozens of other free office tools.

PROFESSIONAL GAME DEVELOPMENT WEB SITES

There are hundreds of web sites devoted to amateur game development, but surprisingly few aimed specifically at professionals.

❱ **GameDev.net (www.gamedev.net)** GameDev is the best web site available for beginning developers and bedroom coders, but it's not just for amateurs. It has tons of articles, as well as book reviews, tutorials, forums, and other resources.

❱ **Gamasutra (www.gamasutra.com)** Gamasutra is *the* web site for professional game developers of all kinds. It also happens to be the home of my popular Designer's Notebook series of articles. It's not a tutorial site for newbies, but you'll find a great deal of useful material there all the same. Don't be afraid that everything will be over your head; it won't, although some of the programming articles can be very technical. Best of all, it has databases of game companies, organized by location and function, and a database of job openings.

FlipCode (www.flipcode.com) Like GameDev.net, FlipCode is aimed at the skilled amateur. It doesn't have the lists of jobs or database of subcontractors that Gamasutra has, but there are plenty of development resources.

Yahoo's Game Programming Directory (http://dir.yahoo.com) Navigate to Recreation > Games > Computer Games > Programming. There you'll find a list of several dozen programming-oriented sites, with the most popular ones listed at the top.

> ❭ **Webring.com's List of Game Programming Webrings (www.webring.com)**
> Navigate through menus to Home > Computers & Internet > Software >
> Development > Game Programming. This will let you find all sorts of webrings,
> each of which concentrates on a particular area of game development.

Console Manufacturers' Web Sites

The console manufacturers are finally becoming a bit less secretive about developing
for their machines. Here are each of their web pages on the subject. Some links on
their pages may only be accessible to licensed developers, however:

Sony PS2 Linux Kit	http://us.playstation.com/hardware/more/SCPH-97047.asp
Xbox Developers' Page	www.xbox.com/dev
Nintendo Developers' Page	www.noa.com

Game Job Postings

Your best bet for game job postings is individual publishers' and developers' web
sites, because they will have the most detailed and up-to-the minute information. The
problem is that there are a heck of a lot of them to look through. For collections of job
postings in one place, you should also try some of the following:

Gamasutra Jobs Page	www.gamasutra.com/jobsearch
GameJOBS.com	www.gamejobs.com
games-match (US)	www.games-match.com
games-match (UK)	www.games-match.co.uk
Mary-Margaret.com	www.mary-margaret.com

NETWORKING RESOURCES

Networking is the key to finding a job. You're much more likely to hear of a position
that really interests you by meeting and talking to other game developers than by
sending in résumés cold to the addresses listed in job ads. Here follows a collection of
resources to help you get in touch with other developers.

Gatherings

Forums and bulletin boards are OK, but the best way to network is to get in the same
room with other developers. Here are some of the places they meet:

❱ **IGDA Chapter Meetings (www.igda.org/chapters)** IGDA chapters connect members in specific geographic areas and help promote regional game development communities. Chapter members network, learn from each other, identify upcoming challenges and issues in their work, and help define the characteristics of the professional community where they live and work. Meetings are almost always free and open to non-members, unless the chapter is conducting an event that it needs to pay for.

❱ **Game Developers' Conference (www.gdconf.com)** *The* annual professional conference for the game industry, held every year in San Jose, California. If you can only get to one event a year, make it this one. The conference is affiliated with the IGDA, so IGDA members get a discount. If you can't afford the price of admission, you can volunteer to work for about 20 hours over the five days that the conference lasts, and that will get in you free. Volunteering is a blast, too—some developers actually do that in preference to attending in the normal way.

❱ **Electronic Entertainment Expo (E3) (www.e3expo.com)** E3 is the industry's annual trade show in America, produced by the publishers' trade association, IDSA. Its primary purpose is for publishers and distributors to show games to retailers, but there are many developers wandering around as well, scoping out the competition. Entrance to the expo itself is quite inexpensive, but the associated conference costs more. Normally held in Los Angeles.

❱ **D.I.C.E Summit (www.interactive.org/dice)** The name stands for Design, Innovate, Communicate, Entertain, and the event is put on annually by the Academy of Interactive Arts and Sciences. It's a much smaller event than the GDC, but is attended by a good many industry bigwigs, which gives it a somewhat "exclusive" feel.

❱ **GDC Europe (www.gdc-europe.com)** The European version of the Game Developers' Conference, presented by the same group. It is a bit smaller than its American counterpart, but growing. Held annually in London.

❱ **European Computer Trade Show (ECTS) (www.ects.com)** The European equivalent of E3, though far smaller. Despite the name, it is a game show, not a general computer show. Held annually in London, in conjunction with GDC Europe.

❱ **SIGGRAPH (www.siggraph.org)** SIGGRAPH is the graphics Special Interest Group of the Association for Computing Machinery, and their annual conference is an eye-popping extravaganza for anyone interested in computer graphics and animation. Highly recommended for artists and high-end graphics programmers, though not necessarily a place to look for jobs in the game industry.

) **Milia (www.milia.com)** Milia covers a variety of digital media, including interactive entertainment. For several years this was *the* cool new place to be seen in the game business. Milia is held at Cannes in France, and a certain amount of the Cannes chic rubbed off on it. More recently the event has lost a little of its hyper-cool image, but there's still a strong game presence.

) **International Game Developers Meetup Day (http://gamedev.meetup .com/)** This is a web site that allows groups of game developers to find each other for regular meetings, in dozens of cities around the world.

Resources for Women

There are many "girl gamers" web sites, but girl gamers aren't really the same as female game developers. I know of only two resources specifically dedicated to issues related to women in the game industry.

) **Women in Game Development (WIGD) Committee of the IGDA (www.igda.org/committees/women.php)** The Women in Game Development (WIGD) Committee was formed to create a positive impact on the game development industry with respect to gender balance and equity.

) **Women_dev mailing list (www.pairlist.net/mailman/listinfo/women_dev)** This is a fairly active mailing list made up of professional female game developers, plus a few students and even a few men—I'm a regular reader myself. Visit the web site for information on subscribing. In order to avoid problems with trolls, subscription is not immediate; you will have to wait to be approved by the listmistress. Approval is automatic, however; there isn't a test!

Resources for Minorities

Unfortunately, at this point I know of only one group for minorities in game development.

) **Culture Rock Network (http://groups.yahoo.com/group/culture_rock/)** A Yahoo Group for professional people of color and culture who want to get into the interactive entertainment industry, or who are already in it. Its purpose is to bring together skills, experiences, ideas and awareness of what is given and how other races and their influence can play a major part of the consumer's gaming experience.

Miscellaneous Resources

Following is a mixed bag of other useful resources for newcomers to the game industry:

❯ **IGDA Students and Newbies Page** (www.igda.org/students/)

❯ **IDGA Breaking In Page** (www.idga.org/breakingin)

❯ **IDGA Education Page** (www.idga.org/academia) Although primarily intended for academics, this is where you can go to find the most recent version of the Curriculum Framework document in Appendix B.

❯ **Salary Information** (www.igda.org/biz/salary_survey.php) *Game Developer* magazine publishes an annual salary survey. You can download a PDF copy.

❯ **Tom Sloper's Advice Page** (www.sloperama.com/advice.html) Designer Tom Sloper has put together an excellent collection of lessons about the game business for newcomers. He also answers letters from wannabes.

Glossary of Game
Industry Terms

I'VE included this glossary to help you understand some of the more arcane terms used by the game industry. Most of them are development terms from the crafts of art, audio, and programming, but there are also legal, business, and a few job-hunting terms as well. If you're a complete newcomer to game development, it will help you to be familiar with these terms before you go to your first job interview. It is by no means complete, however!

2-D graphics Collectively refers to graphical data presented without a 3-D display engine, including backgrounds, user interface elements, and *sprites*. *Textures*, while they are two-dimensional, are normally considered part of the 3-D graphics because they are used to help create the appearance of 3-D models.

3-D acceleration hardware Specialized chips and boards designed to accelerate the display of three-dimensional environments by taking over computing tasks from the CPU. They include a specialized graphics processor, a microprocessor specifically designed for *rendering* 3-D scenes, and extra memory to store *geometry*, fonts, *textures*, and other building blocks of 3-D graphics. The current generation of high-speed 3-D games would not be possible without it.

3-D graphics Collectively refers to graphical data presented by means of *3-D rendering*. 3-D graphics includes *geometry, textures,* and other data. These graphics are usually designed in such a way that they can be displayed from any perspective, as if the player were actually inside the scene.

3-D rendering A collection of software techniques for taking the *geometry* of a three-dimensional scene made up of *polygonal* objects, and displaying it on the screen from a particular perspective. Video games do 3-D rendering in real time, usually assisted by *3-D acceleration hardware*. For movies, which are *pre-rendered,* the scenes can be far more complex and detailed.

A-life Artificial life, a game about managing the lives of simulated living things (people, animals, or fictitious creatures). Unlike most games in which simulated beings are just "units" with few of the characteristics of living things, in A-life games they have complete life cycles. They are born, die of old age (sometimes), reproduce, and require food, shelter, and other needs on an ongoing basis.

Action adventure   An *adventure game* in which there are some action elements and the game moves a bit faster.

Action game   Any game whose challenges consist primarily of motor skills tests: hand-eye coordination, accurate shooting and steering, timing jumps or runs, and so on. Almost all arcade games are action games. Many people unfamiliar with video games believe that they are all action games.

Advances   Money paid to an external developer, usually over time in a series of *milestone* payments, to develop a game for a publisher. When the game is being sold, the developer's *royalties* are withheld until the money advanced has been repaid.

Adventure game   A fairly slow-moving game in which the player takes the role of a person in a world having an adventure of some kind. Adventure games have strong plot lines, distinct characters, and interesting scenery. Their challenges are usually logical or conceptual, based on the player solving puzzles, rather than action challenges requiring physical skill or luck.

Alpha (test)   Alpha is the point in the development of a game at which all the features of the game are present (even if all the data and *levels* are not) and the game can be thoroughly tested. When a game reaches alpha, alpha testing begins. Alpha testing is internal testing, done by the publisher, developer, or a combination of the two.

Alpha channel   Nothing to do with either *alpha testing* or "the *channel*"! In image files, an alpha channel is additional information stored about each pixel in the image to indicate how opaque that pixel is if it is to be blended with another image. The alpha channel is usually stored as a single additional byte on each pixel, with a value of 0 representing totally opaque pixels and 255 representing totally transparent ones. Different values in between are used for representing varying degrees of opacity. A 32-bit image normally consists of one 24-bit image plus an 8-bit greyscale alpha channel.

API   Application Programming Interface. A pre-written software package of routines that a programmer can build into his program to accomplish certain tasks. An API is normally designed to provide an interface between the application program (in our case, a game) and something else like an input or output device.

Armature   A collection of data that defines the skeletal structure of a 3-D model that is intended to be animated. The armature indicates to the software how the joints move and how they are hierarchically related to one another—for example, the position of the wrist in 3-D space is dependent on the position of the elbow, which in turn is dependent on the position of the shoulder.

ASIC   Application-Specific Integrated Circuit. A silicon chip designed to handle a particular data processing or other electronic function, as opposed to a general-purpose chip like a microprocessor which can have many possible uses.

Assembler   A programming tool, a program that converts a file of *assembly language* machine instructions into an *object file*.

Assembly language   A human-readable form of a computer's internal machine language. Each different kind of processor has its own assembly language—68000 assembly language, 8086 assembly language, and so on. Formerly the primary way in which computer games were written, assembly language is now only used for optimizing particularly speed-sensitive parts of the code. An assembly language file is converted by an *assembler* into an *object file*.

Assets   A collective term for the audio, video, animation, and other data files required by a game. Sometimes also referred to as the content. With modern games using hundreds or thousands of files, asset management is now an important issue for developers.

Avatar   Generally, a character in a game who represents, and is controlled by, the player. Mario in Nintendo's *Mario Brothers* games is the player's avatar.

Backstory   The background story that precedes the events taking place in a game and usually explains the situation of the game. The backstory is sometimes printed as an introduction in the manual; more commonly it is shown as a non-interactive movie that the player sees before starting the first level of a game. Occasionally, the backstory is not given to the player in advance, but revealed to her over time during the course of the game (this is the normal procedure for mysteries). In the movie *Star Wars*, Luke Skywalker's secret heritage, which he gradually comes to learn, is part of the backstory.

Beta (test)   When a game in development reaches the point that all the features are present in the software and all the assets have been created, it is said to be "at beta." At this point beta-testing can begin; the game can be tested with all its assets. In open beta-testing, members of the public are allowed to help test the game.

Blue screen   See *matting*.

Bug database   A database of bugs maintained by the testing manager. All bugs found by the testers are logged in the bug database. This tells the programmers what they need to fix. When a fix has been tested and proven to work, the bug is "closed."

Build   A collection of the files needed to play a game—for example, the *executable* program plus all the data files that it reads. This does not mean that the game is complete, however, only that the files needed as of the current time are assembled in one place, and the program will not crash because data is missing. When a build is assembled, the features that have been implemented so far can be tested. It is considered good practice to assemble a working build at regular intervals throughout development (daily, during testing), rather than leave the program in pieces and try to patch it all together at the end. *Milestone* deliveries normally consist of builds.

Bump-mapping In 3-D graphics programming, a technique for making the surface of a polygonal object appear bumpy rather than smooth, without adding additional polygons to the object. A bump map is a greyscale image showing where the bumps are; this information is then used to modify the *texture* on the surface of the object, giving it a bumpy appearance.

Business model A company's plan for selling its products, usually characterized in terms of how it intends to charge for them. If the consumer pays on an ongoing basis to receive new data or information, for example, the business model is called a "subscription model." If they buy each item individually, it is called a "retail model," and so on. Online games are normally sold on a subscription model.

Channel 1) A slang term for the status of a game as it ships from the publisher to the distributors and retailers. "We've got a quarter of a million units in the channel" means that the publisher has manufactured and sold 250,000 copies of a game to distributors or retailers (some of which may have been bought by customers). 2) A single monaural stream of audio information intended for one speaker. Stereo sound can also be called "2-channel" sound. With the advent of home theater systems, some media formats support 5 channels.

Codec Conjunction of "compressor" and "decompressor." A codec is a library of software routines that a program can call upon to compress or decompress data (usually audio and video data) for playback to the speakers and screen. One codec usually handles one particular compressed file format—MP3 files, for example. See *data compression*.

COG See *Cost of goods*.

Color depth The amount of space required to store the color of each pixel in an image. An 8-bit image (a picture with a color depth of 8 bits) can display only 256 possible colors; a 16-bit image can display 65,536 colors; 24-bit images can display more possible colors than the human eye can perceive, and 24 bits is generally considered the largest amount of color depth required for a simple image. Images with 32-bit color depth are usually using 24 bits per pixel for the visible image and a further 8 bits for the *alpha channel*.

Color space   Color may be represented numerically by several different means, which may be more or less suitable for use with different kind of media (video screens, film, printed paper, and so on). Programmers most frequently represent color using the RGB (red-green-blue) color space, because this corresponds directly with the colors of the phosphor dots in a monitor. Printers prefer the CMYK (cyan-magenta-yellow-black) color space, which corresponds to the colors of ink used in four-color printing. There are many other forms of color space representation as well.

Compiler   A programming tool, a program which takes as input a file of program code (a source file) written in a high-level language, such as C++, processes it, and produces as output a file of machine code for a particular machine (an *object file*).

Compression   1) See *data compression*. 2) See *signal compression*.

Conversion   See *porting*.

Cost of goods   The amount that it costs to physically manufacture the actual product, including its box and manual, and ship it to the warehouse. Beware, however: with console games, which are normally manufactured for the publisher by the console manufacturer, the cost of goods is sometimes quoted with the console manufacturer's license fee included, so be sure to check. With a PC game, it means only the cost of manufacturing the physical objects themselves.

Crunch time *or* crunch mode   Any time that the whole team (production, development, or both) is working very hard to meet a deadline; more specifically, the period near the end of the project when everyone is trying to eliminate the last bugs and polish the game to its highest state before release. During this period it is not uncommon for a few people to work 80- and even 100-hour weeks.

Cut-scene   A short, noninteractive scene in a game used to display narrative material, usually part of an ongoing storyline, in between periods of interactive play. These used to be presented with *pre-rendered* movies, but are now more frequently presented using the game's graphics engine. This way the cut-scene can be integrated seamlessly with the rest of the game.

Data compression   Any of a wide variety of algorithms for reducing the amount of space that data require in a storage medium, usually by finding and removing redundancies in the data. For example, the telephone book could be made smaller if it only printed the first names of all the people with the same last name, rather than repeating the last name for each person. Data compression techniques can be divided into two kinds: *lossy* and *lossless*. Data compression is a complex and highly mathematical subject, a branch of information theory. Few programmers write their own data compression routines, however; they rely on *codecs,* which do it for them.

Death march   See *crunch time*.

Debugger   A programming tool that allows the programmer to monitor and modify the internal workings of a program as it runs.

Demo   1) A collection of a job-seeker's previous work, used to demonstrate his or her skills and experience to potential employers. This can take various forms: a portfolio of drawings; a PowerPoint presentation; a computer program; a CD or tape of music or other types of audio; a videotape or DVD of animations or other video data; a web site. A demo is of paramount importance to any job-seeker looking for design or development work. 2) A small computer program, constructed within strict size limits and other rules, that demonstrates extremely skilled programming techniques. Collectively, this activity is part of what is called the "demo scene," chiefly in Europe. This is a hobbyist activity and is not related to commercial game development.

Demo reel   A *demo* in the form of a video tape. Usually used by videographers and animators.

Demo scene   See *demo,* second definition.

Dev station *or* dev kit   A collection of hardware and software tools that allows a programmer to create software for a console machine. A dev station normally consists of a special game console with its anti-piracy features turned off so it can read ordinary CDs, plus a means of connecting the console to a PC so game software and data can be downloaded into it. It may also include special debugging hardware. The dev station for a given console is only available from the console manufacturer, and normally only sold to licensed developers for that machine.

DirectX   An *API,* developed by Microsoft, which allows programmers to control the large variety of audio, video, and input devices available on a Windows PC through a single standard set of routines. It is distributed free of charge, but controlled by Microsoft.

DSP   Digital Signal Processor, a specialized chip for manipulating audio (and sometimes video) data. DSPs are at the heart of the sound boards in PCs, and are also built into game consoles. By handing off certain tasks to the DSP, the main CPU is free to do other things.

Dynamic range   In digital audio, the range of loudness intended to be represented by a certain number of bits of data. For example, one byte is only capable of representing 256 levels of dynamic range, whereas two bytes are capable of representing 65,536 levels of dynamic range. When combining audio recorded at different times, it is important to match the dynamic ranges of each of the samples appropriately to achieve a proper effect. If a quiet sound (billiard balls clicking together) is recorded with the same dynamic range as a loud sound (a door slamming), then, when mixed, the billiard balls will sound just as loud as the door. To correct this, the dynamic range of the quieter sound may be *signal compressed*. The actual volume at which the sound is played is of course determined by the speakers and amplifier.

Earn out   A product is said to earn out when it has made enough money for the developer's *royalties* to recoup the *advances* they were paid to build it. Once the game has earned out, the developer starts receiving royalties for it. Unfortunately, with many games the advances are so high (the game costs so much to develop) that it never does earn out and the developer does not receive any royalties.

Edit suite   A collection of gear, and sometimes the rooms containing the gear, for editing audio and video.

EDL   Edit Decision List. Given a long tape (or file) containing audio or video data from a recording session or video shoot, an EDL is a series of start-points and end-points where the tape should be cut up to select the desired material.

Egoshooter   European term for an *FPS*.

Engine   A subset of a computer program that performs a particular task, usually on an ongoing basis. Engines are designed in such a way that they can be used in several different games, thus saving the cost of redeveloping that part of the code for each game. The most common types of engines are graphics engines (which display 3-D spaces on the screen) and physics engines (which compute the behavior, including collisions) of moving objects in a 3-D space. Some development companies license their engines to other development companies to allow them to make games more quickly.

Executable   A file of machine code that is ready to be run by a computer. This is the end product of the programming process. Files ending in .EXE on Windows machines are executables.

External development   Game development done outside a publishing company, by a development company under contract to the publisher.

External producer   A producer who is producing a game that is being developed elsewhere. If Electronic Arts publishes a game that is being developed by Stormfront Studios, a separate company, the producer at EA is an external producer. Stormfront Studios may also have a person heading up the development team with the title of producer; this person is an *internal producer*.

Fidget   A short animation for a game character who is waiting around for something to do, so he doesn't stand unnaturally still. A character who isn't doing anything should exhibit one of several possible fidgets every 15 or 20 seconds. Also referred to as an *idle animation*.

Finite state machine   In games, a software technique that can be used to create the artificial intelligence for autonomous, or partially autonomous, units. At any given time, each unit is in exactly one of a number of states defined by the finite state machine. For example, a soldier could be in one of the states of advancing, retreating, holding ground, or dead. The state will determine what behavior the soldier exhibits in the game. For each state, a prescribed set of conditions determine under what circumstances the unit will change to a different state. For example, if a soldier's fear attribute goes above a certain threshold, he could change from the state of advancing to the state of retreating, with accompanying changes in his visible behavior. If his health attribute drops to zero, his state changes to dead, from which (presumably) there are no conditions for further change. Game designers work together with programmers to define the finite state machines for all the units that will need them.

FMV   See *full-motion video*.

Forward kinematics   See *kinematics*. A computer animation technique in which the position of a creature's limbs are computed starting from its torso and working outwards along its joints to its hands and feet, the position of each subsequent joint being dependent on the ones that came before it in the hierarchy.

FPS   1) First-Person Shooter, a game in which the player sees the game world from the point of view of a person in that world, and runs around shooting at things with a variety of weaponry. Also sometimes called a *POV shooter*. 2) An abbreviation of Frames Per Second. See *frame rate*.

Frame buffer   A region of memory in which the image that will appear on the screen is *rendered*. Once everything has been drawn in the frame buffer, the graphics hardware is informed that it is ready for display.

Frame rate   The rate at which a computer or other display system displays new frames on a screen, measured in frames per second. Movies have a fixed frame rate of 24 frames per second. American television displays 29.97 frames per second. Many computer monitors are set to 70, 80, or even 100 frames per second to avoid flicker. Video games update the screen at regular intervals, so they also have a frame rate. If the computer has many tasks to do in each frame, its frame rate may drop to the point where the game has a jerky appearance. A high frame rate is a sign of fast, efficient code (or fast hardware).

FRP   Fantasy Role-Playing game. Not all such games are placed in fantasy settings, however. See *RPG*.

Full-motion video   Video data that fills the screen and in which motion can appear in any part of it. FMV is the equivalent of TV; the whole screen may be active. In the early days of computerized video, it was often necessary to display video in a small window, or to restrict areas of motion to a subset of the whole screen, because the processor was not powerful enough or the storage medium fast enough to deliver FMV. With modern hardware the distinction between full- and partial-motion is no longer meaningful. The term is often used to simply refer to video files played by the game.

Full producer   See *producer*.

Genre   A group of games possessing similar gameplay, though not necessarily similar settings. Unlike novels, which can be categorized into genres by their subject matter and setting (romance, science fiction, etc.), games are categorized into genres by how the player plays the game (driving a vehicle, commanding an army, breeding creatures, and so on) regardless of the setting.

Geometry   Collectively, all the *polygons* that make up a 3-D scene or model.

Gold   Not the same thing as in the music industry! In music a record is said to have "gone gold" when it has sold 500,000 copies. A game "goes gold" when it is completely tested, has passed quality assurance, and is ready for manufacturing.

Hardware acceleration   See *3-D acceleration hardware*.

Headhunter   See *recruiter*.

IDE   Integrated Development Environment. A suite of programming tools that all work together seamlessly to help a software engineer write, compile, and debug code. Not to be confused with IDE disk drives, in which the acronym stands for Integrated Drive Electronics.

Idle animation   See *fidget*.

Interactive fiction   Another term for *text adventures*. Interactive fiction is no longer commercially viable, but is now created by hobbyists who are interested in exploring the potential of interactive, text-based literature as an art form. They usually give their work away for free.

Internal development   Development done by a team working as employees at a publishing company. Internal development means that the publisher pays their salaries and has direct oversight on their work. It is generally more costly to the publisher than *external development*, but the additional degree of control is sometimes worth it.

Internal producer   A producer who is in charge of, or at least working to produce, a product being developed within the same company. An internal producer can be within a publishing company, if it is doing *internal development,* or within a development company. A producer at a development company is primarily a development manager and does not have the same obligations or responsibilities as a producer at a publisher.

Inverse kinematics　See *kinematics.* A computer animation technique in which the position of a creature's limbs are determined from an external influence on them. For example, if a creature is reaching out to pick up an object, the position of its hand is determined from the position of the object. The angles of the joints in its limbs are then subsequently computed from this data plus the position of the creature's torso. This technique helps to make the creature's interaction with objects in the world look correct.

JPEG　Joint Photographic Experts Group, an industry standards organization whose role is to define data storage formats for still image data. JPEG normally refers to a *lossy-compression* image file format defined by this group—for example, "a JPEG picture" is a file in JPEG format. The JPEG compression algorithm has the great advantage that you can control how much quality you sacrifice and how much compression you obtain as a result.

Keying　A television-industry term for *matting.*

Kinematics　A computer animation technique in which, rather than displaying a fixed animation that looks the same way every time it is played, the computer computes the position of a creature's arms, legs, and so on, with each step (or other action) it takes. See *forward kinematics* and *inverse kinematics.*

LBE　Location-Based Entertainment. This refers to forms of entertainment, usually computerized but not always interactive, installed in a particular location that the public must travel to. In practice this usually means "ride simulators" and "experiences" of one kind and another in theme parks or tourist attractions.

Level　1) A self-contained mission or scenario within a game, with its own starting conditions and victory condition. The term comes from arcade gaming, in which the game usually proceeds in a series of stages at increasing levels of difficulty. In war games they are often called missions or scenarios. Levels are typically built by *level designers.* 2) The volume at which a sound is recorded (audio level). When mixing sounds that were recorded separately, audio engineers must adjust their levels to make aesthetic sense—a pencil being dropped should not be as loud as a train wreck.

Level designer　A designer responsible for building *levels* (first definition) in a game under development. Level designers are usually junior staff. Given the game's content and gameplay mechanics, they devise a series of levels containing challenges of different kinds, generally using a level editor, a tool specially written for the purpose.

Linker   A programming tool that takes as input multiple *object files* and links them all together to form a working *executable*.

Localization   The process of modifying a game for sale in a different country with a different language. In addition to changing the text and audio, sometimes the code and graphics need to be changed, especially if the destination country has censorship laws that prohibit some of the content in the game.

Lossless compression   A data-compression technique that preserves all the data, enabling it to be decompressed back into a file identical to the original. ZIP archives on PCs use a lossless compression algorithm. See *data compression*.

Lossy compression   A data-compression technique that results in a certain amount of information being irretrievably lost. Lossy compression may be used in cases where the loss of information does not significantly harm the results—in image, video, or audio data where the eye or the ear will not detect the difference. It may not be used with text (which would result in misspellings) or program code (which would result in bugs). *JPEG* is a lossy image compression technique. The amount of degradation to the image (and corresponding amount of compression) is settable by the *codec*. See *data compression*.

Matrix management   A form of company structure in which authority is exercised along two dimensions rather than down a single hierarchy. In matrix management, each non-managerial employee has, in effect, two managers. For example, all the employees on a given project report to a project manager, regardless of what their job is; but they also each report to a manager based on their position—for example, all the programmers report to a programming manager regardless of which project they are on. This system causes conflict and confusion. Some people seem to have forgotten the old adage that "no man can serve two masters." Nevertheless, companies persist in trying it from time to time.

Matting   A video or film technique in which one image is superimposed over another. The most familiar use of this trick is in TV weather forecasting: the weather announcer stands in front of a blue or green screen in the studio, and the weather images are superimposed by special equipment anywhere blue (or green) appears, making it look as if the screen is active.

MDF   Marketing Development Funds. This is money allocated by a publisher to help market a specific game. It's usually spent on advertising, special store displays, and public events designed to attract press coverage.

Memory leak   A programming error, a condition in which a program repeatedly requests more memory from the operating system but does not return it when done, eventually causing it to use up all available memory and crash.

Middleware   Pre-written libraries of software routines that a development company can license for use in their games, generally *engines* of one kind and another. Middleware is now big business, helping to cut the development time in a game.

MIDI   Musical Instrument Digital Interface, a data format for recording the notes played by a musical instrument and storing this information in a file. Note that MIDI does not record the actual sound made by the instrument (its waveform), only which keys are struck (if it is a keyboard instrument), how hard, and for how long. A *synthesizer* uses the information about which key was struck to play back a pre-recorded sample of a musical instrument, creating synthetic music. A MIDI file can store information about multiple instruments at once, and other details such as repetition and drumbeats. MIDI files have the advantage of being very small, and the disadvantage that the quality of the playback depends entirely on the quality of the synthesizer. With the advent of efficient music compression via MP3 files, most games do not ship with MIDI files, but composers use MIDI files to record and edit their compositions. MIDI files are edited with a piece of software called a *sequencer.*

Milestone   A date upon which a development team is supposed to deliver a *build* to the publisher, usually containing certain features set out in the development contract. If the game is being *externally developed,* the publisher's acceptance of the milestone build triggers a milestone payment. Milestone payments are part of an external developer's *advances.*

MIP-mapping   A 3-D graphics technique in which multiple versions of a *texture* are stored in memory at different resolutions. When the camera is far away from the texture, the geometry engine selects the lower-resolution texture to show, rather than trying to shrink the high-resolution texture down mathematically. The results more accurately mimic human vision.

MMOG   Massively-Multiplayer Online Game. A game played over the Internet by hundreds or thousands of players simultaneously.

MMORPG   Massively-Multiplayer Online Role-Playing Game. An *MMOG* that is specifically about role-playing and (usually) character development through combat or other gameplay activities. *EverQuest* and *Asheron's Call* are examples.

MOO   MUD, Object-Oriented. A *MUD* in which it is possible for the players to design and introduce objects of their own, with properties defined by a scripting language.

Motion capture   A technique for converting the motion of things in the real world (usually people) into data that can be turned into animations, generally 3-D models. There are various ways of capturing the data. Motion capture is frequently used on athletes for sports games and martial artists for combat games.

MP3   A *lossy-compression* audio file format defined by the *MPEG* organization. MP3s do for audio what *JPEG* does for still images: they enable the audio to be compressed to different levels with differing degrees of quality loss.

MPEG   Motion Picture Experts Group, an industry standards organization whose role is to define data storage formats for video data (which also includes embedded audio data). MPEG normally refers to a *lossy-compression* file format defined by this group—"an MPEG movie" is a file in MPEG format.

MUD   Multi-User Dungeon (or Domain, depending on who you ask). A text-only precursor to the *MMORPG*, although MUDs typically only have hundreds rather than thousands of players. Most MUDs are noncommercial, built by hobbyists, and free to play in. Because they are text-only, they require a good deal of imagination.

MUSH   Multi-User Shared Hallucination, a type of *MUD* typically designed more for social role-playing rather than combat. *AmberMUSH* is an example set in Roger Zelazny's fictitious world of Amber.

NDA   Non-Disclosure Agreement. A short contract in which one party agrees not to reveal a secret that the other party is about to tell him. Normally, no money changes hands; the party gives their promise to keep it secret in exchange for getting to know what it is. Used all the time in the game industry when people need to talk to others about confidential intellectual property issues.

Object file   The output of a *compiler* or *assembler,* an object file contains machine code, but not in a form that it can be run by the computer. The object files must be linked together into an *executable* by the *linker* first. The term is not related to *object-oriented programming.*

Object-oriented programming or language   A new (in the last 20 years) generation of programming languages and techniques, gradually supplanting older ones, in which programmers are encouraged to think about a program in terms of data structures (called "objects") and various manipulations that can be done to them (called "methods") rather than as one giant mechanism for accomplishing a variety of tasks. This approach is thought to make the program code more understandable and re-usable, and less prone to bugs. C++ and Java are both object-oriented programming languages, containing features to support these concepts not found in older languages like C and FORTRAN. There was initial resistance in the game community to using object-oriented methods because the early object-oriented *compilers* produced somewhat slower machine code, but this is disappearing.

Offer letter   A formal offer of a job. An offer letter should spell out at least your start date, your starting salary, and any other negotiated benefits, such as bonuses, especially if they differ from the company's standard policy. To accept the job, you sign one copy of the offer letter and return it to the company.

Open source   A movement in the software development community to make the source code of applications available for other people to work on. Although this will never become standard for commercial games, it is increasingly popular for tools and middleware.

OpenGL   An *open-source* hardware-independent *API* for displaying graphics in a machine-independent fashion. Its competition is *DirectX* for Windows.

Performance analyzer   See *profiler*.

Persistent world   An online game that simulates a world that continues to exist and change even while a player is logged off. *MMORPGs* are persistent worlds, but a persistent world need not be massively-multiplayer, nor need it be a role-playing game.

Polygon   The fundamental unit of graphical data displayed by a 3-D graphics *engine*. A polygon is a region in 3-D space described by three or four points called *vertices*. The points make up a triangle or quadrilateral (usually abbreviated "quad"); polygon is a generic term for either. Three-dimensional models are built up out of hundreds or thousands of polygons to create a surface. Some game engines are designed to work with triangles, others with quads. Most modeling tools are capable of producing either.

Polygons per second   A measure of the speed of *3-D acceleration hardware*. The more polygons an accelerator can display per second, the more detailed a scene it can display before having to reduce the *frame rate*.

Porting   Also called conversion. Taking a computer program that works on one kind of computer or operating system, and making it work on a different kind of computer or operating system. Because games tend to be much more hardware-dependent than other forms of software, this is a highly skilled occupation.

POV shooter   Point-Of-View shooter. See *FPS*.

Pre-rendered   A still image or movie whose appearance has been computed in advance rather than on the fly. The rendering has taken place at the developer's studio before the product ever reaches the customer, so it is not possible for the customer to interact with or change the scene. See *rendering* and *3-D rendering*.

Producer   Sometimes also called Full Producer. A person responsible for the administrative and managerial aspects of creating a game as a product. Producers used to work only for publishers, but now the title is sometimes being used at development companies to refer to the head of the development team. See *internal producer* and *external producer*. Associate and assistant producers are positions below producer; executive producer is above.

Product manager   A marketing position, a person responsible for the marketing of a given product.

Product plan   A publisher's plan, usually extending 1–3 years into the future, of all the products or types of products that they want to release during that time. Also known as an *SKU* plan.

Product sense   A quality, possessed by good producers, of knowing when a game will be a fun and profitable product, and how to modify it to make it fun and profitable if it isn't.

Profiler   Nothing to do with tracking down serial killers! A profiler is a programming tool, an application that monitors the behavior of another program to determine which parts of the program are using the most CPU time. Modern profilers can also monitor the program's use of the machine's graphics and audio processors. Also called a performance analyzer.

Project manager   Also called schedule coordinator or scheduler. A person responsible for keeping track of the schedule and progress on a project. This is not always a leadership position.

Pseudo-code   A way of quickly describing an algorithmic process to a programmer, by writing it down as if in real program code, but without observing the necessary rules of syntax to make it readable by a *compiler*. Game designers sometimes write little pieces of pseudo-code to explain to the programmers how they want a given process to work. The programmers then convert the pseudo-code into real code.

QA   Quality Assurance, sometimes also called Quality Control. Use of the term varies. Occasionally it simply means normal product testing (either playtesting or bug testing), but it also can mean the final checks before a game is declared *gold*.

Raw (audio, image, and such)   Uncompressed data recorded directly from a hardware device such as a digital camera, with no header information or other details. Modern hardware is now smart enough to perform some compression and produce data in industry-standard file formats, so raw data is seldom seen any longer.

Raytracing   An image *rendering* technique that involves treating every pixel on the screen as if it were being lit by a ray of light, and computing backwards into the simulated scene to see where that ray of light came from and what color it should be. If the scene contains mirrors or lenses, multiple light sources or shadows, raytracing accurately reproduces these effects. At the moment the technique requires too much processing power for a video game to do it in real time, but it is used to generate pre-rendered video.

Recruiter   A person hired by a company to help them find qualified talent for their open positions. Recruiters are paid by the company; if one helps you get a job, you don't owe her anything. Also known colloquially as a headhunter.

Reel   See *demo reel*.

Rendering   A computerized process of converting the *geometry* that represents a scene or spatial location into a visible image of the scene. Put simply, rendering creates the picture from the data. See *3-D rendering* and *pre-rendered*.

Reserves *or* reserves against returns   A fund the publisher keeps in order to repay distributors and retailers for copies they return for a refund. The publisher also withholds some of the developer's royalties and puts them in this fund.

Returns   Copies of a game returned from the retailer to the publisher for a refund because the retailer cannot sell them. Frequently, the publisher simply allows the retailer to destroy them rather than sending them back.

Royalties   Any payment somebody gets as a percentage of the revenue generated by sales of something. Development companies get royalties from the publisher on the wholesale sales of a game that they developed, typically 15 percent or more of the price. However, they don't begin receiving royalties until the *advances* have been repaid to the publisher and the game has *earned out*.

RPG   Role-Playing Game. A game that is mostly about developing the skills and strengths of one or more characters through combat and other activities. Generally based on the *Dungeons & Dragons* model or similar. Sometimes also called an FRP.

RTS   Real-Time Strategy game. A game, almost always a war game, in which play takes place continuously rather than in turns, hence "real-time."

Sample   1) A single number that records the amplitude of a sound wave at a given instant in time. See *sample rate* and *sample size*. 2) A recording of the sound that a musical instrument uses to play a single note. This information is stored inside a *synthesizer* to reproduce the sound of the instrument. The sound need not be recorded from an actual musical instrument, however; any object that makes noise can be used as an "instrument."

Sample rate   The number of times per second that a digital recording device measures and records the amplitude of the sound waves it is receiving from the microphone. Compact discs use a sample rate of 44,100; that is, they store two 16-bit values (one for the left and one for the right channel) 44,100 times per second. The higher the sample rate, the more accurately a digital device can reproduce the original analog sound. Digital Audio Tape uses a sample rate of 48,000.

Sample size   The number of bits that a digital recording device stores every time it records a sample. Samples are usually in whole numbers of bytes—8-bit samples, 16-bit simples, and so on. Compact discs use 16-bit samples. The greater the sample size, the more accurately the original analog sound may be reproduced—and the more space is required to store it.

Schedule coordinator *or* scheduler   See *project manager.*

SDK   Software Development Kit. A library of software routines provided to a programmer to help with some particular task. You can license an SDK from the PKWARE company to enable your program to read and write ZIP archives, for example.

Sell-in   The number of copies of a game sold by the publisher to the retailers. Not a terribly useful number, since what really matters is getting it into the hands of the customers.

Sell-through   The number of copies of a game sold by the retailers to the consumers, i.e., the number of copies actually in players' hands.

Sequencer   A computer program for generating and playing music, usually recorded in a *MIDI* file. The sequencer reads the file and drives a *synthesizer.* There are also hardware sequencers that can control a variety of devices; they are used to generate the music in dance clubs.

Shader language   A special type of computer language designed to be executed by a graphics processor in *3-D acceleration hardware* as part of the *rendering* process, to change the appearance of the *geometry.* Shader languages enable programmers to modify the appearance of 3-D scenes using the graphics processor rather than the machine's main CPU, which frees up the CPU for other work.

Signal compression   In audio engineering, manipulating a waveform so that the quietest sounds in a given soundtrack are louder, and/or the loudest sounds are quieter. "Compression" in this case means compressing the *dynamic range* of the waveform into a narrower range.

Sim   A simulation of some kind. The term is more frequently used to refer to vehicle simulations such as flight simulators and car racing games than to process simulators like *Sim City.*

SKU   Stock-Keeping Unit. This refers to a single, indivisible item that a company sells, an object or collection of objects that is not broken apart to sell separately. A game console, including its manual, cord, and controller all make up one SKU, because you never would never break up that group; they should all be sold together. However, if you also want to let customers buy additional controllers, you can package controllers by themselves as a separate SKU. If a game is made for multiple platforms, each will be a separate SKU with its own unique SKU number so you can keep track of how many you're selling on each platform.

SKU plan   See *product plan.*

Source file *or* code   A file containing human-readable program code, written in a programming language. A programmer spends most of his or her time editing source files. The source code is read by a *compiler* or *assembler,* which produces as output an *object file.*

Sprite   A small 2-D image of an object or character that can be drawn on the screen at different locations over time to give the impression of movement. A sprite normally has a variety of associated animations depicting various things the character can do (walking, jumping, attacking, and so on). In old side-scrolling games all the characters and enemies were sprites.

Storyboard   A series of quick sketches, often made on paper, that illustrate the progression of a visual display of some kind. In the movies they are used to plan shots; in games they do the same thing, but also map out user interfaces and the general flow of a game.

Synthesizer   An electronic device capable of reproducing the sound of one or more musical instruments. Synthesizers are built into all the audio cards used in PCs, enabling the PC to act as an instrument. Early synthesizers did this by using mathematical algorithms to create an approximate reproduction of the sound that real instruments produce when played, in a process called FM synthesis. The results were not very successful, however. Modern synthesizers contain a digital recording, called a *sample* (second definition), of the sound that a real instrument makes, and they manipulate the sample mathematically to change its pitch and duration for each note. This process is called wave table synthesis, and is often indistinguishable from the real thing to the untrained ear. Synthesizers can hold 100 or more samples at a time, each from a different instrument. Synthesizers are controlled by programs called *sequencers.*

Texel   A pixel that is part of a *texture.*

Text adventure   An *adventure game* with no graphics, played entirely with written descriptions of the action and locations, and driven by keyboard commands. Now commercially obsolete, but still being created as a hobby by the *interactive fiction* community. Infocom was the best-known publisher of text adventures.

Texture   Nothing to do with real-world textures, which is the feel of a surface, detectable by touching it. In computer graphics, a texture is a 2-D image that is mapped onto the surface of a *polygonal* object in an 3-D environment in order to create the appearance of its surface. If you model the shape of a tin can as a cylinder, you can then apply a label to the can via a texture. Without a texture all you can do is color and shade the cylinder.

Ultimatte   A device used in video production for *matting*.

UV   A pair of numeric coordinates that specifies the relationship between a *texture* and the 3-D model it is texturing. When you change the UVs, the texture slides around on the surface of the model.

Vertex   A point in three-dimensional space that defines part of the surface of a 3-D model. Three vertices make a triangle; four make a quadrilateral, or quad; both of these are *polygons* that form part of the *geometry*.

Wave file   A data file containing recorded digital audio.

Wave table   A collection of *samples* (second definition) of different musical instruments, stored inside a *synthesizer*.

Work-for-hire agreement *or* work-for-hire contract   A contract between a publisher and a developer, or between a developer and a subcontractor, to do work for a flat fee, rather than for *advances* against *royalties*. Work-for-hire agreements are frequently used with *localization* work and for music, writing, and other subcontracted tasks.

Z buffer   A region of RAM memory that stores the "distance" between each polygon in a scene and the hypothetical camera, in order to determine which ones are farthest away. *Polygons* are *rendered* into the *frame buffer* from back to front so that the ones at the back are obscured by the ones in front.

Index

How to Get a Job Making Video Games

INTERNATIONAL CONTACT INFORMATION

AUSTRALIA
McGraw-Hill Book Company Australia Pty. Ltd.
TEL +61-2-9900-1800
FAX +61-2-9878-8881
http://www.mcgraw-hill.com.au
books-it_sydney@mcgraw-hill.com

CANADA
McGraw-Hill Ryerson Ltd.
TEL +905-430-5000
FAX +905-430-5020
http://www.mcgraw-hill.ca

GREECE, MIDDLE EAST, & AFRICA
(Excluding South Africa)
McGraw-Hill Hellas
TEL +30-210-6560-990
TEL +30-210-6560-993
TEL +30-210-6560-994
FAX +30-210-6545-525

MEXICO (Also serving Latin America)
McGraw-Hill Interamericana Editores S.A. de C.V.
TEL +525-117-1583
FAX +525-117-1589
http://www.mcgraw-hill.com.mx
fernando_castellanos@mcgraw-hill.com

SINGAPORE (Serving Asia)
McGraw-Hill Book Company
TEL +65-6863-1580
FAX +65-6862-3354
http://www.mcgraw-hill.com.sg
mghasia@mcgraw-hill.com

SOUTH AFRICA
McGraw-Hill South Africa
TEL +27-11-622-7512
FAX +27-11-622-9045
robyn_swanepoel@mcgraw-hill.com

SPAIN
McGraw-Hill/Interamericana de España, S.A.U.
TEL +34-91-180-3000
FAX +34-91-372-8513
http://www.mcgraw-hill.es
professional@mcgraw-hill.es

UNITED KINGDOM, NORTHERN,
EASTERN, & CENTRAL EUROPE
McGraw-Hill Education Europe
TEL +44-1-628-502500
FAX +44-1-628-770224
http://www.mcgraw-hill.co.uk
computing_europe@mcgraw-hill.com

ALL OTHER INQUIRIES Contact:
McGraw-Hill/Osborne
TEL +1-510-420-7700
FAX +1-510-420-7703
http://www.osborne.com
omg_international@mcgraw-hill.com

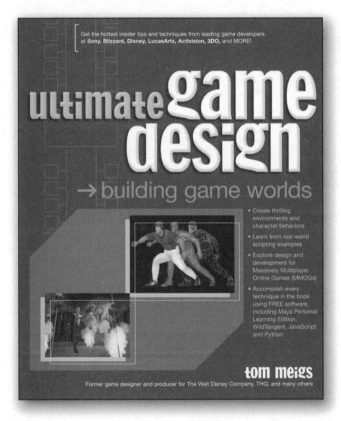

BREAKINGIN
PREPARING FOR YOUR CAREER IN GAMES

THINKING ABOUT YOUR FUTURE? THINK ABOUT A CAREER MAKING VIDEO GAMES!

START HERE

www.igda.org/BreakingIn

The interactive entertainment industry is not just where today's hottest PC and video games come from. It's also where thousands of interesting people make a living as programmers, artists, producers, musicians, managers and more. If this is the kind of career you'd like to explore, do yourself a favor, and find out more online: www.igda.org/BreakingIn.

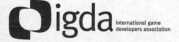

igda
international game
developers association